In the Shadow of Your Wings
New Readings of Great Texts from the Bible

Norbert Lohfink, s.j.

Translated by Linda M. Maloney

A Michael Glazier Book

THE LITURGICAL PRESS
Collegeville, Minnesota

www.litpress.org

BS
511.3
.L6413
2003

A Michael Glazier Book published by The Liturgical Press

Cover design by David Manahan, O.S.B. Illustration: detail, *The Ustyug Annunciation,* 12th cent. icon, The Tretyakov Gallery, Moscow.

Portions of the present book were originally published as *Im Schatten deiner Flügel. Grosse Bibeltexte neu erschlossen.* © Verlag Herder, Freiburg im Breisgan, 1999. ISBN 3-451-27176-1.

Scripture quotations, unless otherwise noted, are from The New Revised Standard Version Bible ©1989 by the Division of Christian Education of the National Council of Churches of Christ in the U.S.A. Used by permission. All rights reserved. Translations marked by an asterisk (*) follow the author's own; the asterisk is omitted when the independent translation is clearly indicated by the text.

© 2003 by The Order of Saint Benedict, Collegeville, Minnesota. All rights reserved. No part of this book may be reproduced in any form or by any means, electronic or mechanical, including photocopying, recording, taping, or any retrieval system, without the written permission of The Liturgical Press, Collegeville, Minnesota 56321. Printed in the United States of America.

1   2   3   4   5   6   7   8

Library of Congress Cataloging-in-Publication Data

Lohfink, Norbert.
   [Im Schatten Deiner Flügel. English]
   In the shadow of Your wings : new readings of great texts from the Bible / Norbert Lohfink ; translated by Linda M. Maloney.
      p. cm.
   "A Michael Glazier book."
   Includes bibliographical references (p.) and index.
   ISBN 0-8146-5146-1 (alk. paper)
      1. Bible—Cristicism, interpretation, etc. 2. Christian life—Catholic authors. I. Title.

BS511.3 .L6413 2003
220.6—dc21
                                                              2002073959

For my brother Gerhard

On his 65th Birthday

Contents

Foreword   vii

Chapter 1: Death at the River Frontier. Moses' Incomplete
   Mission and the Contours of the Bible. 1

Chapter 2: "Go from your country . . ." The God of the
   Patriarchs and Matriarchs. 15

Chapter 3: Conquest or Return? Reading Joshua Today 27

Chapter 4: Jeremiah and the Sacred Heart of Jesus.
   The "New Covenant". 44

Chapter 5: Hosea and Wrath. Some Suggestions for Reading 57

Chapter 6: The Psalter and Meditation. On the Genre of the
   Book of Psalms. 75

Chapter 7: The Loneliness of the Just One. Psalm 1 91

Chapter 8: Introspection and Cosmic Mysticism. Psalm 36 98

Chapter 9: Peace Poetry in Israel. Psalm 46. 111

Chapter 10: Three Ways to Talk about Poverty. Psalm 109 119

Chapter 11: The Old Testament and the Course of the
   Christian's Day. The Songs in Luke's Infancy Narrative 136

Chapter 12: Children of Abraham from Stones. Does the
   Old Testament Promise a New Covenant Without Israel?. . . . 151

Notes. 171

General Index 177

Scripture Index. 182

Foreword

In the eighth chapter of this book I will attempt to interpret Psalm 36, that incredible document of a movement from a mysticism of human introspection to a mysticism of the presence of God in the world and society. At the midpoint of the psalm the sustaining image suddenly reverses. The sun-god, sweeping through the heavens as the all-illuminating guarantor of earthly righteousness, becomes the divine mother bird who takes her chicks protectively under her wings. Ultimately righteousness can only enter this chaotic world through rescue. The further shifting of the image shows *where* that happens. For even the image of the hen is only transitory. It leads further to the cherubim who stand spreading their wings above the Ark, in the Holy of Holies of the Temple on Zion.

Righteousness from rescue, rescue in the place of praise and adoration—*these* are the contexts to which the Bible, the basis of the lives of Jews and Christians, belongs. That is what I wanted to suggest when I chose for this collection of essays (originally all public lectures) the title from Psalm 36: "In the Shadow of Your Wings."

Here historical questions and informative material play a relatively minor role in comparison with other previous collections of mine. They are not entirely absent. Nor have I undergone one of those exegetical conversions that are increasingly common, leading to an ascetic restriction to a timeless "pure" text or a mania for late historical dating and thus devaluation. However, for the most part these chapters give attention to the present text, the only one available to us in the context of our own tradition. This is the text that is read publicly in the Synagogue and in the Church. Ultimately, that is the only text we have to interpret, if we want to be theologians.

My concern is always with individual texts and themes, and I do not always draw out the lines of connection to the whole Bible. However, I believe that one can also interpret "canonically" in this way. The framing essays may indicate my overall view of the canon.

In addition, in organizing the material I have generally followed the succession of the biblical books in the canon. After some consideration of the Torah and two prophetic books, and before turning briefly to the New Testament, I concentrate particularly on the Psalms. In my own dealings with the Bible they have become more and more important to me, especially as a result of many years of weekly conversations on the Psalms with the Little Sisters of Charles de Foucauld during the years of their theological studies in Frankfurt. Of course the special points of view in light of which I have approached the individual texts and themes are strongly influenced by those who have, in the several cases, invited me to lecture, and by the questions that were in the air in each context. Yet I hope that the variety that results is still representative, and that many readers will find at least something in the book that is helpful and perhaps even encouraging.

I dedicate the book to my brother Gerhard on his 65th birthday. I admire the clarity with which he was prepared to draw consequences for his own life from the things he, as an interpreter of the Bible, recognized. And I am full of gratitude to him for having cared so tenderly and faithfully for our old parents in the last years of their lives.

Rome, at the Pontifical Biblical Institute, 1 March 1999
Norbert Lohfink, S.J.

Chapter One

Death at the River Frontier

Moses' Incomplete Mission
and the Contours of the Bible

Twenty-two times in the book of Deuteronomy Moses opens his mouth to speak: twenty-two times, corresponding to the twenty-two letters of the Hebrew alphabet. Now, in chapter 34, he has finished speaking: The Torah is written down, hands have been laid on his successor Joshua (ch. 31), the song "Give ear, O heavens" has been sung (ch. 32), the blessing of the departing man has been spoken over the twelve tribes (ch. 33), he has ascended the mountain at God's command, and there

> the LORD showed him [let him *see*] the whole land: Gilead as far as Dan, all Naphtali, the land of Ephraim and Manasseh, all the land of Judah as far as the Western Sea, the Negeb, and the Plain—that is, the valley of Jericho, the city of palm trees—as far as Zoar. The LORD said to him, "This is the land of which I swore to Abraham, to Isaac, and to Jacob, saying, 'I will give it to your descendants'; I have let you *see* it *with your eyes,* but you shall not *cross over* there." Then Moses, the servant of the LORD, died there in the land of Moab . . . but no one knows his burial place to this day. (Deut 34:1-6; emphasis added)

This is purely objective language, coolly viewing from outside. But what an abyss lies beneath! The *seeing* alone is the primitive cultural legal act of the transfer of property through inspection, still present in Roman law. In the company of witnesses one would ascend a tower, and from that height the seller would show the buyer the piece of land with its walls, angles, and trees. In the sight of those standing around, the buyer cast an eye upon it all. By this inspection the land became his or her property. Seeing a land then, in this passage, means acquiring it. But in Moses' case this happens immediately before his death: all he gets is a look. He wanted to see the land differently, namely by crossing the Jordan with the rest of the people.

Only a few days before, he had argued with his God about it. He tells of it himself in Deuteronomy 3. He had taken courage from the fact that he was able to lead the people in taking possession of the land east of the Jordan. Perhaps God had repented and was ready to take back his earlier wrath (1:37)? So Moses prayed: "Let me *cross over* to *see* the good land beyond the Jordan, that good hill country and the Lebanon" (3:25). He meant a different kind of seeing, namely viewing and experiencing up close, not from a tower or a mountain. But God said no:

> "Enough from you! Never speak to me of this matter again! Go up to the top of Pisgah and *look* around you to the west, to the north, to the south, and to the east. *Look well,* for you shall not *cross over* this Jordan." (3:26-27; emphasis added)

The whole book of Deuteronomy is stretched between these two texts about seeing the land. To enter and see the promised land—or to see it from the mountaintop and then die immediately: this, Moses' fate, will be our subject; this border situation, when everything hoped for is in sight and yet still beyond the river that separates us from it.

The Exodus was Moses' task, but it is only half done.

We will see clearly how great the tension is here when we remember that the entry into the promised land is the second half of the Exodus from Egypt. Because in these chapters we will be thinking "synchronically" about the canonical Bible, it will be well if we go back beyond Deuteronomy itself. Already at the burning bush (Exodus 3) the whole plan is clear. God speaks from the fire and says that he has come down "to deliver them (Israel) from the Egyptians, and to bring them up out of that land to a good and broad land, a land flowing with milk and honey" (Exod 3:8). The two things are just as closely bound together in the credo that, according to Deuteronomy 26, the head of an Israelite house will speak when bringing the first fruits of the harvest to the Temple: God has led us out of Egypt and brought us into the land, and now we bring forth our harvest (Deut 26:8-10). A single arch extends from Egypt to the new land. There was nothing worth mentioning in between.

But Deuteronomy has to see the whole thing in a different light as well. It began with the story of the spies. Immediately after leaving Horeb, Israel did not trust (Deut 1:32), and so it could not enter the land. For that reason it had to wait forty years, until the whole generation that came out of Egypt had died in the wilderness. None of those who are now to enter the land had come out of Egypt. One group came out, but a different group will enter in. Moses, too, must first die.

But the extent to which that goes against the whole picture painted in Exodus is clear from what is said about Moses' successor; in fact, none of what happens in Deuteronomy would be necessary otherwise. The covenant in Moab has to be made only because, with Moses no longer there, the entry into the land has to have an organizer. For a change of leadership to take place, the whole thing has to be put on a new basis. That is the only reason why Moses has to proclaim the Torah all over again and write it down, and why the tribes have to pass between the halves of the slaughtered animals and swear again that they will live according to the Torah.

We are not even in the institutional context of a monarchy, in which succession to the throne after the death of a king is both a central issue and a matter of course, practiced and customary. In the period of the judges, now about to begin, Israel is not a monarchy. It exists as a society without a head. Joshua is not the first king of Israel, just as Moses was not a king. Moses had the unique charism of a founder. Joshua is just the part of Moses that Moses himself can no longer be because he must die too soon. When he has completed the rest of Moses' task he can die without having to install a successor to himself. The idea does not even occur to him. He is only Moses' successor so that he can complete the task the books of Deuteronomy and Joshua speak of so often that they are almost pushy about it: conquering the land and dividing it among the tribes. Once that is done, Israel no longer needs a human head—at least until a new epoch begins in which (to its own ruin) it wants kings and political organization "like other nations" (1 Sam 8:5). Thus when the question of a successor appears at the beginning of Israel's history only in the case of Moses, it is undoubtedly because Moses' (unique) task has not yet been completed.

There is an issue here, the most fundamental issue in the world. The Exodus has not yet reached its goal; Israel is not yet in its land. Moses was supposed to have taken care of that. But now he must die with only half of it completed. At the very end of chapter 34 there is something like an obituary for Moses. If only it could have been written of him that he led Israel out and in! But it did not happen. Only the Exodus could be called his work, although that alone made Moses the greatest of all the prophets:

> Never since has there arisen a prophet in Israel like Moses, whom the LORD knew face to face. He was unequaled for all the signs and wonders that the LORD sent him to perform in the land of Egypt, against Pharaoh and all his servants and his entire land, and for all the mighty deeds and all the terrifying displays of power that Moses performed in the sight of all Israel. (Deut 34:10-12)

The miracles in Egypt and at the Sea—but no miraculous entry into the land. He was meant for that, too. But he could only behold the land from afar. He will not cross the Jordan.

Moses' death as a literary boundary marker

The question why this fracture occurs in Moses' existence and in the history of Israel's beginnings forces us to reflect on the power of sin and our solidarity in guilt. But that is not our subject at present. Instead, I want to turn our thoughts in another direction, to show that Moses' death on the threshold of the promise about to be fulfilled also has literary-theological significance. This rupture of meaning generates within the Sacred Scriptures a fundamental structure for the whole Bible, and indeed for Jewish-Christian existence. The Exodus, that is, God's fundamental action, breaks in two at this point in a literary sense as well, and theologically it becomes a structure in two pieces that has to be brought together again and again.

On the literary level there is a fracture here. For "children's Bibles," which have influenced Christians' idea of the biblical world for generations, the history of Israel simply continued, even though in the mean time Moses had died. Modern biblical scholarship, once it had discovered the sources of the Pentateuch, took it as a matter of course that those sources simply continued into the book of Joshua; it became more common to speak of a Hexateuch than a Pentateuch—if the literary-critical divining rods did not probe even farther, into the subsequent historical books. When Martin Noth discovered the Deuteronomistic History, of course, a crevice appeared between Numbers and Deuteronomy—but from Deuteronomy onward the history continued uninterrupted until the Babylonian exile at the end of the second book of Kings. Nowadays the Pentateuch theory is wobbly, and not everyone feels entirely confident about the Deuteronomistic History either. But in place of them the vision of a late-Deuteronomistic historical work extending from Genesis to 2 Kings is beginning suddenly to dazzle some Old Testament scholars. In the workshops of our liturgists, who are undertaking the praiseworthy endeavor of improving the sequence of pericopes for the Sunday readings, the popular phrase nowadays is "salvation history." In the project they are currently discussing, the history of Israel and the world extends in a long line of carefully selected pericopes from Adam and Abel to Qoheleth and the Maccabean martyrs. But Moses' death on the frontier, before the completion of the Exodus, makes all that, literarily speaking, a heap of irresponsible garbage. There is no continuous line. In the very centerpiece of all the existing narratives that make up salvation history there is a built-in fracture that, from the logic of things, is totally unexpected.

It was created quite deliberately. For at least Deuteronomy and Joshua were, in their pre-history, a single book at one time. The carefully crafted depiction of the transfer of power from Moses to Joshua is presented in a complex of narratives that is not yet aware of any demarcating line between the two books. Thus even the premature death of Moses and the completion of his work by another could still be submerged under an appearance of continuity. But now there are some boundary markers here.

We see it in literary terms by the fact that Deuteronomy 34 is not only linked directly to Joshua 1, but in exactly the same way to the book of Isaiah, and to the Psalter, and in a somewhat less clearly marked fashion to other individual building blocks of the Old Testament canon. I need to explain this point of view a little further because it can scarcely be called common knowledge.

The Pentateuch as a manual for the actors in the book of Joshua

The book of Joshua, no matter how clearly its first sentence reflects the connection to the preceding event of Moses' death, nevertheless immediately proceeds to make it clear that it regards what has gone before as a matter that is complete and closed. It begins with a word of God to Joshua, and within that speech by God we read:

> Whatever happens, be strong and courageous beyond measure! Be careful to act in accordance with the Torah that my servant Moses commanded you! Do not turn from it to the right hand or to the left, so that you may be successful wherever you go. Let not this scroll of the Torah depart out of your mouth! You shall meditate on it [*lit.* mumble it] day and night, so that you may be careful to act in accordance with all that is written in it. For then you shall make your way prosperous, and then you shall be successful. Have I not commanded you: Be strong and courageous? (Josh 1:7-9*)

The passage ends as it had begun, a clear indication that the text is a secondary insertion in an older book. Such insertions were often shaped in such a way that they end with the phrase to which they were attached at the beginning, so that the older text can continue without interruption and without disturbance from the insertion. So it is here.

But what does this insertion do? It makes the Bible self-referential. It alters everything historically done and said in its narrative world up to this point, making it a closed entity that is presented to the protagonists of the subsequent action as an objective book, and then as a given, model world to be internalized subjectively in a continual murmuring to oneself. (Mumbling texts was the technique of meditation then in use.) The continuing time line from creation to the death of Moses, which in and of itself would simply go on, has become something new. It has been given an endpoint. Everything before is now a unit, immediate to the present now approaching, and when the present continues forward it ceases, dissolving slowly into the darkness of the past.

In the few sentences of the inserted passage we can clearly see how the concept of Torah is newly defined, step by step. At the beginning it is the Torah that Moses had commanded Joshua to observe. Was that the Torah that he proclaimed to all Israel in the book of Deuteronomy? Perhaps it was individual instruction given only to Joshua. But presently it is "the scroll of the Torah." This, a reference back to Deuteronomy 31:24, clearly means the written covenant text of Deuteronomy 5–28, which Moses entrusted to the priests and elders of Israel after proclaiming it to the whole nation (Deut 31:9). But still more: in the intertextuality of the whole Old Testament, in which, for example in the books of Chronicles, the expression "scroll of the Torah" refers to the whole Pentateuch, the expression "Torah scroll" in Joshua 1 may ultimately have the whole Pentateuch for its reference. At the canonical level it is then no longer important whether the Torah in one case is called the Torah of Moses and in another the Torah of God, because the reference is always to the five scrolls of the Pentateuch. The book of Joshua, even though it appears to follow seamlessly on Deuteronomy, at the same time sets itself radically apart from the whole Pentateuch. That is the point that interests me.

This opposition between a model world in the form of a book and the history that flows out of it, or also sins against it, beginning now and continuing into the future, shapes the whole complex of books from Joshua to 2 Kings. The Torah scroll quickly disappears from view; little is made of it, and only at the end of the books of Kings, under Josiah of Judah, is it rediscovered in the course of renovations in the Temple. Josiah is a final figure of hope. The land into which Joshua had led Israel has already shrunk to Jerusalem and the small territory of Judah surrounding it. But Josiah's cultic reform leads him along the same paths that Joshua followed during the conquest: first in the center, then southward, and finally to the north. But he cannot stem the evil tide. Israel is not destroyed, but the land is taken from it, the land to which the Exodus had led. Israel must go into exile. The second half of the Exodus, which Moses did not lead, is annulled at the end of the books of Kings.

*The direct connection of other text complexes
in the canon to the Torah*

The book of Isaiah is rooted in the life of the prophet Isaiah from the era of the kings, but it unfolds its larger discursive situation in the horizon of the exile, in the Deuteroisaianic chapters. Nevertheless, if we look closely we see that the book follows directly on the end of Deuteronomy. The appeal to heaven and earth to bear witness (Isa 1:2) takes up Moses' song, "Give ear, O heavens," from Deut 32:1, and the address to Jerusalem as "rulers of Sodom" and "people of Gomorrah" in Isa 1:10 refers to the impending exile that is sensed in Deut 29:23 [MT 22], where the same two cities are named. In the same breath Jerusalem is called to listen to "the Torah of our God." Then it is made clear what the Torah is concerned about: not sacrifices, but justice for the oppressed. In the second chapter a new and different Torah appears: the Torah for the nations, who will receive it in the time of the eschatological pilgrimage of the nations to Zion. The tension between these two Torahs will be the content of the whole book of Isaiah. What concerns us here is simply that this book, with its programmatic beginning, is immediately in touch with the end of Deuteronomy and of the entire Pentateuch.

The same is true of the Psalter. It begins in Psalm 1 with the image of the man who

> does not follow the advice of the wicked,
> or take the path that sinners tread,
> or sit in the seat of scoffers;
> but his delight is in the Torah of the LORD,
> and he murmurs his Torah day and night. (Ps 1:1-2*)

The last phrase agrees verbally, to a great extent, with the formula at the beginning of the book of Joshua. In the closely related Psalm 2 there follows, much as in the second chapter of Isaiah, the theme of the nations in the messianic time. It is true that at first it is introduced in the ancient imperial style, and the key word Torah is not found. But then the man from Psalm 1, who now shines as the anointed king on Zion, suddenly ceases to wield his war club; instead he proclaims a message to the kings of the earth. The Torah he thus pronounces calls on them to submit themselves to the service of the God of Israel.

In this address we find the appeal: "be wise" (Ps 2:10). This is the same verb that appears twice in the same form and the same tense at the beginning of the book of Joshua (Josh 1:7, 8), where we have to translate: "so that you may be successful." Our language cannot combine the two nuances of meaning that are conveyed by the single Hebrew verb, but for the Hebrew ear there is no difference here. I have no doubt about the intertextual cross-reference.

Thus the Psalter also situates itself, analogously to the books of Joshua and Isaiah, immediately after the death of Moses, directly following the five scrolls of the Torah. In addition we can say, on the same level of observation, how far these text complexes that attach themselves to the end of the Torah extend.

Just as the beginning of Joshua, together with the end of the second book of Kings, constituted a frame around a major historical work, so the last book of the minor prophets, Malachi, in its final chapter, clearly closes with Torah motifs. Thus Isaiah, as a continuation of the Pentateuch, begins the whole complex of the prophetic books.

In the Psalter the first two psalms correspond to the great concluding *hallel* (Pss 146–50), in which scholars have long seen a reference back to Psalms 1 and 2. Here, then, the whole collection of 150 psalms, as a textual whole, is attached to the Pentateuch.

In the remaining books of the Hebrew or Greek canon this kind of direct reference to the Pentateuch is not so clearly marked. Nevertheless, they are certainly anything but pearls on the string of a continuing chain of history. From the exile on, Israel made no attempt at a continuing historical report within its canon. The great variety of genres alone makes most of the so-called "Writings" appear as individual pieces. As such they are open to a direct relationship to Torah, and within the body of these texts it is frequently given expression.

Non-linear connections between books

Thus the death of Moses holds a key position within the canon. Here begins something like a multidimensionality that is not determined by the course of time alone. We are entering a virtual space. The canon is not linear. Its books are networked together like the items in a database, in which one may move from any series directly to any point in another series. Here in the canon we can at least refer directly back from any text complex to the one text complex of the Torah, and the Torah is immediate to each of them.

Isn't it interesting that it is easiest to illustrate an ancient reality in terms of the newest computer technology? But that can be explained. The computer is replacing the book as a system of text storage. Books are linear; their pages are counted in order. When, around the turn of the era, the codex gradually replaced the scroll, it represented progress. It was easier to find individual parts of the text more quickly. It was no longer necessary to unroll the scroll; you could just page through. However, this progress was accompanied by a disadvantage. What was now found in a codex was formerly written on several, perhaps many scrolls. Scrolls were stored upright in small baskets. But the baskets, the basis of any ancient library, did not impose a linear succession on the rolls standing in them. Thus in any text complex comprising several scrolls there could be an interplay of much more complex non-linear relationships among the individual scrolls than the later codex allowed. So, for example, in a kind of branching process, various writings could be simultaneously linked to a first document. The book, as an instrument for organizing texts, had to grow into the multidimensionality of electronic storage before these potentials for meaning in the ancient scroll system could be revived. Besides all this, a non-linear networking corresponds to the internal organization of the human brain.

Meanwhile, however, the book has accustomed us to think of literary entities in linear terms. In the case of the Old Testament canon this linear thinking is reinforced by the fact that our canon, in book form, actually follows the course of history up to the end of the books of Kings. After that the system falters. But by then it has already long since activated the unilinear historical mentality that dominated the minds of people in the modern era, to which is added the expectation of an evolutionary curve of progress. This way of thinking spontaneously, although in a manner more or less forced, causes unilinear time to appear to continue even after the books of Kings, so that we may find some order in the books that follow.

If these writings do not deal with a particular period, because they are not works of history, they are mentally located within a kind of latent historical frieze for the period when, according to the opinion of modern literary historians, they were written. Thus, for example, in the German liturgists' project for revising the Old Testament readings in the Sunday lectionary the book of Qoheleth is placed near the very end. Apparently it is assigned to the third century B.C.E. That is, in fact, probably when it was written. But nobody seems to notice that it relates to King Solomon, who lived 800 years earlier, and intends to reflect his experience of the world. And placing it in the time of Solomon would also be wrong. The book of Qoheleth by no means intends to represent history. It relates directly to Torah, attaching itself to the Torah's beginning by taking death as its central theme, asserting forthrightly that the human being must return to the dust from which he or she was taken (Qoh 12:7; cf. Gen 3:19).

According to the organizational principle dependent on the time of composition that is applied to Qoheleth, the pericope project should have placed the creation account in Genesis 1 not at the beginning of the series of readings, but somewhere in the post-exilic period. So it seems we are to be presented with a sequence of pericopes containing this built-in misconception—based on nothing but an obsession with linear history.

It would be better to stick to the facts: The Old Testament canon is not a historical frieze and cannot be made to be one. Of course the canon contains historical descriptions, but even in the largest section of those, extending from creation to the Babylonian exile, there is a clear break after the death of Moses. What then follows stands equal to, though in competition with and alongside other, for the most part not historiographical text segments of the canon, and all of them are ordered to the first five scrolls, the Torah, as their fundamental textual reference.

The Torah is a "canon within the canon," or, to put it in terms of the history of religions and cultures, it contains the basic myth, the "primitive age," the "cultural memory," what happened *in illo tempore,* "in those days," and not a "communicative" historical memory, which in oral cultures extends back only about three generations, but since the introduction of writing and archives can be traced from more distant times in the past up to the present. Such a general historical memory was apparently not in the interests of those who constructed our canon.

Old Testament canonical structure as fundamental theological statement and instruction for liturgical action

Theologically, however, this means that we may not introduce the Old Testament into our proclamation of faith as if it were a historical account, most certainly not in cultic action that is essentially performative. What the Old Testament presents is a "primeval history," revolutionary within the story of religions up to the historical point of the crossing of the Jordan, and it then integrates within a multidimensional space the continuation of the greatest variety of commentaries on what has gone before.

However, only the first half of the ultimately decisive event of the primeval time, the Exodus, has been retained within the founding myth. That is what is theologically so exciting. The second half exists in the Torah only as a project and a promise. It is the primary subject of the remainder of the canon, which is a polyphonic commentary on it. It is full of alternatives, one of which is described in the historical work extending from Joshua through 2 Kings. That was a failed experiment; at the end of it Israel is again outside the land.

In chapter 20 of the book of Ezekiel, Israel's history in its land is retold from an exilic perspective, and it all sounds as if Israel had never been in the land at all. The time in the land was still a time in the wilderness, and now Israel, by contrast, is in the "wilderness of the peoples" (Ezek 20:35). The real entry into the land is still to come.

In the prophetic books, when we read them in their final form, the entry is always still to come. Everywhere in the Old Testament canon, in one way or another, we find reflections from every possible angle on this threshold existence.

As long as the Torah alone constitutes the full continuous reading on the Sabbath in Israel's synagogues, and as long as, at the end of the year's readings, the reading of the death of Moses is not followed by reaching for the scroll of Joshua, but instead by a return to the beginning of Genesis— as long as that is the case, all Israel knows that it is still caught up in the fate of Moses: across the Jordan, still in the wilderness. Not only Moses, but all Israel can only look across, but cannot cross the river. That is the enduring situation of listeners in the Synagogue. The canonical structure and the order of readings in the Synagogue correspond. And so it must be.

Continuation, relativization, and reduplication of the Old Testament canonical structure in the New Testament

The Church has a different canon. In saying this I am not referring to the difference between the Hebrew and Greek lists of books, which involves both numbers and ordering. In my opinion they do not vitiate what I have developed up to this point.

Given the difference between the Torah and all the remaining books, it is certainly possible for the Torah to have spawned additional growth. If the immediacy of the different segments of the canon to the Torah is the fundamental datum for organizing the texts, and not the linear succession, there can be variations in the ordering as the books are listed or in the transition to written codices.

In this regard I do not believe that the so-called Septuagint canon shifts the weight toward the prophetic books and eschatological expectation. Rather, the insertion of the Hebrew "writings" at appropriate points in the list reveals the stronger sense of genre among the Greek-educated librarians in Alexandria. It is possible that in the case of the more extensive Greek Bible there was at first a more conservative situation in play. Whereas in the homeland the development had already reached the stage of recognizing Torah, Nebiim, and Kethubim as Sacred Scripture and granting only to the Torah the special rank of a "canon within the canon," it appears that in the Greek-speaking world for a long time only the Torah was acknowledged as Sacred Scripture in the strictest sense. Philo of Alexandria had the most extensive Greek Bible, and yet he commented only on the Torah, whereas Qumran had already developed commentaries on the Psalms and Prophets. Thus the special place of the Torah had by no means been eliminated in Alexandria: quite the opposite. That special place has been retained in the still more extensive Christian canon.

But does not the addition of the New Testament change everything? Here, since I am crossing the boundaries of my own field, I can of course only propose theses and offer conjectures that others who are more competent in these questions may want to pursue.

In the first instance the whole New Testament is nothing more than a further set of texts within the multidimensional sphere of "commentaries" on the Torah. It is still a question of where and when Israel's Exodus ends. But at the same time the New Testament is not just one commentary among others. It is the definitive commentary. In Jesus of Nazareth, God brought the Exodus to its end for Israel and also in its consequences for the nations, which had long been foreseen by the prophets. To that extent the New Testament stands, great and powerful, over against the Old Testament and relativizes its own foundational text with a new one.

John baptized across the Jordan, in the wilderness. But Jesus, with his first disciples, crossed over the Jordan to the west. In the land he proclaimed that the reign of God had come, and it did come in the signs and wonders in the land that Moses' epitaph could not report. That is how the gospels begin. (Even in John 3:23, 36, where the Baptizer also works in the land west of the Jordan, he only begins to do it after Jesus has crossed the Jordan ahead of him.) The gospels thus also link directly to the situation that existed when Moses died, on the bank of the river. But since the resurrection of the dead begins at the end of the gospels, we are sure that the Exodus has reached its goal.

But now something occurs that is analogous to what happened with Moses. I will describe the literary reflection: the point at which we can see what is happening is the division of the Lukan writings. In the New Testament canon its two parts are no longer placed together, and in the oldest lists we have the Acts of the Apostles was not even placed after the gospels.

At the beginning of Acts the disciples stand looking after their disappearing Lord. We know exactly how they feel: can it be that with him the land into which we thought we had finally entered is also vanishing into the world beyond? The angels have to shout at them: ". . . why do you stand looking up toward heaven? This Jesus, who has been taken up from you into heaven, will come in the same way as you saw him go into heaven" (Acts 1:11). What a striking analogy to the death of Moses! But one thing is different: they know where he has gone, and they know that and how he will return. So the entry has been accomplished. And yet for those who stand looking upward it has been delayed again. Again we find that we are not standing, unveiled, *in illo tempore*. Again a retrospective "primeval history" has to be written, to which the "commentaries" can be attached.

Therefore in the New Testament, the definitive commentary on the Torah of the Old Testament, we again find the structure of the basic canonical text with its character as primeval history, plus a further set of texts as commentary. The basic text is the fourfold book of the gospels; the remaining writings are commentary on it, again attached in a multidimensional format. Because Jesus has departed and will come again, time again stretches out ahead, and what is laid down in fourfold fashion in the gospels can again be realized in a multitude of ways.

Reflecting the full structure of the canon in the Sunday Liturgy of the Word

The internal structure of the New Testament canon has never been called into question in liturgical use anywhere. The two readings, one of them from the gospel, were always fixed elements; they cannot even be done away with on the feast of the Ascension, where the narrative proper to the feast actually occurs in the first New Testament reading rather than in the gospel.

It is just as important that, even in our Church in which for more than a millennium there was no Old Testament reading on Sunday, the gospel still remained in the second place. That was not because the gospels are not the oldest writings in the New Testament; it was modern biblical scholarship that found that out. Nor was it because a kind of rhetorical climax had to be achieved by placing the gospel last. Ordinarily it would be in the nature of things that, when the given relationship is between text and commentary, the text itself should be read first, and then the commentary on it. From that point of view the gospel ought to be read first. The surprising sequence of New Testament reading, then gospel, is rather the ruins of an ancient structural plan that began with the reading from the Old Testament. The Old Testament reading and the gospels were like the two foci of an ellipse.

Our latest liturgical reform restored that for us. It did nothing more than return to the origins. However, in details its lectionary is highly problematic. It is simply a scandal that in the German-speaking countries—though this is not universal throughout the world—there is a rubric in the missal that, in order to reduce the number of readings, permits the omission of the Old Testament reading "for pastoral reasons," and this quite frequently occurs. Nevertheless, it is worth emphasizing how much more clearly the structure of our Liturgy of the Word now corresponds to the structure of the canon of Sacred Scripture.

But—and here the course of my thinking brings me back around to the death of Moses and the break between the Torah and the rest of the writings in the Old Testament canon—it still does not follow the precise structure of the canon. As our liturgists are now, quite correctly, thinking about whether improvements could be made in the concrete selection of texts for the—finally restored—reading from the Old Testament, with better choices than in the hasty product of the first attempt, they should immediately throw their ideas about a catechetical introduction of the congregation to the history of Israel into the shredder. Instead, they should listen to Georg Braulik. In the Festschrift for Hans Bernhard Meyer he has shown that in the churches that have retained an Old Testament reading from the outset, and where we *de facto* obtain the oldest witness to the order of readings from the Old Testament in the liturgy, namely in the Nestorian and Jacobite churches in Syria, the first and proper Old Testament reading is not just any text, but, except in the Easter season, always a reading from the Torah. Then there is space for readings between the Torah reading at one end and the gospel reading at the other, with at least two such readings in the middle. Here was the place for readings from the other books of both the Old and New Testaments.

That corresponds to the real canonical structure. Georg Braulik derives from this a suggestion for a three-year course of readings from the Torah, proposing for the intermediate reading that there be a selection of two alternative texts, one from the Old and one from the New Testament, one related to the Torah reading and one to the gospel. Depending on which of the principal readings the preacher will choose as basis for the homily, he or she could then choose one or the other of the intermediate readings. Our Sunday Liturgy of the Word must really be constituted in that or some similar fashion if we do not want to smuggle just any kind of modernisms and sloganizing into our liturgy, but rather to orient ourselves to the structure of the biblical canon itself.

It could be that we would then enter more truly into that crucial situation of listening that is appropriate to our real location between "already" and "not yet." Deuteronomy 34, the death of Moses, who already sees the land but cannot cross the Jordan, must be allowed to proclaim its true, important structural message for Christian existence. But the text can only proclaim it if we restore to the Torah its proper position in our liturgy.

Chapter Two

"Go from your country . . ."
The God of the Patriarchs and Matriarchs

Abraham was led into an unknown country. His God said to him: "I will give this land to you and your offspring." But he, and his son Isaac, and Isaac's son Jacob lived in this land, which was *their* God-given land, as foreigners, as tolerated resident aliens. The Bible repeatedly emphasizes this in its stories of the primeval ancestors. Only much later did their descendants possess the land as their own.

Centuries in Egypt, the Exodus, forty years in the wilderness—all that happened in between. The ancestors and the early generations of Israel had encountered the true God. One of the most gripping experiences they had was that this was a God who makes people foreigners. Is that not peculiar?

On the other hand, we also experience being strangers in our world. Some feel this more sharply, others less so, but everyone has the experience. Perhaps I can just describe a little of how I have experienced this feeling in the last few years. In doing so, I am not saying that this is any kind of special religious experience.

Stranger in one's own land, stranger in one's own house

I live in Frankfurt am Main, my home town. It is a city of soaring skyscrapers, while deep beneath them lies a world of chaos. All the same I love it; after all, I was born there. Every day I have to go downtown. I used to go by car, but then parking grew scarcer and scarcer, ecological awareness expanded, and the streetcars improved their schedules. So for a number of years now I have been going by streetcar. But what do I see around me? Every skin color, every imaginable language, the faces of all nations, newspapers in unknown tongues, clothing from every continent, and sometimes

I ask myself: is there one other German face in this car? It is not that I don't like this mixture of peoples, but suddenly I have the feeling that I am a stranger, or more precisely that I am a foreigner in my own land.

And then there are all the other factors: I am getting older and am now retired, but I still live in the college where I have lived and worked for decades. I am beginning to notice that I am not current with everything that is happening there. My fellow residents who are still fully engaged in work are talking about people and things I don't know. Not only that: they have new ideas, new feelings. I notice that new generations are coming on board. And suddenly I feel myself a stranger in the place where I used to be completely at home. A stranger in my own house, one might say. This intensifies the experience I spoke of before, of being a foreigner in my own land.

Why have I written all this? It may be that some readers have had comparable experiences. Perhaps we have come a little closer together in our common knowledge of what it means to be a stranger, even and especially where we really should be at home.

This is certainly a more poignant feeling of strangeness than what tourists experience when they travel, for example, from the flatlands to the mountains, where they are overjoyed at entering at least once and for a short time into a world that is foreign to them. It is even a different experience from that of refugees, who in these times are coming in waves, now from one direction, now from another. They flee to a foreign land under intense pressure. They really would have greatly preferred not to have this fate forced upon them. The strange experience I am talking about, though, is that of being a stranger where one really should feel at home.

I think that we have the same kind of experience, in fact that we may feel it most deeply and with a special kind of shock and horror, when we come in contact with the God who spoke to our ancestors Abraham, Isaac, and Jacob, and called them by name.

As far as our image of God is concerned, nowadays we really have almost only *one* task: to free ourselves from our own God-images and to learn who the real God is. The real God is not the golden base of our own souls. The real God is not the distant Unimaginable and the eternal Silence behind the universe. The real God is certainly not a demon. The real God is the living God, the one the Bible shows us. One of the colors in that picture, especially in the stories of the patriarchs and matriarchs, is this: that contact with this God makes people strangers in their own world.

How that occurs, what happens, and what it means—being made a stranger by God—is what I want to explore here.

Up to now I have painted this being-a-stranger as something negative and burdensome, as I have experienced it recently and as many other people certainly do also. But let us not presuppose even that much. We should not exclude from the outset the possibility that this business of being made a stranger by God may have a thoroughly positive aspect as well. We want simply to seek in the biblical narratives about the patriarchs and matriarchs for instruction about what it means to say that God can make strangers of us: what kind of darkness is involved, but also what kind of light it may contain.

Abraham leaves home

Our topic constitutes the very beginning of the narratives of the ancestors in Genesis. It is true that there is a preceding transition from the primeval history to the patriarchal/matriarchal history: the genealogy of Shem (Gen 11:10-32). That forms the bridge. At its end is Terah, the father of Abraham, Nahor, and Haran. Terah was already a mobile man: he planned to move from Mesopotamia to Canaan.

However, that was a self-chosen migration. It did not succeed. Halfway there, in Haran, the tribe stopped and did not go farther. Nevertheless: Canaan was already an old family dream. A move away from home, into the unknown, had some meaningful associations for this family. Perhaps it was simply a matter of necessity, which drives most migrants even now. But there is also the lure of the strange and the new.

As I have said, the migration did not succeed. Moreover, the genealogy ends with the statement that Abraham's wife Sarai was barren. Childlessness, when not desired, also makes one a stranger, in that culture even more than today. A family becomes a dead branch on the tree of the larger clan. It becomes marginal, because the future is withdrawn from it. It no longer belongs to the "normal" state of things, and so acquires a species of strangeness for the others, the ones who are "normal."

The transitional text in the second half of Genesis 11 is thus not only a genealogical bridge; it brings us very close indeed to the first motif that will shape the ancestral narratives. We are already being secretly prepared for the leaving of the homeland, for estrangement from the family. All this exists only in the briefest remarks, the bare bones of facts without any narrative flesh on them, certainly without any evaluation. Nevertheless, we as readers are somehow prepared for what will come at the beginning of chapter 12.

Now, however—and this is what is new—God takes this business of estrangement in hand:

Now the LORD said to Abram,
"Go from your country

and your kindred
and your father's house
to the land that I will show you." (Gen 12:1)

How God says this to Abraham, we are not told. Later there will be visions by night and divine appearances. Here, at the beginning of the story of Abraham, everything is concentrated on the matter at hand, the thing Abraham is called to do. Perhaps this narrative reticence is important for us. If Abraham were introduced here as a visionary, we, if we do not have a vision, might feel that we are dispensed from the possibility that God could call us into a foreign world.

In any case Abraham does not act on the basis of calculation, and not even out of a yen for change; he receives a call from without, unexpected despite all that has happened in his family's prehistory, and that call tears him away from all his attachments. He is to "go," to "go forth."

This going forth, this letting go, is specified in three ways: country, kindred, father's house. Terah, his father, had emigrated with his whole household. They had left their home country, but the clan constituted a kind of portable homeland. The Hebrew world for "kindred" *(moledet)*, while it implies the idea of physical relationship, often gives the impression of carrying with it the notions of common childhood experience, common socialization. Language, culture, memories, the multitude of human relationships within a broader kinship—all these can be more enduring and sustaining than a landscape or familiar towns and streets.

But Abraham is to leave all that. Still more: he is to leave his father's house, which represents the family in the narrower sense. This man who sees no future within his own family because his wife cannot give him children is now to sever his connection with the last stem, the one on which he had grown, the reality for whose more fruitful branches he still could have lived a useful life.

This threefold step—from his country, from his cultural community, from his closest family—reveals even in its language, through intensification, the radicality of the alienation that Abraham's God demands of those who worship him. It is something different from what Terah had started when he attempted to lead a large group of people with their own cultural identity on a well-planned migration to a different territory. This move, too, has a goal, though in a very restricted degree. Abraham does not know where he is to go. There is a goal. God knows it, but does not name it. God will show it to Abraham on the way. Only then will Abraham see, with astonishment, that it is that very land of Canaan to which his father Terah had intended to travel on his failed, humanly-planned migration. But now, as he is leaving, he does not know that yet.

So he must go forth without immediately entering in. He simply has to "take a hike." And when we say "hike," we are not talking about a mountain hike from which we come home again at evening, or at least stop over in a hut. It is walking without knowing where one is headed.

That is to say, God *does* give some information in advance. The text goes on. We read the first part of what God said. Of course, the information is not exactly what one would like to hear. All it says is: "I will show you the goal of your going forth." But it continues:

> I will make of you a great nation,
> and I will bless you,
> and make your name great,
> so that you will be a blessing.
> I will bless those who bless you,
> and the one who curses you I will curse;
> and in you all the families of the earth shall be blessed. (Gen 12:2-3)

To begin with, this turns upside down Abraham's fate as it has been thus far: the dead branch of the family shall, if he agrees to be completely sawed off, become just the opposite. He is to be full of blessing, that is, full of God-given, life-producing powers. He will be so in a way that bursts all normal measures. The genetic zero shall become a powerful nation, known and admired everywhere—for that is what the great "name" means. And still more: the fate of all nations will depend on their attitude toward this people, and the end of God's ways with what Abraham shall become will be blessing for all.

There is nothing greater than this. Here God tosses Abraham into the tide of a universal plan for history. But we may never forget: this is said to a person who is at the end of his hopes, and whom God is tearing radically away from the last thing that still sustained him. And it is a glimpse of the distant future. The more glowing it is, the more hesitant are the near future and the next steps of the one who is being alienated from everything, and the more shrouded in darkness.

The irritating darkness of the alienation into which God can rip someone is thus not without some light. But it is a light that stands like a star somewhere in the night sky, beautiful to look at, but powerless to help us in any way to see the path on which we are to take our next steps.

When we read beyond these first verses of Genesis 12 we discover an Abraham who is continually being shown the night stars of heaven, but whose feet move tentatively forward and often take false steps from which his God has to snatch him back more than once.

Even when he knows that he has arrived in the land of promise, he cannot settle there. He wanders about in the land as a nomad, remaining a foreigner to the people of the land and to the land itself. And what kind of false paths does he have to follow before he begets a son to whom the initial promise can be attached! At the end of his life he is still so much a foreigner in the promised land that he sends his servant Eliezer to Haran to find a wife for the son of the promise among his former relations.

This is the human fate of someone snatched by God into foreign places! In our century we have seen so many migrants who have gone into strange lands, and through them we can more easily sense something of Abraham's fate than our fathers and mothers could in more orderly times when the world was not so much on the move. Beyond this, we may know not only from tales of the past and legends of the saints, but even from our own lives and from the paths followed by young people entrusted to us how God can snatch people from their human origins and their own life-projects and draw them slowly on long, tentative paths that lead only to the land that God promises them.

Perhaps some of us are also connected with new Christian groups who are having this same experience today, in their search for new forms of Christian life and Christian community. We know how they can suddenly stand face to face with the question of leaving everything that formerly was dear and natural to them, solaced only by distant stars in the heaven of promise, and setting out on a tentative path, on which they can scarcely make out their next step, and how in doing so they more and more become strangers in the world of their own origins, often even persecuted and branded as sects.

The call into foreignness as a Christian path and a God-driven Christian destiny, then, is something that touches us in our own time and world as well. The God whom Abraham encountered was the God who, by touching people, makes them foreigners in their world. That is not just a statement about the way God deals with us. It is a description of the very experience of God.

Real personal knowledge, after all, is not just a matter of knowing someone's name, having superficial information, being able to describe particular characteristics of the person. It grows from within and very indirectly to the extent that we have a common story. This is most obvious in the case of people who love one another. The longer they love and the longer they live together, the less they can say about each other, it seems. That is not because they no longer know or understand each other; it is precisely because they understand each other so deeply. Of course, as our understanding of another deepens, our awareness of his or her uniqueness, and thus incomprehensibility, grows. But there is something else going on. We do not understand the other through direct insight. In human encounter we learn to know the other more and more at depth as we come to understand more and more deeply what the other thinks about us, what she or he trusts us with, hopes for from us. By discovering what the other projects through me into the world I come to understand who and what she or he is.

It is no different with God. The more we learn through experience what God promises us, but also what God expects and demands of us in our next, tentative steps, the more is it clear to us, at a point deep within us, who God is. In this sense it is quite central to our genuine knowledge of God that we, like Abraham, discover that God is the God who calls us into strangeness and allows us to exist as foreigners in a world that understands us less and less because we are growing more and more beyond it.

However, I want to say explicitly that this does not imply some kind of program of detachment from the real world. Abraham was not called to be a desert ascetic in order to become spiritual: by no means! His calling was about land, people, and a blessing of fruitfulness. But right within this concrete reality of life is where the foreignness happens when God touches a person, or a group of people, and begins to lead them. In the concrete experience of being led in this world one gradually learns what it means to say that our God is a God who makes strangers of us.

What sustains us then is the power of faith. In it we can trust this God who deals with us so oddly. Thus knowledge of the God who makes people into foreigners is in a very deep sense a testimony of faith, which cannot be had otherwise. We have to surrender ourselves to such paths. The story of Abraham can teach us that. In this way we learn who the God of Abraham, Isaac, and Jacob is.

But we are by no means finished with the subject of "being made strangers by God." The narratives of the ancestors show us some very different faces of our theme.

Jacob flees into foreign places

Abraham was no great moral hero, either. He followed the call and he never gave up believing in the promise, no matter how much he sometimes wavered. But all his mistakes and all his wavering were part of the whole story: that he traveled to a foreign land, and as a foreigner moved through the land that was supposed to be his own. It was different with Jacob, the other major figure among Israel's ancestors. He had to undergo another and completely different experience of the God who leads into strange places. Let us spend a little time with him.

What is new with Jacob, in contrast to Abraham, is the sin of the one who is called and a different way of being a stranger, one that is connected with that sin. The biblical story of Jacob is pointed to this new theme from the outset. The promise once given to Abraham is revealing its first stages of fulfillment. Childless mothers bear children. A new family from which a people can arise is already in place. They are still in the land of promise, although only as tolerated aliens. But within the common world of promise, within this "holy family," if you will, the family that joins together in bearing—even in constituting—the foreignness into which God has dragged them, there now arises an *internal* division, an *internal* conflict.

The ancient symbol that human imagination has contrived for the deepest division that can exist between people who belong together is that of twins. And right away, here are twins in the biblical narrative. Rebecca, the wife of Isaac, bears twins in her first lying-in. The later strife is distantly foreshadowed at their birth: one comes out first, but the other tries to hold him back by grasping his heel. Esau, the firstborn, who according to the cultural model of the time was solely responsible for carrying on the line of promise, is so bamboozled and taken for a ride by Jacob, the second son, beginning in childhood and conclusively when the two become young men, that the blessing of the aged father Isaac finally comes to rest on Jacob—with the result that Jacob, who inherits the right to the promise and puts Esau in second place, can no longer even hope to stay in the land promised to the family, though the family itself is still wandering about in the land as foreigners (Genesis 25–27).

We learn of a division, brought about by sin upon sin within the people of promise, a people just now beginning and scarcely possessed of any foreseeable future. But the God of Abraham will not abandon this plan. God writes straight with crooked lines. Ultimately our divided and splintered Christianity is much closer to the deep conflicts of Jacob's generation than to the problems of the ancestor Abraham, who received the first call and followed it in faith.

God does not overlook sin or act as if it had not happened. God forces Jacob to bear the consequences. Sin plays itself out. God accompanies the chosen one on the path carved out by sin; God accompanies Jacob, who is now the bearer of the promise, even though he has achieved it by betrayal and sin. The brother he betrayed pursues him and intends to destroy him. The complete twin theme storms across the land. Jacob, the weaker, must flee. So begins the new experience of foreignness, which Jacob, the disturber of God's plans, must undergo.

Jacob flees to the "people of the east," to the old, pre-Abrahamic tribal relatives; there he is received, he marries into the clan, he becomes rich, and in the end he has a large family, but he is in a foreign land, not in the place where he is supposed to carry on the promise. Those who are led by God into foreign parts cannot simply return to their former home. If they do, it will become for them, in an awful way, a very different kind of foreignness.

We really should go through all these many-layered stories in Genesis 28–31, and then those about the difficult and strange return in Genesis 32–35. Of course we cannot do that in such a short space. Everything Jacob has done in the past, all his sins, all his betrayals, now fall back on him. Others do to him what he had done to his brother. He has the wool pulled over his eyes well and properly by Laban, his father-in-law, and Laban's two daughters; they exploit him; he is helpless in a foreign land, cheated, with no one to help him, handed over to the wiles of his own relatives.

Of course there is no real relationship here any more; Abraham had abandoned it. These others remained in the old world and certainly never understood fully why Abraham separated from them. Even though Jacob, in his own behavior toward his brother, had already adopted their style of living, he no longer belonged to them. He was marked by his Abrahamic ancestry. He did not flee to those who were his own; he fled to the family from before, long since become strangers. That kind of foreignness can be harder than one without such a prehistory.

So he wanders for twenty years among the people of the east, as a stranger; he serves seven years for the woman he loves, and when the wrong one is slipped him at his wedding he serves another seven years for the right one. He only gets free in the end by fleeing in secret and extorting his right to return home.

That is the foreignness of the chosen people, which they also fashion for themselves by their sins. It is marked by a new and greater distress, and yet it is strangely permeated by an enduring divine blessing. We need to read the stories of Jacob from that point of view, too.

Even during his flight Jacob's God comes to him at Bethel and assures him that he will return home and that the promises will endure. Even in the foreign land the blessing is always there, even when it grows out of the tricks of the betrayer, and in the end, when he flees, he is a man rich in flocks and the head of a family with eleven, and then twelve sons, the ancestor of a nation that will be named after Jacob/Israel. The strange reconciliation with his brother Esau is successful, and Esau retires to a neighboring land east of the Jordan, leaving the land of promise to Jacob.

In these stories we meet the God who sends us, in our sins and because of sin, into a new, utterly ambiguous foreignness. The one-time home to which we, in our sins, tried to return becomes for us a new and bitter foreignness, but when we accept and acknowledge this new foreignness that we ourselves have created, even that becomes a promised blessing, and we can return to the land of promise. All these confusing connections are brought together, as in a mighty symbol, in that night-battle at the Jabbok (Genesis 32), where readers even today cannot tell who wins: Jacob or the angel with whom he fought.

In any case Jacob, the sinner and betrayer, much like and yet very differently from his ancestor Abraham, comes to know the God who can make people into foreigners. There is no returning from that exile. The attempt to return in guilt creates new strangeness. But God carries God's history forward even through that. It may be that the Jacob stories in Genesis are the Bible stories that the Church today ought to read most carefully.

But we have not yet finished with the theme of the God of Abraham, Isaac, and Jacob, who makes God's own people into foreigners. There is still a third figure of foreignness to be found in these stories in Genesis. We now come to Joseph, who was sold into Egypt.

Joseph is sold into a foreign land

Jacob's return does not put an end to the conflict within the family that is to become the people of God. Former deeds are still falling back onto the patriarch's head. Now he must see how the old war between brothers continues to seethe in the power struggles among his own sons, so that the son he loves most, the one for whose sake he endured so many years in a foreign land, becomes a new victim. Joseph is sold into Egypt by his brothers, and so thrust outside the realm of the promise (Genesis 37).

Here is a new image for the experience of becoming a stranger within God's saving work in history. Now God does not make a single person into a foreigner in order to begin the work of salvation in this world. And God does not follow as the sins of the chosen one thrust him into a new exile, as in the case of Jacob. This time other people force an innocent person outside the sphere of the promise in order to get rid of him. Joseph is sold as a slave, loses his identity, and really becomes a foreigner—foreign to his family, which is the place of the promise.

And God is also at work here. We have to read the long story of Joseph in light of the end. Then it is clear that what happened, and was only resolved through such great agony, even though it arose out of the most brutal hatred between brothers, was at the same time a saving act of God, who desires to bring about good.

For in the very moment when Joseph, in tears, makes himself known to his brothers, when they are utterly confused and confounded, he tells them: ". . . do not be distressed, or angry with yourselves, because you sold me here, for God sent me before you to preserve life" (Gen 45:5).

This is followed by another dramatic climax. When Jacob dies the brothers fear that the old father was the reason why Joseph did not take vengeance on them. Now they expect it, and they send messengers from afar to beg him again for forgiveness. Joseph weeps again; once more he calls his brothers to him, and again he says:

> "Do not be afraid! Am I in the place of God? Even though you intended to do harm to me, God intended it for good, in order to preserve a numerous people, as he is doing today." (Gen 50:19-20)

Here, then, we have a clear dissociation between human ideas and divine ideas about the same event. The former are evil; the latter, God's ideas, are directed to preserving life. The ultimate winner is God. But despite all the differences between human and divine thinking we cannot close our eyes to the fact that both, in acting, used the same means and traveled the same road: an innocent person was sold into foreign lands, thrust down to the lowest level of foreignness, becoming a slave in a foreign land and among a strange people who could again sell him for money as if he were only an object. Can anyone be more foreign, from a social perspective, than when he or she falls between the millstones of a world that deals in human beings? It was into that kind of foreignness that God brought the innocent one among the brothers.

The Bible emphasizes and appreciates that Joseph really became a foreigner. First he was torn from all his own ties and relationships in order that, having been sold, he might be transported to a strange land. There he had no other choice than to transform himself, first as a slave, accommodating himself to the new world. The more he rose socially from his inferior situation, the more he was transformed into an Egyptian. That must have been a deep internal shift. It must have been deepened especially when he founded an Egyptian family. When his brothers came to Egypt they did not recognize him. That is how different he must have become. He knew them, so it must be that the old world of his youth and his own family remained alive, deep within him. But the Egyptian overlay must have thrust it all very deep down. In this story, then, Joseph became a foreigner in a multiform and intricate way.

It is very important to this story that Joseph did not give up his God. This is made clear in a flash when Potiphar's wife tries to sleep with him (Gen 39:7-10). His will to hold fast to his God breaks suddenly through. And his God is also with him. We cannot read the whole story of Joseph's rise out of the depths of the Egyptian prison to the highest administrative office in the land in any other way than as a continual chain of miraculous moments of divine guidance. Joseph did not read them any differently, and thus at the end of it all he could summarize it in a single sentence: God desires to preserve the life of many.

This God allowed him, through the guilt of others, to become the lowest and most helpless foreigner in a strange world, but at the same time God effected the salvation of many people from hunger through the suffering of an innocent person. Here, with Joseph, we see for the first time that the promise to Abraham includes a blessing for all the tribes of the earth. We also get an inkling that God is a God who does not shrink from demanding of a human being the highest degree of alienation—in Jesus, the ultimate alienation of death on a cross.

Let me conclude. Of course I have by no means been able to exhaust all that the book of Genesis tells us about the God of Abraham, Isaac, and Jacob. There is still so much more in these deep stories, and we have to read them over and over again with new eyes. But perhaps I can apply a single observation: we are never disappointed when we seek the God of salvation who desires good things for all creatures, but we seem to be led far away from images of God that we desire to create out of a golden fund within our own souls or that we shape according to our own banal, liberal, impoverished ideals. The encounter with God destroys the world in which we have made ourselves at home; it changes us at depth and tosses us into a new destiny. We may be utterly terrified, but at the same time we experience a dimension of happiness that we never suspected could be.

Chapter Three

Conquest or Return?
Reading Joshua Today

Oslo 1994: it was like the dawn of hope. Can there yet be peace in the "Holy Land"? Since then the situation is again such that no one can tell what may happen. Why, we wonder, is everything about this question so unspeakably grim? We know that somehow it has something to do with the Bible. But if that is the case, then we European and American Christians are not mere observers. We, too, live out of the Bible, no matter how seldom we give it a thought. So I, as an Old Testament scholar, will presume to ask the question: "Does the Bible say anything about who owns the Holy Land today, and how the people who live there now should behave toward one another?"

If we put the question this way there is only one thing to do: look closely and see what the Bible says—especially what place, on the whole, the Bible assigns to violent force. Of course that will not give us a complete view of the conflict, and certainly will not furnish any political advice. But it may help us to understand. It may even force us to reflect a little on ourselves. Ultimately the task is to find the hermeneutic concealed in the Bible itself for the texts that drive the participants today.

First I need to limit the question. On the basis of the media reports, often highly simplified, we almost always accept what is happening as a hot point in the conflict between the Judeo-Christian civilization of the West and the Islamic civilization of the Middle East. Palestine appears to be a boil on the surface of the globe, the point of a feverish eruption that may soon engulf the whole body: the clash between a culture that has experienced the Enlightenment and what is basically a medieval fundamentalism. That is how the Islamic world sees it, and we accept their schema of friend and foe.

But this theory of the conflict in Palestine cannot be accurate, for the people of Palestine are not only Muslims. There are many Arab Christians who are often completely missing from the picture. They are the most destitute victims of the conflict, as is clear from the fact that their number is steadily shrinking. Many see no way to save themselves and their families except by leaving their homes and emigrating. A few decades ago, Bethlehem was still a Christian city—Arabic, Palestinian, but Christian. Now there is no longer a Christian majority. Everyone who could manage it has emigrated.

Because this is about the Bible, I want to set aside the usual schema altogether. I will eliminate the Muslim majority of Palestinians, which forms our picture of the population, from my reflections. That group is not shaped by the Bible, at least not directly. I will speak only of the Israelis on the one hand and the Christian Palestinians on the other.

These two groups are located within the biblical field of gravity. There is more reflection recorded on the Israeli side. There is an argument about what the Bible really says—parallel to the political divisions in Israel as well—right up to the biblical reasons given for the murder of the Israeli Prime Minister on November 4, 1995. Yitzhak Rabin was not alone; he had a large portion of the population behind him. He sought peace, seeing it as the real Judaism. Thus his murder also indicates dissension over the Bible. The Christian Arab side is more muffled, more confused. It has few intellectuals, and it does not have its own tradition of theological reflection on the Bible. There are almost no offers of help from Christian theologians in other places, and those that exist scarcely penetrate this suffering world. But for that very reason, theologians from other countries need to think through these questions.

Popular hermeneutics, Palestinian and Israeli

Let me first attempt to describe the average conception of the Bible in each of these two groups—the Christian Arabs and the Israelis—in the context of the present struggle. As far as the Bible goes, what is mainly at issue is the book of Joshua and its depiction of the radical destruction of all the residents in the land, the "seven nations" (cf. Deut 7:1), through the *ḥerem* ("ban," "dedication to destruction"). This cruel conquest of the land took place in every detail at God's command, as the book of Joshua repeatedly emphasizes. The theory behind it is found in the book of Deuteronomy, and consequently we must keep that book in view as well.

How did Arab Christians read the book of Joshua in the past? They were small farmers in the countryside, craftsmen or merchants in the towns; they were the women of those families. They liked to listen to the Old Testament at worship or in religious instruction classes. They knew it well. It told about their own homeland. They knew the places that were conquered in the book of Joshua; maybe they even lived in one of them. As a matter of course they identified with the Israelites who entered the land under Joshua's leadership. They felt themselves to be successors to those Israelites. God had given the land, back then, to the Palestinians of today. The history of Israel was their own history. At some point these Jews had become Christians. Probably no one, or scarcely anyone, considered the idea that they were descended from Philistines or other non-Jewish inhabitants of the land in ancient times. They had some vague notion that there was still a Jewish people living in small groups in Palestine and dispersed throughout the whole world, and that these people's heart was still attached to the land, that in spite of the long time that had elapsed they still thought of themselves as people driven from their homeland—but that had nothing to do with the Arab Christians' understanding of who they themselves were.

Then the Jews arrived in great numbers. The state of Israel was established. The various Arab-Israeli wars were fought. In the end the whole land was in the hands of Israel. At this point our Arab fellow Christians experienced a rupture in their relationship to the Bible that still shapes the picture today. They suddenly realized: this is a different people, who lay claim to the same holy books as their Bible. They identify, just as we do, with the Israelite conquerers of the land in the book of Joshua. In their eyes we, the established inhabitants of the land, represent the seven nations whom Joshua exterminated at God's direction. The shock was so great that the normal reaction of Christian communities today is: we don't want to hear any more about that book; it is not to be read in our worship services. Away with the Zionist Old Testament!

Alongside this picture we should place a model of the Bible-oriented Israelis. In the first phases of the Zionist immigration these were for the most part not Torah-observant Jews. There were some of those, but the Zionist immigrants were more likely to be emancipated, educated civil libertarians, perhaps agnostic, perhaps imbued with anarchist or socialist ideas of the previous century, especially those involved in the kibbutz movement. But even in this non-religious milieu the Bible quickly became the most important book. It was the classic document of Ivrit, successfully developed out of ancient Hebrew to be the language of Israel. It helped the immigrants to feel at home in the hills and valleys of the land as they had in their old homes. It awakened love for this land, to which they may at first have fled purely as a refuge from the perils of Antisemitism and the Shoach. For the next generation, born in the land, it was the classic school textbook. Most Israelis know large chunks of it by heart.

Later there came new waves of Jewish immigrants, some from Arab lands. They brought a greater measure of religious zeal than the first waves. Those who returned from Yemen may be seen as typical. For them the book of Joshua, which for the previous immigrants was only a geographical guide and a classic of their native language, had religious authority. The inhabitants of the land against whom Joshua once fought merged in their minds with the Palestinians who attempted to prevent Jewish settlements in the land and created bloodbaths with their suicide bombs. The book of Joshua offered a model for how to behave toward such people in the land. At least one could claim the right to armed defense of one's own settlements not only as an emergency measure but also on the basis of the Bible. Was one not, in fact, obligated to prevent a Prime Minister from violating the command of God given on Sinai: "Take care not to make a covenant with the inhabitants of the land to which you are going" (Exod 34:12; cf. Exod 23:32; Deut 7:2)? That was exactly what Yitzhak Rabin had done, and therefore a law student of Yemeni descent, Yigal Amir, felt obliged to "execute" him in the name of God at the end of a peace rally.

But it is not just a question of such extremes. More important is what perhaps half or more than half of the ordinary Israeli population feels today, even many who wept over this murder. It can be stated this way: The Bible expects us to fight for this land, just as Joshua and the people of the twelve tribes once did. We not only have a right to settle there: we are required to do so.

Thus two completely opposite ways of applying the same book of Joshua, and with it the whole of the Old Testament, to oneself and to one and the same land of Palestine stand opposed to one another. It is no help at all to tell both sides something like: "Let the Bible be the Bible and think more about tolerance and human rights!" Obviously we have to think constantly of tolerance, justice, and the obligation to keep the peace. But neither of these groups is prepared to let the Bible be the Bible, neither those who read in it a promise of the land to their people nor the others who now refuse to read it in their worship, although they suffer greatly from it. On both sides the people's existence is much too deeply rooted in the Bible for that to happen.

It is clear that both mentalities are not as inaccessible to mutual understanding as appears to the parties involved, if only from the fact that they both have to work hard to find a basis in their own traditions for the way they deal with the book of Joshua.

There is a hardcore group of traditionalist Jews with a mystical style of devotion who reject the state of Israel altogether. According to them the land will not be given back to the people of Israel through human might, but only by God, when the Messiah comes. This attitude has good roots in the classical Jewish tradition of biblical interpretation. For example, Moses Maimonides, the greatest Jewish scholar of the Middle Ages, explicitly refused to see God's commandment to Joshua to destroy the inhabitants of the land as applicable to his own time. It was still fully valid, but it did not refer to just any inhabitants of the promised land; it applied only to seven named nations, and they no longer existed. So much for the rootedness of present Jewish reference to the book of Joshua in the Jewish tradition.

On the other side, we must ask where in all of worldwide Christianity we would find anyone who shares the conviction that the Christians who now live in the Holy Land have a different relationship to their land than Christians in other lands throughout the world have with respect to their native lands. Are there any Christians who think that Palestinian Christians have taken on the role of the nation of Israel in some special way? I see nothing of the sort, nor do I find it in the classical theological traditions of Christianity. Perhaps there is a connection between this and the fact that in recent years Christianity has not developed a particularly notable solidarity with Palestinian Christians. In fact, there is scarcely any to be found.

Hence we must admit that there is a lack of tradition on both sides, both in Christian Palestinian indignation about the "Zionist" character of the Old Testament and in the new Israeli interpretation of the book of Joshua in their confrontation with the Palestinian inhabitants of the land.

One other thing should be noted: both interpretations of the book of Joshua and the whole of the Old Testament are as similar in their basic position as they are opposite in their end results. That position is, ultimately, fundamentalistic, but to avoid that negative label I would prefer to say that on both sides the book of Joshua is being read "typologically." That is: at the time when the Israelites first entered their land there occurred the "type" of an event that has recurred in our own time in its "antitype." It is the immigration of a people chosen by God into the land of Palestine, then as now. Hence according to the typological view it is true that the way things happened before is the way they should happen now. God's commandments at that time are also God's commandments for today. Because the book is read in this way the Jewish settlers, on the one hand, can find their legitimation in it, while on the other hand the Christian Palestinians feel so rejected that they are no longer willing to read the book of Joshua as the word of God in their worship services. Both find in it the basis for their convictions about divinely willed violence.

The hermeneutical question, then, seems to me to be: is it the sense of the Bible that the book of Joshua be read typologically with regard to present problems? The answer, in my opinion, must be given in terms of biblical scholarship, and not merely in light of a modern hermeneutics that we might find it comfortable to fling over it. The answer is: no. Now let us see why that is so.

First I want to ask in what sense the book of Joshua could be at all relevant to the present struggle in Palestine, in terms of the book itself and of the present historical hour. I will first proceed in terms of history.

The promise of return that concerns us today has no prototype in the book of Joshua

Israel's seizure of the land as depicted in the book of Joshua, as a single campaign by the people of the twelve tribes involving the destruction of all the inhabitants of the land, never happened. In spite of the scholarly controversies about Israel's early period that are constantly bubbling up, there is general agreement on this point. The migration of the people and the complete conquest of the land and radical elimination of the seven nations described in the book of Joshua, in the striking narrative form it now has, stems at the earliest from the time of King Josiah of Judah in the seventh century B.C.E. It certainly contains older elements of tradition, but they are erratic, and they have been deliberately manipulated, systematized, and generalized by the authors. The narrative technique was inspired by certain topoi in the Assyrian royal inscriptions. We cannot even suppose that the composition was intended to present a "historical" reconstruction of Israel's beginnings. Thus no one can say that it happened the way it is described.

What was the authors' intention at the time? If I am right in placing the fundamental conception of the book of Joshua under Josiah, the book made its statement at a time when Israel, at the end of the royal era, had once again lost almost the whole of its land, with nothing left except the city of Jerusalem and a few remnants of the land of Judah surrounding it. In the form of a grand saga of the beginnings, the book said to its addressees of that time, in a broadly sketched symbolic portrait: By the will of your God, the whole land belongs to you. God would leave it to you, and to the extent it has already been lost would restore it to you, if only you would radically trust in God. God is victorious over all opponents, on behalf of all who trust in God.

It is necessary to read this whole depiction from the margins; in its totality it begins at the opening of Deuteronomy, with the failure of the attempt to conquer the land described in the narrative of the spies, directly after Israel has left Sinai. Moses explicitly states that this was because of a lack of faith (Deut 1:32). The successful conquest under Joshua was a pure gift of God, as the summation by the narrator at the original end of the book of Joshua emphasizes (Josh 21:43-45). The key point is the radicality of the wars described, which is the narrative symbol for the radicality of Israel's trust in God and not a historically-understood assertion of a military scorched-earth technique at the beginning of Israel's history. All that is part of the original intention of the book, and is not a reinterpretation later imposed on it.

It is true that at the end of the seventh century, under Josiah, there existed the intention to win back the lost parts of the land, since the Neo-Assyrian empire was collapsing. But Josiah could scarcely have had in mind a campaign of conquest and destruction. His intention was rather a process of annexation, carried out quietly and with a wink of agreement from the neighboring powers, especially Egypt. In this last case it appears to have failed, as shown by Josiah's death at Megiddo in the year 609. Apparently Egypt regarded the whole Syro-Palestinian region as its sovereign possession in which individual states could lay claim only to as much territory as Egypt permitted them. Josiah evidently exceeded those limits. Under such circumstances there could have been no thought whatsoever of real military actions.

In order that there might be no mistake, and so that it would be clear from the outset that the techniques of war depicted in the book of Joshua were not valid for the present time of Josiah, the book of Deuteronomy, which was combined with the book of Joshua even in this early stage of the history of their composition, made some clear theoretical statements. While it is true that Moses commanded the destruction of the seven peoples of the land in the name of God at the time of the conquest (Deut 7:1-2 and frequently thereafter), in Deut 20:10-20 he established a law of warfare that drew a clear distinction between later wars and the unique war of conquest under Joshua (Deut 20:15-18). The latter touched only the seven peoples, and for all later wars such a strategy of elimination was expressly forbidden. In Josiah's time the seven peoples had long since disappeared. Some of them were in any case only matters of rumor and may never in fact have existed. Hence there should be no doubt that, even at the moment when the book-complex of Deuteronomy and Joshua was first conceived, the destruction of the inhabitants of Palestine was reported not as a model for current or later imitation, but with the intention I have described above.

Soon after the book of Joshua was completed in its formal and critical basic structure, in 587 B.C.E. Jerusalem was destroyed by the Babylonians. The elite of the land were deported to Babylon. Israel's autonomous existence in the land promised to its ancestors had come to an end. A literary reflection of the new situation is found in the books of Deuteronomy to 2 Kings, a complex unit developed during the period of the Exile. This complex of texts is effectively a look backward at seven centuries of failed history. At the end Israel is no longer in its land; God's promise of the land was made in vain. The books are intended to explain how this collapse of all the promises came about. The high point of the portrayal is the existence of Israel as a state. The kings drove Israel into the abyss because they broke it away from its God and from full reliance on God alone.

Within this historical work interpreting the past, the book of Joshua has a fixed function in service of the principal statement. At the beginning of this course of history it presents a brilliant contrast to what later occurred when Israel took form as a state. It depicts a faithful immediacy to God, concentrated in the time of the beginnings, mediated only by Joshua, not by a state. In this immediacy of faith Israel acquires its land—that is, its happiness. Then, in light of later epochs, it is shown how the people frittered away what they had won.

On this literary level also, then, there is nothing to be found that would signal any further insistence on the historicity of the things depicted in the book of Joshua. The older description was simply taken over and given a broader function in the new complex of statements. At this literary level there can be no question of any idea of a return to the land. To that extent any notion of an intended typological statement regarding the future is simply inappropriate.

The Babylonian Exile was a radical caesura in Israel's history. It could even have been the end of that history. But prophets appeared, promising a new beginning and a new future. There was a movement of conversion that took those promises seriously and thus contained the possibility for a new beginning. In this connection the theme of "land" was, of course, acute once more. The leaders were exiled abroad. Where would the future of the people of God take place? Somewhere else? Or in the land once promised, inhabited, and then lost through their own sins? The promise of the land to Abraham, Isaac, and Jacob, presumed by the Deuteronomy of Josiah's time, was effectively finished. Or was God maintaining it, and was it still valid? Would there be a return, a kind of new entry into the old land?

The prophets of the Exile promised that return. God would again gather Israel from among the nations in which it was scattered and replant it in its old land. In fact, from the time of the conquest of the Babylonian empire by Cyrus the Persian groups had repeatedly returned from the diaspora to the homeland. Around the rebuilt Temple in Jerusalem there arose a new Jewish community life. It was only the destruction of the Temple by the Romans in 70 C.E., and ultimately the Islamic conquest of the land half a millennium later, that again broke apart Israel's presence in its land. From then on there were only tiny, oppressed Jewish groups living there, but they were no longer normative for the place—until the Zionist return movement began.

It is important for the historical assessment of these things that since the Babylonian Exile all of Israel has never returned to its homeland. From that time onward a large portion, ultimately the vast majority of the people has lived in other nations, believing the prophetic promises that some day the hour of return would strike for all of them. If we look for the foundations of the belief in this return to the land so long awaited, now occurring before the eyes of our generation, they are not to be found in the promise of the land to the ancestors, to Abraham, Isaac, and Jacob. That is only indirectly a part of this context, as a provisionally failed prehistory. The Zionist movement, to the extent that it places value on biblical foundations, is sustained by the exilic prophets' promise of return, after the catastrophe had already happened. That is how the early Zionists always understood it. It is by no means automatically the book of Joshua that sets the standard for the return. It is not a matter of a historical process supposedly depicted there and to be analogically repeated. Joshua belongs within the context of the first promise of the land and its fulfillment, not in that of the promise of return.

In addition, the prophets' promises of return contain no trace of a typological reference to the book of Joshua comparable, for example, to the consistent typologies of a new Exodus that we find in these same prophets, such as Deutero-Isaiah. At any rate, the few remote plays on it do not refer to the element of the population-destroying war of conquest. According to the prophetic texts that announce the return, that event is always a divine miracle having nothing to do with warfare. Nowhere do we find a post-exilic command of God to reconquer the land militarily.

There are only two small texts, Obad 17-21 and Zech 9:13-16, that appear to depict the repossession of the land in images of struggle. In Obadiah 18 we find the image of fire from which, it is said, there will be no escape. The key Deuteronomistic word *yāraš*, "take possession," is also key in this verse. But it is all the more striking that the other words associated with it in Deuteronomy and in Joshua, especially *ḥerem* ("dedication to destruction") are absent. Thus from the context fire and the inability to escape it can certainly be read as metaphorical. In no way can this passage be read as an instruction for action.

Nor is that the case in Zech 9:13-16. It is true that this text follows immediately after a statement about the final return from afar to the homeland, which will occur in the time of the Messiah (9:11-12). But the statements about war that follow in the text (9:13-14) do not refer to fighting against the inhabitants of the land, but rather to struggles with the "sons of *yāvān*," that is, the Greek world empire. However, here in a context in which the coming messianic king is depicted as absolutely peaceful (9:9-10) it appears that the idea of a final eschatological battle has been inserted, with the full reign of peace to follow afterward. This is probably because the peaceful king in 9:9 was described as "victorious." It has something to do with the return of the last "prisoners" from the "waterless pit" of the diaspora (9:11), but at most in a temporal and not a causal sense. In this scenario Israel has already been restored for a long time to the whole of its land (cf. 9:1-8).

To conclude this historical review: the book of Joshua depicts the fulfillment of the promise of the land to the patriarchs, but the gathering of the people of Israel in their ancient land in our century is not—biblically speaking—to be associated with that promise. It answers rather to the promise of return given to Israel, once again scattered among the nations of the earth. It has *nothing* to do with military conquest. A typological repetition of the conquest under Joshua is never in view in the biblical text in this context. In fact, the presentation in the book of Joshua itself, at the time when it was written, was not intended as a historical report, but as an image of radical trust in God.

The entire Bible read as "canon" does not make the book of Joshua a set of instructions for today.

The question of the proper hermeneutic for reading cannot be settled through historical observations. Neither Jews nor Christians read the Bible simply for historical information, as testimony to a historical development from which we might be able to draw lessons. We regard this book as the word of God. When we listen to it read in worship, when we pray or sing its texts, we apply it immediately to ourselves, taking it at least in some respects out of its original context.

This is the very point at which we find the origins of typological reading of the Bible, and this is where it is appropriate. Certainly the current typological treatment of the violent conquest of the land under Joshua arose, both for Jews and for Christian Palestinian groups, out of that kind of reading of the Bible, no matter how great a role archaeological and historical interests may have played, especially in Jewish circles. Hence we have to ask ourselves whether this kind of immediate and synchronic reading of the Bible does not lend the book of Joshua and its statements about destruction a new kind of authority.

In my opinion that is not the case, if we read carefully enough. Even when read canonically and synchronically the biblical text itself forbids an interpretation of the book of Joshua as a direct typological instruction manual for the return of Israel to its land. Within the book complex Deuteronomy-Joshua itself, in the prophets of the return, in the Old Testament canonical structure as a whole, and finally—at least for Christians—in the New Testament, a set of four barriers or restraints has been set up, one after another, to prevent such a reading.

1. Most important is the barrier set in the books of Deuteronomy and Joshua against a typological reading of the command to destroy the peoples of the land. The decisive statements are not in the book of Joshua, but in Deuteronomy, which proposes the theory. The book of Joshua only tells how it was carried out.

At the heart of the book of Deuteronomy, within the history told by the book's narrator, Moses makes laws. These are directly addressed to his audience within the story, the generation of Israel in Moab, not the readers of the book. But these are laws, that is, instructions for behavior that are valid from the time of their promulgation onward. So they apply to the readers as well.

This is a phenomenon similar to typological thinking: such laws are valid for Israel in perpetuity, that is, today as well. But Moses makes distinctions within the laws themselves. Some of them begin: "When you come into the land and live there, then . . . ." That means that these laws are attached to the land. When Israel is not in its land such laws do not apply. Something similar is true of the commandments to destroy the peoples of the land. According to their formulation and context they are valid for the moment when Israel under Joshua conquers its land. Moses says nothing about their validity in a repeated or similar situation centuries or millennia later. These are not even laws in the strict sense of the word; they are instructions for action in a particular, unique historical situation.

Even so, to prevent anyone from interpreting them typologically Moses builds something like a prophetic view of the future around the book of laws, all within the narrative world. As early as ch. 4 of the book of Deuteronomy he announces that Israel will be driven out of the conquered land because of its sins (4:25-31). Then in the threats in the chapter of sanctions (28:47 and following) and in 29:16-29 [MT 29:15-28] he takes up those prophecies again, and in ch. 30 he even promises a return to the land after exile and conversion (30:1-10). Thus Moses himself is a kind of prophet of the return.

Especially relevant for our question is the text of Deut 30:1-10. It is part of Moses' speech in 29:2–30:20 [MT 29:1–30:20] which, within the narrative world, draws together the ritual texts of the making of the covenant in Moab.

Two things strike us at the very beginning of this speech. In the review of the conquest of the northern lands east of the Jordan in 29:7-8 [MT 29:6-7], despite the frequent borrowings from the language of Deuteronomy 2 and 3, every single element of the destruction of the peoples is avoided. In addition, when the human partners to the covenant are listed in v. 11 [MT 10], "those who cut your wood and those who draw your water" refers to the Gibeonites of Josh 9:27, the only group of people who, according to the book of Joshua, managed to avoid being dedicated to destruction. The participants in the making of the covenant and, beyond them, the later readers are thus set at least mentally within a world in which destruction of peoples is not at issue.

From 29:22 [MT 29:21] onward Moses looks prophetically into the future—first, in 29:22-28 [MT 29:21-27], to the Exile. Here, in the rhetorical construction of a future scene, "all the nations" of the world appear on the world stage as an interpretive choir, with the descendants of Moses' current audience forming only a small part of the whole (v. 24; MT 23). They will all ask the reason for the catastrophe and will answer themselves, moving toward a confession of faith in YHWH, the God of Israel, who does justice within history. Thus in light of the catastrophe all distinctions between Israel and the other peoples disappear. What made the seven peoples so dangerous—that they could bring Israel to turn away from its God—is here reversed. The time will come when all the nations, together with Israel, will confess this God as the one who acts in history.

Then follows the prophecy of return in 30:1-10, sustained throughout its palindromic structure by the word *šub,* "turn," "return," "restore," "bring back," repeated seven times (30:1, 2, 3a, 3b, 8, 9, 10). The culminating statement in the text is not about return, but about the "circumcision of the heart" associated with it, accomplished by God. Its effect is that Israel can finally and enduringly love its God with its whole heart and soul (30:6). But before this, 30:5 has to speak of return. The accents set in 30:1-10 can only be fully perceived in an intertextual reading, with the reference texts especially ch. 4 and the last part of ch. 28, which together with Deuteronomy 29–30, as I have said, represent a future-directed frame around the laws. However, other passages of Deuteronomy also contribute. Formulations from those texts are taken up and incorporated. This reading technique also, of course, takes account of texts not referred to in the proof context, because non-reference or non-incorporation can also be a statement, namely a statement of omission.

It is true that Deut 30:1-10 speaks of "nations" or "peoples," but first of all, in vv. 1 and 3, only of the nations among which Israel was scattered, and from which it will then be gathered. God's "gathering" Israel from there (30:4) recalls the Exodus from Egypt (cf. 4:20). But nothing is said about the warlike actions of God at that time (cf. the long descriptive series in 4:34). Apparently no divine act of violence needs to be mentioned in connection with this gathering of Israel from among the nations.

The statement about the return to the land itself is formulated as a deliberate reflection of Deut 7:1, the introduction to the first appearance of the command to destroy the peoples of the land. The crucial word *yāraš*, "take possession of," also recurs, but there is nothing said about destroying the peoples of the land. While in 7:1 God clears away "many nations" from before Israel, according to 30:5—and the same word root is used, so that the text of 7:1 echoes in the ears of the hearers—God makes the returning people themselves "numerous" in their land.

In 30:7 there is talk of curses that God removes from Israel and imposes on others. But those others are "your enemies and . . . the adversaries who took advantage of you." Thus nothing is said about whole peoples, certainly not about the peoples of the land into which Israel is returning. The reference is probably to the oppressors of the Exile. Since there is a clear reference to Deut 7:15 and 28:60, there is also no thought of war and destruction; the background idea is the "diseases of Egypt" (28:60). Thus here again there is no notion of violent actions carried out by Israel in connection with the return.

In summary, we must say that for the readers of the whole book of Deuteronomy a typological application of the instructions for the destruction of the peoples of the land in connection with the conquest under Joshua is excluded not only as regards later wars following the conquest (cf. the war rule in Deuteronomy 20), but at least as clearly for Israel's return from the Exile. Thus a barrier is set up in the two interconnected books of Deuteronomy and Joshua against any typology of destruction on the model of Joshua.

2. For the prophets of return, as I have already said, Israel's return to its land is not only described as a pure divine miracle. Alongside the statements about the return are others that again work as a barrier against all attempts that may be made, despite the obstacles, to transfer the Joshua narratives through typological application.

First, there is the fact that these same prophets do indeed often predict gruesome and bloody fates for the nations of the world in times to come. The judgments pronounced over the nations are by no means mild. But it is all the more amazing that they are not directly connected with Israel's return to its land. They stand alongside it, but do not connect. This is again an eloquent statement by omission.

But then we find another group of texts in this context, having to do with Israel's relationship to the nations at the time when Israel will return to its land. At the end of the ages the nations will confess the one God, and the pilgrimage of nations to Zion will begin. In Jerusalem they will learn to beat their swords into plowshares (Isa 2:2-5//Mic 4:1-5). But that means the beginning of a positive relationship between Israel and the nations. It can even be said of them that when they "diligently learn the ways of my people, to swear by my name," they "shall be built up in the midst of my people" (Jer 12:16). They, too, will "possess the land" (Ps 25:13).

It is true that, as regards the groups from among the nations who will dwell with Israel in the land in time to come, the statements are at odds with one another. Often these are individual late additions to the primary texts that, depending on their authors and those authors' hopes and expectations, point in different directions. Thus the completely positive statement of Jer 12:16 contrasts with Isa 14:1-2 and 61:5, which seem to refer instead to a subjected group of people acting as servants. However, the very end of the book of Isaiah appears to say that there will even be priests and levites from among the nations on Zion (Isa 66:21). In any case, even in texts that seem to indicate a class distinction and a relationship of servitude there is nothing said about destruction or extermination.

The late prophets of the Old Testament thus see the Israel of the future days of promise restored to its land and enjoying prosperity there. This is accomplished through a broad communication with the other nations, who in the mean time have come to revere the true God, and that communication extends to those nations having a share in the land of Israel, even though it is decisively Israel's land. Such a sphere of promise surrounding the promise of return is undoubtedly a second barrier placed by the Old Testament against the application of a typology of Joshua-style violence.

3. Thus there arises a further question. The Old Testament is made up of its individual books, arranged in a particular order. Does this arrangement of the books alter the situation and give the book of Joshua a higher rank? But the third barrier arises precisely here.

The most fundamental canonical structure is created by the deep caesura between the book of Deuteronomy and the book of Joshua. Deuteronomy is the last of the five books of the Torah, which ends after the death of Moses. The book of Joshua is no longer part of it, and hence it is decidedly not part of Israel's exemplary "primeval history." This is also reflected in the order of Sabbath readings in the synagogue. There the Torah is read. After the death of Moses the reading begins again with the creation; it does not continue with Joshua. Through this delimitation the book of Joshua becomes the beginning of a description of an initial period in the history of Israel in its land, a period that is long since ended and cannot return in the same form because it was a failure.

For the "basic myth," contained in the Torah alone, the "gathering of Israel" in its land is still in the future. It is to be thought of as a return. Thus in a sense the Torah looks past the book of Joshua, directly to the return to the homeland. Thus the whole canonical structure of the Old Testament, through its innermost basic structure, also calls into question any typological understanding of the Joshua narrative.

4. Of course this is absolutely true of the Christian canon, expanded and modified by the New Testament. By no means is the New Testament untouched by the whole question of the "land"; in fact, it is a central question there also. The historical Jesus apparently regarded the "gathering of Israel"—no matter how he interpreted it—as his personal mission, and he rejected any kind of Zealot violence for that purpose. The evangelists underscore this. According to the writings of the New Testament, the time for the pilgrimage of nations to Zion has arrived with the advent of Jesus of Nazareth. The Sermon on the Mount is to be preached to the whole world (Matt 28:20), and according to it the meek will "inherit the land" (Matt 5:5).

What does this mean for those who believe in Jesus as Messiah—in the land of Israel and throughout the world? According to the letter to the Ephesians the "twoness" (of Jews and Gentiles) is made "oneness" in the Church because the dividing wall of hostility is broken down (Eph 2:14). The people of the nations cease to be strangers and aliens in the midst of Israel; they are fellow citizens within the holy people and members of the household of God (Eph 2:19)—and according to Old Testament usage the "house" of God means the "land."

This point of view is fully at home within the statements about Israel's return and the pilgrimage of the nations in the exilic and post-exilic prophets. The book of Joshua, by contrast, is not honored with a single quotation in the New Testament, which as a whole contains almost four hundred Old Testament citations. This is indeed a fourth and last barrier against a typological reading of the picture of violent conquest in the book of Joshua.

Be it well noted: if the New Testament statements are more than metaphors then it is true above all that this land was originally Israel's. On the basis of the New Testament it would by no means be legitimate to refuse the children of Israel the right to settle anywhere in the land, so long as they act justly. But at the same time, the nations are made companions of Israel. They receive a legitimate share in Israel's gifts, among which is the land. This obviously does not mean that now all the nations should move massively into the land of Israel, and certainly not that they should oppress Israel there. The New Testament aims entirely at peace and has no thought of resettlement, but that peace also includes an encounter in the land of Israel.

Certainly it would never have occurred to the New Testament writers that the Jews who were Jesus' disciples must for that reason abandon the land of their ancestors. In the New Testament the Jewish Christian community in Jerusalem is the mother church for the new communities among the Gentiles. Paul brings to the "poor" in Jerusalem (a biblical name of honor!) the gifts of the nations promised by the prophets when he carries his collection to Jerusalem.

It makes no sense with regard to the Palestinian Christians of today to do research on the origins of individual families and then rely on these details. But that there is a broad genetic and historical continuity between Jews who accepted faith in Jesus and Jews who converted to Islam on the one hand and the present Christian and Muslim Palestinians on the other hand is not something that should be concealed or kept secret, even if the Arab Christians are not "Jewish Christians" in the strictest sense (which would include a certain degree of Torah observance). But are we not touching here on the theological basis of Palestinian Christianity?

Palestinian Christians in their function as "Jewish Christians"

What I am going to say in conclusion can of course only be the thought of someone who argues on the basis of a Bible that includes the New Testament. But nowadays it has to be said to almost all Christians as if it were something entirely new.

We Christians have suppressed the idea that we have our salvation only through a sharing in the gifts of Israel, and as a result are thoroughly related to Israel. In turn, the people of Israel are practically unaware that the pilgrimage of nations to Zion that is prophesied in their sacred scriptures has long since begun. Thus we have the dreadful consequence that, through a typological interpretation of the book of Joshua that is false in itself, Palestinian Christians are written in where the book speaks of pagan and utterly sinful peoples, the "inhabitants of the land," the "seven nations"—and many Israelis see the Palestinian Christians in that position, as do many Palestinian Christians themselves.

At least the Palestinian Christians must simply refuse to agree to such an identification. It is right that they should insist on their inherited rights and their rights as human beings, but that is not yet something at the level of faith. On that level they must seek themselves once more in the New Testament, in the Jewish Christians of Jerusalem. Then they, from among all the nations, would have a special assignment on behalf of the entire Church, namely to be the link to the Jewish people that still awaits the Messiah because it cannot see that he has already come, and that nevertheless, despite this whole salvation-historical confusion, remains God's people.

We Christians outside the promised land have the duty, on behalf of the abandoned and helpless Arab Christians, to become aware of this biblical situation, to think it through and tell of it, and then to apply it to our Palestinian fellow Christians. It is the most important aid we can give them, because it is an assistance already given in the Bible to enable them to recover their identity. I am also convinced that it is only through such a route into the land promised to Abraham and since become a "Holy Land" for so many people and groups, a route that goes to the depth of things, that the peace we all desire can be won.

We Christians read the writings of the prophets, just as the Jews do. We look to the future with them. We await the fulfillment of the promises, and at the same time we know that the fulfillment has already begun. The breathtaking struggle between the Palestinians and the Israel that has returned to its land is taking place in this context. It is imbued with infinite suffering on all sides. It takes place against a background of guilt on all sides. We too, if we do not make adequately clear how our Christianity depends on its Jewish connections, take ever more guilt on ourselves and make all these things still more difficult.

These knots in history are such that only One can untie them: the Lord of history. He alone can give us renewed hope that, through and despite all tears, he will bring to fulfillment the words spoken by his prophets.

Chapter Four

Jeremiah and the Sacred Heart of Jesus
The "New Covenant"

In a postconciliar world in which many of the older forms of devotion have been suppressed it is refreshing to find that in the Canisianum in Innsbruck the great Sacred Heart tradition of the Tyrol is still being maintained, and in an intelligent manner. That same Canisianum has been instrumental in our century in alerting both Church and theologians to the antiquity and the biblical-patristic basis for devotion to the Sacred Heart of Jesus.

We only have to think of Hugo Rahner, who in his later years was rector of the Canisianum. At the beginning of the century Karl Richstätter had already pointed out the prehistory of the modern devotion to the Sacred Heart in medieval mysticism. But then Hugo Rahner, in the midst of World War II, demonstrated in a number of essays that even before the medieval Heart-of-Jesus mysticism there had been a great patristic theology concerning that Heart from which flow streams of living water. He traced the beginnings of this line of tradition in Asia Minor almost directly to the Fourth Gospel, especially John 7:38 ("out of the believer's heart shall flow rivers of living water") and 19:34 ("at once blood and water came out").

You ought to know what those articles meant at that time. The liturgical movement, which first became fully the official concern of the Church decades later as a result of the Second Vatican Council, was then surging powerfully upward from the Church underground. It was by no means, as in later times, primarily pastoral or catechetical in orientation. It certainly had no intention of destroying anything. Its only intent was to reawaken life drawn from the fullness of Christian liturgical celebration, and of course to restore its primeval Christian purity and symbolic power. But in the process it was almost inevitable that, for example, devotion to the Sacred Heart would be seen as a late modern embellishment of the Church year, and so would become suspect. Therefore it was very important to show, if possible, that this devotion came from the early patristic days, which were universally admired, and even that it opened access to a central symbol of that early period. Hugo Rahner succeeded in doing that.

I, too, grew up within the liturgical movement, and when I was a Jesuit novice shortly after the war some forms of devotion to the Sacred Heart, which suddenly surrounded me, seemed rather odd to me. I still remember how an older Jesuit pointed out Hugo Rahner's articles to me, and how they helped me through that conflict.

What is really strange is that at that time no one seemed able to go back any farther. Hugo Rahner and the others who at that time helped to uncover the true dimensions of devotion to the Heart of Jesus obviously knew that the phrase introduced by the evangelist John, "out of [the believer's] heart shall flow rivers of living water," had to come from the Old Testament prophets. But which ones? It was not a literal quotation, but a kind of abbreviated citation of a whole group of passages. We can now say without hesitation that it refers on the one hand to various promises of the end-time that speak of a spring flowing out of the Temple, and on the other hand to the wilderness stories in the Pentateuch that tell of water flowing from the rock. It was probably not possible, given the state of research, for anyone at that time to give countenance to such a biblical-theological overview, which can be best demonstrated from texts in the Targums.

It is typical that in the same volume of the *Zeitschrift für Aszese und Mystik* in which Hugo Rahner published his articles an Old Testament scholar wrote about the earlier bases for devotion to the Heart of Jesus. This was Gustav E. Closen, one of my predecessors at Sankt Georgen in Frankfurt. He consulted the Old Testament and found three small texts in Jeremiah 30, Psalm 22, and Psalm 16 that he regarded as messianic prophecies. In reading these pages one cannot avoid the impression that these three verses have been hauled kicking and screaming into the picture in a final, desperate effort to provide some proof. But if the mystery that so fascinated the Heart-of-Jesus mysticism of the Middle Ages and the Sacred Heart devotion of the modern period stems from the revelations of the Old Testament, it cannot be concealed in dubious texts of messianic prophecy that even the Church Fathers scarcely regarded as such. Its light must emerge from texts that are at the center of Old Testament theology.

It has always seemed to me that we ought to inquire further in this direction, and the need is greater today than ever, now that we Roman Catholics have gained a much closer relationship to the Bible, and the newer forms of biblical scholarship have opened new ways of access to it, and because we are obliged to give an entirely new account of our Christian path in dialogue with our Jewish contemporaries. In the course of the years I have discovered something in the Old Testament on the basis of which, I feel, we could again approach the great tradition of Sacred Heart devotion, even if we cannot demonstrate a continuity of tradition through the New Testament, the age of the Fathers, and the Middle Ages. Devotion to the Sacred Heart could, however, be newly connected to questions that are urgent for us today.

Hugo Rahner, as he indicates at one point, felt confident in writing his articles about the Sacred Heart because the Church had long since introduced the motif of the stream of water from the Savior's heart into the Daily Office for the feast of the Sacred Heart. In a similar way I may note that we find the Old Testament passage that is the focus of what I want to say as a reading for Lauds in the Roman Daily Office for the feast of the Sacred Heart.

This is the great passage in the book of Jeremiah about the new covenant, Jer 31:31-34. I want first to present the text, then put it in its biblical-theological context, and finally show how, contrary to first appearances, it leads us to the center of the tradition of devotion to the Sacred Heart and lends it dimensions that are otherwise obscured.

Jeremiah 31:31-34: The promise of a new covenant

The text in itself is rather short. It is the only one in the Old Testament that promises a "new covenant." There are, of course, similar statements, but none that speaks of a *"new covenant."* To that extent the text is extremely important for us Christians, who are convinced that we are living in the *"new"* covenant. It also constitutes a high point in the book of Jeremiah, and in fact in the whole of Old Testament prophecy, as well as in the Old Testament covenant theology rooted especially in the Pentateuch. All the more interesting, then, is what the text says about the new "covenant." Here is the text itself:

> [31] The days are surely coming, says the LORD,
> when I will make a new covenant with the house of Israel and the house of Judah.
> [32] It will not be like the covenant that I made with their ancestors
> when I took them by the hand to bring them out of the land of Egypt—
> a covenant that they broke,
> though I was their husband, says the LORD.
> [33] But this is the covenant
> that I will make with the house of Israel after those days, says the LORD:
> I will put my Torah within them,
> and I will write it on their hearts;

and I will be their God,
and they shall be my people.
34 No longer shall they teach one another, or say to each other,
[a man to his neighbor, a man to his brother]
"Know the LORD,"
for they shall all know me,
from the least of them to the greatest, says the LORD;
for I will forgive their iniquity,
and remember their sin no more.

The first thing that has to amaze us, when we hear it as Christians, is the human partner in both "covenants," both the old and the new. It is not, as we would expect at least in the case of the New Covenant, humanity, and most certainly not, as we postmodern contemporaries might perhaps wish, the single, autonomous individual. It is the people Israel. Only this people, but Israel really as a people, is God's partner in the "covenant."

When the beginning of the text says that God will make a new covenant "with the house of Israel and the house of Judah" it appears even more limited and detailed. But at the time of the Babylonian Exile, when this text was formulated, the end of the history of both divided kingdoms, "Israel" in the north and "Judah" in the south ("house" is here practically equivalent to "state"), was still in the very recent past, and the texts that preceded this one spoke of the return of both groups of exiles. Thus the double expression "Israel and Judah" simply clarifies that this is once again the one, entire people of God with whom God will make the new covenant. Consequently, in what follows the common name "Israel" is used for the whole: "this is the covenant that I will make with the house of Israel." Still it is important for us that this great promise is decisively for the people of God, Israel.

Otherwise the text is made up of contrasts. There was the *old* covenant, from the time of the Exodus from Egypt, that is, the Sinai covenant. Now contrasted with it is the *new* covenant—"after those days." The prophetic words that preceded this had spoken of the still-future return from the Babylonian Exile and of the new existence of the returnees in the old land. That will be in "those days." Now the perspective extends still farther. We are now in the most distant future, at the end of the ages, at the time the early Christians will say has arrived in Jesus of Nazareth.

But the contrast extends still further. The old covenant has been *broken*. That does not mean that it no longer exists. When someone breaks the marriage covenant, that in itself does not annul it. It continues to exist. But it is in crisis. Everything depends on what the two partners do next. Will the wronged partner cause further consequences to ensue? Or is she or he ready to begin anew with the other partner? to continue the old relationship? That would mean, to begin with: does the wronged partner forgive what has been done to her or him? How does the incomprehensibly great God, totally impenetrable to our understanding, react? Does God say to Israel: "That was the end"? God could say that, for God is, as we say, the *"Lord."* But at the end of the text we hear that God does not say it. God forgives the guilt and no longer remembers the sin. Thus over against the breach of the covenant stands *pardon,* over against the broken covenant a renewed one. Is that it? No, still more—again a contrast appears.

This very strange and different God not only renews the old, but says "new," "greater," "different," "better"—because no longer breakable. That is the true and deepest contrast in the text. It is rooted especially in the word *"new"*—a *"new* covenant." It is not conveyed simply by contrasting sets of statements, but instead through a description of the new covenant that clearly indicates, for those who are acquainted with Israel's Bible, what is new and different about the new covenant, beyond the enduring old one.

The new covenant, to begin with, is by no means something completely different from the first covenant at Sinai. How could it be, since God had so uniquely joined God's very self to this people from the beginning? A part of what the text says about the new covenant was therefore a valid aspect of the covenant with the ancestors at the Exodus from Egypt. Even then God had given this people a *Torah,* a "law"—but we would do better to call it a just social project delightful to God and to human beings. Israel's covenant duty was to live according to that Torah, and God's corresponding action was to be bound to this one people out of all others throughout history: God would be *Israel's God,* and Israel would be *God's people.* This covenant relationship was true of the first, and constitutes the second as well. That is the continuity; it is not yet the new thing.

The new thing is, so to speak, packed around it in the text. God does not simply say that he will *give* Israel its Torah *again.* That happened at Sinai. God gave the tables of the covenant and Moses developed them into laws. That was done again and again through the prophets, who in a sense carried on Moses' line. Instead the text says that God will give the Torah *in a new way,* placing it *in the midst* of Israel, and that means *in their hearts.* At Sinai the Decalogue was written on stone tablets, and one could learn the Ten Commandments by tracing them with one's finger. Now God writes the Torah on the tables of their hearts. That is new.

And it has unheard-of consequences for Israel's dealings with the Law. Israel was and is still today a learning people. One must *learn* the Torah in order to know how to live. Still more: one must learn it in order to *learn to know* God. For how else could anyone know God except by seeing how God forms our world, what God desires for us, how God wants us to be?

This is a description of "love." Love is, in great part, knowledge—but a very strange kind of knowledge. We come to know the truth about the other by taking slow and tentative steps into the way in which the other sees us.

So the covenant in Israel had to be handed on from generation to generation through instruction. Each new generation (and each individual in Israel, again and again through the different phases of her or his life) had to try to know God ever anew and ever deeper. This took place as people continually instructed and assured one another about God's Torah. That was the only possible way for Israel to remain in this unique relationship, the covenant with the God of the Exodus from Egypt.

But in the new covenant, according to the promise given us, it will be different. There each one already has God's Torah written on her or his heart, and thus each one already knows the whole from inside. That endlessly weary and in the end not entirely functional system of learning the Torah is no longer the ultimate recourse.

That is what is new in the new covenant promised in Jeremiah, in contrast to the Sinai covenant. It is not a different Torah. There is no shaking of Israel's election. But there is something that in its fullness is only to be found between the lines: this covenant can never again be broken. Where human freedom has its true place, in the heart—there is the law dug in; there is embedded, through the law, the infinitely lovable image of the one who gave the law; there can exist nothing else but the joy of this partnership; there one can no longer even want to escape; there exists, at last, an indissoluble marriage with all its delights.

The new covenant never needs to be renewed, for God's Torah has been woven into human freedom itself. The promise is that at the end of the ages God will cause this to happen in the house of Israel.

Perhaps it has become evident what kind of an unbelievable utopia exists in this text from Jeremiah 31. This statement about individual hearts proposes a new society in which the sustaining institutions of the previous society lose their old functions. No one needs to be socialized any more; everyone is already that way. The text proposes a society based on the rightly-directed freedom of the heart. The heart, as the locus of a no longer tentative and certainly no longer deviant freedom, is the golden coin that buys this society. It is the miracle that sustains it. Everything depends on the miracle of this changed heart. Only God could create such a thing. Has God done so?

Let us set that question aside for now, because I want to clarify, in the second part, the kind of central need, of Israel and of humanity as a whole, that receives its response here.

The Old Testament theological context of the saying about the new covenant

First let us have a look at the prophet Jeremiah. We do not know whether our text about the new covenant is his or not. Probably we owe it to his school, who meditated on and expanded the words of the prophet. Jeremiah himself was deeply marked by Israel's sad fate. He is one of the gloomiest souls in the Old Testament, very much as Michelangelo depicted him in the Sistine Chapel. It was his task to announce the end of Judah and Jerusalem, the end to half a millennium of salvation history. Nobody listened to him. He was persecuted for what he said, tortured, almost killed. Then he saw the end itself, and was carried off to Egypt with the refugees; we lose all trace of him there.

To formulate what Jeremiah saw directly out of our text: he saw that Israel had hardened itself against God's Torah, and that hope was no more, because the people's hearts refused to change. So he could only predict destruction.

He thought again and again about the reasons why the love story between God and God's people had to end that way. The explanation crystallized for him in the concept of freedom bent on evil, or, to use his imagery, in human hearts hardened in the wrong. For him the human heart in its freedom is almost as great a mystery as the unfathomable God:

> The heart is devious above all else; it is perverse—
> who can understand it? (Jer 17:9)

Freedom means the ability to respond to God's Torah. But if we do not do it, our hearts are changed, and at some point the heart itself becomes unchangeable. It can no longer escape from sin; it can no longer recognize God:

> The sin of Judah is written with an iron pen;
> with a diamond point it is engraved on the tablet of their hearts. (Jer 17:1)

That is one of the sayings of Jeremiah that is countered by the words about the new covenant. Why are people so different from animals?

> Even the stork in the heavens knows its times;
> and the turtledove, swallow, and crane observe the time of their coming;
> but my people do not know the ordinance of the LORD. (Jer 8:7)

Why must human freedom, superior to every animal instinct, lead people into faithlessness and down to the abyss?

At this point we encounter the vision of a Torah that through an incomprehensible creative act of God is written, in place of Judah's sin, on the tablets of the heart and need no longer be taught externally, so that one could act against it—when God will miraculously make human beings again equal to the animals in that from their innermost selves they can both know and desire what is right at any time—of course in freedom, and from the heart, because these are human beings . . . .

The creation of a heart that is free and yet deeply marked by God's Torah: that would be the end of Israel's history of wickedness and Judah's constant breaking of the covenant. There seems to be a contradiction here, but it is precisely this new thing that the saying about the new covenant as God's new creation for God's Israel at the end of the ages promises. It is only this new covenant that can exist forever unbroken.

This view of history, so pessimistic in its analysis of human reality and so optimistic in its hope for God's eschatological miracle, is one of the multiform figures within the Old Testament doctrine of justification. This teaching, which has seemed for such a long time to stand between the churches, which has rekindled discussion in the last few years and is still in motion between the Lutheran World Federation and the Roman Catholic Church, is really at the center of every theology. That human beings in themselves are incapable of achieving a right situation before God, that all their attempts fail and that God alone, in divine forgiving grace, can effect the creative work of new love, is expressed here in the book of Jeremiah in the saying about the new covenant that consists of a Torah written on hearts.

The whole Old Testament is shaped by the doctrine of justification: I say this in the face of everything that is continually being proposed about the so-called nomism of Judaism. The very heart of the Old Testament writings, the Pentateuch, whose central content is the great law of Sinai, is, if we look at it carefully, a single doctrine of justification. God makes a covenant with Israel at Sinai. While Moses is still on the mountain the people is already falling away from its covenant God and dancing before a golden calf. Moses pleads; God forgives and renews the covenant (Exodus 32–34). When it departs from the mountain this people, despite having broken the covenant, is a covenant people out of pure grace. The journey through the wilderness is a long series of grumblings and revolution, but at the same time a story of divine aid and miracles given in spite of it all. When Israel finally stands on the bank of the Jordan and will soon enter the land promised to it, Moses can only say:

> It is not because of your righteousness or the uprightness of your heart that you are going in to occupy their land; but . . . in order to fulfill the promise that the LORD made on oath to your ancestors, to Abraham, to Isaac, and to Jacob. (Deut 9:5)

As the whole context shows, this is all about Israel's clear unwillingness, from the very beginning, to keep the Torah, the great gift of the covenant. It is only God's faithfulness, beginning with the primeval ancestors, that keeps the story moving forward.

Therefore we must see clearly how this continuing story in the Old Testament is described as a whole. It turns out that the book of Jeremiah and its point of view stand within a great choir. The book of Joshua, which follows the Pentateuch, describes how Israel entered its land, but it only begins a series of books that ends with the catastrophe of the Babylonian Exile that also forms the context of the book of Jeremiah.

If we see this, it is relevant that Moses, the figure of the covenant-making, did not lead Israel into the promised land. It is significant that the book of Joshua is not part of the core of Israel's sacred books, the Torah. In essence it had gradually become clear, at least to the Israel of the Exile, that despite seven centuries of life in the land Israel had never really entered into that land—because the full possession of the promise did not consist merely in ownership of territory, but in the existence of a society that enjoys the prosperity in that territory that is guaranteed for it by the social project that has been given to it. The reader of the Pentateuch must realize, by the end of the five books, that the history that is now beginning is not yet the true covenant history, but only an evil variation of it.

Deuteronomy itself contains, in its third and fourth chapters, a prospect of the failure of the history in the land that is about to begin, and its ending in exile. Here already Moses looks forward to the time beyond the Exile when scattered Israel will again be gathered and brought home, oriented anew to the Torah by its God. Indeed, we already read here the following statement (in which, despite the singular, Israel as a people is being addressed):

> . . . the LORD your God will circumcise your heart and the heart of your descendants, so that you [we may add: by force of nature, so to speak] will love the LORD your God with all your heart and with all your soul. (Deut 30:6)

Of course, even though the saying about the "new covenant" does not appear here, this is very close to the words of Jeremiah.

Suddenly the Israel that stands with Moses, soon to die, on the bank of the Jordan is transparently clear. It is not only the Israel of that time. It is just as the much the Israel of the Exile; in fact, many Jews are convinced that it is also the Israel of today. Never, even when it has returned to its land partly and for a time, has Israel truly and fully entered the land. It is profoundly significant that in the lectionary system in the synagogue only the five books of Moses are used as the first reading. When the reader reaches the death of Moses each Fall, the reading does not continue with Joshua, but begins again at the creation of the world. Israel is still standing on the bank of the Jordan. It has never yet really entered the promised land. The covenant, which God has never revoked in spite of all Israel's infidelity, has not yet reached that point at which hearts are transformed in such a way that it has become a *new* covenant in the sense of the book of Jeremiah. The Torah must still be learned; Israel still needs, year after year, its Day of Atonement.

At this point our New Testament scriptures take a different path. And that brings me to the third part of my remarks.

The heart of Jesus as the place of the new covenant

Christian faith tells us that with Jesus the new covenant of the book of Jeremiah has entered the world. We even are so bold as to call the Christian part of our Sacred Scriptures simply "the New Testament," which means "the new covenant."

However—if what I have attempted to say above is true, we should shudder to the bone at this formulation of our Christian self-understanding. Could we *only* regard ourselves as Christians *if* our hearts have been so transformed that they are entirely fixed on God's Torah, in complete freedom but at the same time in a way that is practically instinctive, with the reliability of a homing pigeon? Is God's will for society really written into the center of our freedom? Does no one need to teach us any longer? Do we no longer need leadership? Do we have no need to repent of anything? And if someone could really say that his or her heart had been transformed, are our society and our world also transformed? Have we really achieved complete prosperity? And before all that, there is the other question: are *we* the people of Israel, for whom the promises were made? Was any of that promised to *us*?

We cannot flee from that shuddering shock by saying that these things are not to be understood so *literally,* that they are all simply images of inner, invisible grace—or by saying that the same words and images have a *different* meaning for us, and that we should not think too strictly in continuity with the Old Testament. Those would be evasions. For the words of the book of Jeremiah about the new covenant and the Torah in the heart join a great many other prophetic promises of salvation that the New Testament also says have come to pass and been fulfilled.

Consider only the promise of the outpouring of the Spirit at the end of time. When the Spirit really was poured out on the day of Pentecost, according to the Acts of the Apostles, the Church had its beginning. When the gifts of the Spirit continued to be given to the Christian communities the Church continued to exist throughout time. When the Spirit leapt over to the Gentiles it was a sign to the primitive community that the promises could be claimed by other peoples alongside Israel. This is only one example.

The promise of the new covenant is thus valid. Christian faith tells us that since Jesus of Nazareth it has been fulfilled. Therefore, since then, there *must* be a heart on which the Torah is written in such a way that it unites the greatest degree of freedom with the fullness of desire for God's will.

I am saying that there is such a heart. It is just *one* heart. It is the heart of *Jesus*.

That brings us to the point we have been aiming toward from the beginning. In the heart of Jesus of Nazareth, that is, in the freedom of the one man Jesus that at the same time is God's freedom, the God of Israel has at last, at the end of the long period of waiting, in the midst of God's people, caused that heart to exist in which God's Torah has become second nature. The heart of Jesus is the first and at the same time the perfect realization of the new covenant.

This we can also demonstrate. All we have to do is read the gospels. Jesus did not teach like the scribes, but like one who had authority (Matt 7:29; Mark 1:22). He brought a new teaching, with authority (Mark 1:27). When people approached him with halakic questions or even tried to trap him, he answered with complete confidence. When someone asked him about the Mosaic writ of divorce he could simply say that it was not so from the beginning, but was only introduced because of Israel's hardness of heart (Mark 10:5-6; Matt 19:4, 8). In the Sermon on the Mount, in Matthew's gospel, he shows himself the second Moses who takes away not a single iota of the Torah, but at the same time interprets it anew, radically and eschatologically.

Beyond that, there is his way of life. He travels through the land and simply says what he himself has experienced in the depths of his person: the reign of God has come. Where is it? Wherever else it is, it is certainly in his own heart, in which there is not the tiniest resistance to God's will. And so, because of him, everything is different. Not only do human spirits fly to him; their bodies are made whole as well. Even the wind and the waves obey him. The freedom that moves entirely in harmony with the will of God transforms the world. This, at last, is the heart that was promised, the heart in which God's Torah is embedded, so that no one any longer needs to teach this one. Here the promise of a new covenant is fulfilled.

It was not, of course, fulfilled in all the hearts in Israel at the same time. In this one heart the new covenant from God has come to Israel. But to begin with it was fashioned only in a single heart, which was then to be the source from which all the children of Abraham, and indeed all humanity, could drink in freedom from the living water of the new covenant.

That was not part of what Jeremiah said. His words envisioned the immediate and complete end of time, when God will be all in all. There was no reflection about *how* God would bring about the new covenant. It was not said there that God would present the highest degree of divine freedom within God's people as a final story of freedom.

As a story of freedom it need not be a story of immediate and universal acceptance; it could also descend to diabolical depths as a story of an ultimate and violent "no" to God's most urgent offer. And it was so. Every form of "no" to God's offers in the history of humanity concentrated itself in an eschatological and final refusal of God's greatest love. That infinitely precious heart was pierced by a lance. God drew it, as a pierced heart, into divine glory, where it still beats for us and with us, and continues to make it possible for us to receive, through it, a share in the new covenant.

The heart of Jesus *remains* the irrevocable realization of the new covenant in our world. There is no other. *Only* this heart needs no further instruction, only it needs no one to say: "know the Lord." It knows him at the fullest depth that the word "know" can have. However, this "only" represents a limitation. The promise of Jeremiah was made to the *entire* house of Israel, not only to a single heart. But even today, two thousand years later, we cannot say that the other part of the promise has been realized, the part that says "they shall *all* know me, from the least of them to the greatest." In this sense the words of Jeremiah about the new covenant are *not yet* fulfilled among us, even today.

It used to be common to say simply that the Old and New Testaments were related to each other as promise to fulfillment. Such a statement necessarily ignores the continuing existence of Jews, who as a whole and most obviously in later generations cannot be identified with those who crucified Jesus. Judaism continues to live out of the promises of the prophets and awaits their fulfillment. It cannot see that Israel has been eschatologically transformed, and certainly not that the world has been. And rightly so, for the saying about the new covenant is by no means completely fulfilled. On the other hand, the truth that the new covenant is already present, at least in one single heart, is something that we Christians can never question. Nor can we deny that in faith, despite the stoniness of our own hearts, we can share in that one heart, so that not only the one heart is justified before God, but we ourselves in it, and precisely in its fidelity to the Torah even unto death, even to the piercing of that heart. Our justification comes from faith alone, a faith that depends on that heart.

We thus stand at the critical point of dialogue between Jews and Christians. Everything else, no matter how important, especially our confession of our historical guilt in regard to Judaism, is in the end immaterial. We only have to listen, over and over again, when the Jews tell us that it is not yet evident in this world how God's promise of a new covenant can be already fulfilled. We have to tell them that nevertheless, once upon a time in history in their very midst, the heart that was promised, the one on which the Torah is inscribed, did beat, and that we can live from it, even in the midst of the bitterest struggle between light and darkness. This mutual witness is so important because we Christians dare never forget that it is a Jewish heart to which alone we can attribute the new covenant and from which alone we live, just as we dare never forget that the promise of the transformation of hearts is given originally and primarily to the descendants of Abraham, whom we must encounter with the highest respect and love, even if they cannot believe in their brother Jesus of Nazareth. We believers from among the Gentiles are nothing but naturalized citizens among the citizens proper, the elect, and fellow members of the household of God.

Here I will stop, perhaps a little abruptly, with only a very brief final remark. One especially important feature of the modern veneration of the Sacred Heart according to Margaret Mary Alacoque was the idea of reparation. Reparation was the reaction to the fact that this miracle of the new covenant, the Heart of Jesus, was so little accepted. Reparation signified a passionate desire to react in faith to that non-acceptance. How can we do otherwise, once it is clear to us what this most sacred Heart of Jesus means, and that nevertheless two millennia have passed and the promised final hour of history has not been fully accomplished?

Chapter Five

Hosea and Wrath
Some Suggestions for Reading

The book of Hosea doesn't make it easy for us. It is simpler to come to terms with some of the other prophetic books; there are paragraph titles, some of them with time indications, for example in Jeremiah or Ezekiel. A lot of oracles have introductory and concluding formulas: "Thus says Y{HWH}" and "the word of Y{HWH}." That sets them apart. The book of Hosea has no paragraph titles. There is nothing to mark off the individual oracles, either, and there are no other structural marks. Here I am thinking of compositional cycles like the oracles of the nations in Amos 1–2 or the visions in Amos 7–9. In contrast to those, the book of Hosea seems amorphous. As Jerome said: "Hosea is disconnected and seems to speak only in aphorisms."

The book is undoubtedly put together, like the other prophetic books, out of existing oral prophetic material, but the material has been more thoroughly reworked. It has been stripped of its husk, perhaps even reduced to chaff. At any rate the material has been reduced to its basics and then freely reassembled in a new order. Apparently there was no interest in the preservation of an original major text or in referencing the original situations in which the words were spoken. A new text was created. The old text was largely decontextualized, apparently on purpose. The transition to written form was certainly nothing like making a tape recording.

This may have something to do with the fact that Hosea is just the second of the writing prophets. Only Amos is older. Thus there was no such thing as the genre "prophetic book." The genre was only developed in the wake of Amos and Hosea. The books of Hosea and Amos may well have developed independently of each other. In that case the new genre "prophetic book" was born twice, and with different faces. The form of the book of Amos then inspired followers, while the form of the book of Hosea remained a dead branch on the evolutionary tree. Only in the post-exilic history of the genre do we find variants that are closer to Hosea, for example late in the book of Isaiah.

Therefore in the form that the book of Hosea took the prophetic words are not preserved in their original shape. But the passion of exegesis in our century (and in the previous one) was devoted—for the whole of the Old Testament, including this part—to the reconstruction of the original building blocks, or at least to the later history of redaction. That interest broke its teeth on Hosea. Only recently has Old Testament exegesis's interest in origins been expanded, if not entirely reversed. The question of the book as it presently exists, with the text it now has, has come to the fore: the issue of the book as it is, not how it came to be. At the present time this new question is racing forward like a hermeneutical forest fire. But the fire broke out in the valley of narrative prose, and no sparks have yet reached the prophetic hills. There is not even a tongue of flame licking at Hosea.

For if the book of Hosea represents a special type of prophetic book in which, through a writing process without precedent, an entirely new textual reality was created out of prior prophetic material, it is astonishing that there appears as yet to be not a single study that even asks the questions about Hosea that, at least in the English-speaking world, constitute the homework of beginning college students studying the narrative books of the Old Testament. It seems to me that it is time to apply such questions to the book of Hosea, and that is what I will do in what follows. The result will, of course, be nothing more than an experiment.

Precursors

Of course I have been painting the situation pretty much in black and white. Synchronic views are no longer quite so rare, even in the case of Hosea. As early as 1933 Umberto Cassuto experimented with them in a structural analysis of Hosea 2, in Hebrew, as his contribution to the memorial volume for Hirsch Perez Chajes. Since then there have been a large number of synchronic analyses, at least of Hosea 1–3. However, similar analyses of the rest of the book are a good deal rarer, and for the last part, Hosea 12–14, there is nothing at all of this sort that is very persuasive.

Nevertheless, it is beginning to appear that the book of Hosea is by no means just a heap of textual rubble. Formally, at least on the surface, in terms of repetitions of words, forms, and motifs, linguistic configurations, and textual linkages the book appears to be surprisingly well constructed throughout, displaying a systematic intertextual web. Thus the book itself becomes a new context for the decontextualized prophetic words out of which it is constructed. The semantic conclusions from this finding, however, have yet to be drawn.

Still, the analysis of the superficial structure is only a small part of what needs to be done. Since James Muilenburg's presidential address to the Society of Biblical Literature in 1969 this approach has borne the name of "rhetorical criticism." In 1989 Roland Meynet published a manual on "analyse rhétorique," tracing its history back to Bishop Lowth in the eighteenth century and offering some very useful methodological suggestions. But this kind of "rhetorical analysis" is only a beginning stage of the synchronic examination of texts. Even ancient rhetoric, from which the name of this approach is taken, would demand more. For example, the approach requires the use of everything that is called "narrative analysis" in the case of narrative literature, as well as what is called "structural analysis."

It may be, however, that something like narrative analysis of the book of Hosea has already been attempted, even though under a foreign passport and a false name. Hans Walter Wolff, introducing the concepts of "kerygmatic unity" and "inaugural sketch" to Hosea exegesis in his 1961 commentary on the book, *de facto* incorporated Hosea into the category of narrative literature, probably without being aware of it, and removed it from the genre of public discourse or preaching. In narrative literature it is entirely possible to present a story by means of a series of fragmentary speeches, letters, diary notes, etc., allowing the readers to reconstruct the tale reflected in them. Goethe, for example, used that technique in *The Sorrows of Young Werther*. What, after all, is Wolff's "inaugural sketch" but a narrative of that sort about the appearance of Hosea? We only read what came from Hosea's lips, but the leaps from one saying to the next within the text have the effect of narrative spaces. They compel the reader's fantasy to reconstruct the suggestions, questions, replies, and cries of the hearers and those involved—in effect, the whole scene.

Thus at the end of such a "kerygmatic unit" one has lived retrospectively through a whole scene. The curtain falls. But then it immediately rises again for the next prophetic scene, which may take place years later. The intervening time remains obscure, but the reader's fantasy imagines it as time in the life of Hosea and the Northern Kingdom that is not told, but that nevertheless has passed. That is all the more easily possible because, Wolff supposes, the "inaugural sketches" in the book of Hosea are arranged chronologically. The various later additions to the text, which he of course considers also, are not such as to change anything in the genre-true basic structure of the book, which depends on the "inaugural sketches." Thus for Wolff the book of Hosea becomes a biography of the prophet, one whose literary finesse would make it a worthy entry among modern novels. When we get to the end of the book we have journeyed through a prophet's life.

It is like abstract painting: the canvas displays only the firm lines of the prophetic words, and they are in hard, almost expressionistic colors. Everything else is added by the creative reader.

Hans Walter Wolff would certainly reject this interpretation of his presentation, and rightly so, because his intention was entirely different. When he spoke of the "inaugural sketches" that Hosea's sympathizers wrote soon after the prophetic beginnings, and that were handed on by a circle of disciples until they were finally made into a book by the Deuteronomists in exile, he was attempting a historical-critical reconstruction of the book's prehistory. His central concern was with the "primary Hosea traditions." The genre of "inaugural sketch" brought him with razor-sharp precision to the origins, and yet explained the jumpiness and inconsistency of the texts. The historian in him, and in us, could rejoice—the historian who is looking for bedrock. Many readers of Wolff's commentary must have felt a warm wave of comfort slipping down their backs. I was a student when the fascicles of the commentary were being published, and I still remember how much I liked the idea of the "inaugural sketches." We would now say something like: finally, the hidden camera has been revealed, and we can take our seats at the scene when Hosea appears.

It is only now, more than thirty years later, that I can see that something very different took place. It was not the historian, but the person who likes to spend nights reading long novels whose hunger was being satisfied. The idea of "inaugural sketches" made it possible to devour this "shattered" prophetic book as if it were a novel. More precisely, it may not even be the book of Hosea that was the novel, but Wolff's commentary. It acted as a kind of frame in which the author appears as the researcher, takes the reader by the hand, and with impressive scholarship allows her or him to relive the story of Hosea through the rescued "inaugural sketches."

In spite of their fascination, I later bade farewell to the "inaugural sketches," and so did many others. The text as we have it does not permit us to postulate this handy original form for the book of Hosea. We have to stick with what Wolff wanted to get away from "in light of the consistent connections of words," namely that "individual sayings that were originally handed down independently" were "later made into a literary composition." Whether that compositional work was done by Hosea himself, as Francis I. Andersen and David Noel Freedman postulated in their 1980 commentary, or whether Hosea's disciples did so, at least as regards the broad foundations of the book, very soon afterward, as for example Jörg Jeremias, who certainly studied and confronted Wolff's work most closely, asserted in 1979 in his article for Ernst Würthwein's Festschrift, or whether the forging of the book took place only centuries later at the hands of certain "Deuteronomists" who had only bits and pieces of Hosea-sayings and packed them together in layers like an onion, as some of the newest doctoral students propose—all that can remain an open question here, no matter how much my own sympathies rest with Jörg Jeremias, even though I would like to reduce the number of his proposed exilic and post-exilic additions.

In any case, from a diachronic point of view we should posit what I sketched at the beginning: a new text has been created out of finely minced, decontextualized textual material. There is no evolutionary continuity between the oral traditions and the present text, between the genre of the first things written and that of the definitive book. Wolff, without wanting to, tried out a possible beginning-point for narrative analysis of the book of Hosea. His way proved untenable, but we have to try again along different paths, and without a doubt we have to begin precisely with a strong process of decontextualizing.

The basic communicative structure

The decontextualizing, however, is not so extensive as to raise the synchronous question whether there is any such thing as a book of Hosea at all. Rather, the book is characterized throughout by the tension indicated by its very title (1:1). On the one hand it contains that word of YHWH "that came to Hosea son of Beeri" at a very concrete historical moment defined by the names of the ruling kings. On the other hand, the names of the kings listed in this verse are extremely rudimentary as regards the region in which Hosea worked, the Northern Kingdom, where only Jeroboam II is mentioned, while for the Southern Kingdom there is a full list of all the kings who could possibly be named. Apparently the book was expected to be read by people who were familiar with the history of *Judah,* not that of the Northern Kingdom—Judeans, in other words.

These "readers" (the technical term for them is "the implied reader") who help to construct the text's world could not belong to Hosea's generation. The words of Hosea, whose basic import is directed to the entity "Israel" (= "Ephraim") have their thrust expanded or encircled, in units neatly distributed throughout the book, by text elements that a diachronic view identifies, at least in part, as "Judahite glosses." By this means the text as a whole is oriented to a readership called "Judah." Almost all these texts have the basic structure: "What is here said to Ephraim is just as true for you, Judah." At least they can be read that way.

At the end of the book even this "just . . . as" is surpassed in favor of a full identification. The great legal argument in the last part of the book is, according to the way it is announced by the author in 12:3, "YHWH's indictment of Judah," even though the verses that immediately follow and the etymologies of the names in them clearly show that "Israel" once stood in the raw material out of which the book was shaped, and although from here until the end of the book we find only the names of Israel, Jacob, and Ephraim. Through the process of identification that the book of Hosea has set in motion for the readers by means of the Judahite glosses, Judah, by this point near the end of the book, has become identical with what is called Israel, Jacob, and even Ephraim (by the same kind of *pars-pro-toto* language as in the use of the name "Judah"), while earlier, when the Northern Kingdom still existed and the reality of the People of God had not yet been shrunk to Judah alone, it could only have been identified with a part, a group within Israel.

That the word of God proclaimed in the book nevertheless remains the word that YHWH in an earlier age "spoke through Hosea" (1:2) is possible because Hosea never appears in the text-world as the *author* of the book. In a few verses of ch. 3 he functions, briefly, as a first-person narrator. But at that point in the book it is already clear that another voice, an authorial voice, dominates his, so that he himself is only one first-person narrator cited by another. But we will have more to say about that later.

Hosea is central to the book, but not as author. He is central as the "responsible subject" of the book, to use a term that Jan Assmann has used for Egyptian teaching. Ultimately the subject of the speech in the book is God. The divine "I" appears lexematically or morphologically in 89 of the 197 verses of the book. Because of the context, other verses are also part of the divine discourse. But God says it all "through Hosea" (1:2). We even learn some personal facts about Hosea, at least his symbolically significant marriage history and his sufferings as a prophet.

Like almost all the narrators in the Bible, the book-author in the text-world keeps himself as well hidden as possible. He does say a good deal, as I will show. But he never presents himself. As I will also show, no one can regard him, like the other biblical narrators, as an "omniscient author." He comments on the words of God, and in doing so he sometimes makes mistakes. We have to locate him at least in a post-Hosea generation. In 1:1 he mentions Hezekiah of Judah, so he cannot be earlier than that, and may be later. But since there is no reference at all to Babylon or a Babylonian Exile, we cannot place him too much later than Hezekiah, at least not as far as the text-world is concerned.

Since the book addresses a Judah that is identical with the People of God, and since the writing of the prophetic words and their projection on Judah imply their validity for an open future, God does not speak universally in this book to all humanity, but certainly to everything that in the future will belong to what at that time was called "Judah," that is, "Israel."

This gives us a synchronous description of the fundamental communicative structure of the book. Even we readers today, in whose biblical "canon" the book is to be found, can find our places in it. Now let us turn again to the question of genre, which we were discussing earlier when we spoke of Hans Walter Wolff.

Genre: Narrative

In the classic "introductions" to the Old Testament the term "prophetic books" is ordinary usage. This genre is apparently self-evident, because it is not given any further explanation. When push comes to shove we may find the word "collection." By calling them "collections" it seems that we categorize the prophetic books as a precursor phenomenon to the sub-literary genre of "compilation literature," important in the late Middle Ages and the early modern period and still alive in various guises today—jokebooks, cookbooks, etc. Without wanting to touch on any other prophetic books, I would like simply to state that the book of Hosea can scarcely be called a "collection." Material is not only collected here, it is also given a new form. But how?

A textual framework like what "rhetorical analysis" has uncovered especially in Hosea 1–3, and that presumably can be more clearly demonstrated by further work on the book as a whole, makes a text a unity. It also marks out sections and subsections. But it is not a characteristic of a particular genre. In this way the linguistic surface of a great variety of texts can be analyzed in detail, but the only conclusion that follows is that here we have an entire text, not only a loose congeries of individual texts. That is, we can simply falsify the assumption that this is a "collection."

There are some indications that the book of Hosea is an imitation, on a grand scale, of the oral genre of "public speech." In that case a single great literary "speech" would have been composed out of fragments of many individual public speeches by the prophet.

This is an attractive idea. The Homeric epics, which were composed in this same eighth century B.C.E. and were likewise first steps over the threshold between orality and written text, between traditions shaped by internal social forces and literature, are, as regards the initial stage of the genre, major literary parallels to the oral epics of the bards, each created anew at the time of utterance, but of course much shorter. The Attic tragedies, arising out of the Dionysian dithyrambs, were still unique performances even in the fifth century, although their texts could be purchased. In the fourth century, however, there were literary tragedies that were never performed in the form in which they were read. At the latest, Isocrates' *Panegyric* (380 B.C.E.) is the purely literary fiction of a speech before all the assembled Greeks that was never given. A literary genre of "fictive speech" was therefore indeed in the Mediterranean air as a model for the reworking of prophetic traditions.

In the case of Hosea, in particular the key word *rib,* "strife," "pleading" favors such an assumption. It appears in characteristic fashion near the beginning of all three parts of the book (2:2 [MT 2:4]; 4:1; 12:3). It is not true, as is often supposed, that this key word sets us in the framework of a fictive legal proceeding in which YHWH, as the accuser, appears against his people. But that is not necessary. The analogous speech need not also be an analogy of judgment. In real life the prophets did not normally appear before tribunals. It is only a question of a public speech as such, with its characteristic generic features. The main purpose of a public speech is to win over and change the minds of its audience. That is exactly the point of the root *šub,* "turn around, think anew," which appears near the end of all three parts of the book (3:5; 11:11; 14:1, 2, 7 [MT 14:2, 3, 8]). These passages nourish the suspicion that the three proclamations with *rib* refer not only to small snippets, but in each case to whole sections of the book.

Shall we, then, regard the book of Hosea, in terms of its genre, as a major literary "speech" to a fictively assembled Israel-Judah?—or in any case as a chain of three such "speeches," each building on the other?

Something of this sort seems to be true of this book, and yet I do not think that we have really arrived at its genre. In particular, chs. 1–3 are not really comprehended by this designation of the genre. If it were so, God would have to be speaking from the beginning, but that is not the case. In the first chapter an author *narrates,* and again in the third chapter we find *narrative,* this time by Hosea. As long as he is talking about his own life he is not the mouth of God. Finally, in 2:2 [MT 2:4] God does not announce his own *rib* against Israel. He only calls on the children (that is, individual Israelites) to begin a pleading with their mother (i.e., Israel). In Hosea 1–3, in other words, in contrast to the remaining two parts of the book, it is questionable whether the text can be read in any sense as the words of a *rib* against Israel.

On the other hand, this is the beginning of the book, and a book's beginning lays down the pattern for the book, and also for its genre. If we trust the beginning we come back to the genre of narrative, even though in a singular form.

In fact, YHWH's speaking *"through* Hosea" (1:2a) really "begins," according to Hosea 1 (cf. again 1:2a) with YHWH's speaking *"to* Hosea"

(1:2b, 4, 6) and ordering him to marry and to give names to his three children. Thus here God is not speaking through prophetic words, but through a family history permeated by the darkest kind of divine words. The book's author tells the story; thus in Hosea 1 the reader moves into the "narrative."

As soon as that has happened, there follows a crisis of understanding in 1:10 [MT 2:1]. The narrative, which gets more and more succinct as it proceeds, reaches its climax (also as regards its content) in 1:9 with the third naming. That verse is a quoted divine speech. We expect the author to continue in the past tense. But he does not do so. What follow are predictions of the future, introduced by "and it will come to pass." At first we think that the quoted words of God are continuing here. But that cannot be so, because from here on we find no "I" from God, and as to content, what God has just said is contradicted. The three damning names of the children are turned on their heads and reversed, in a glowing proclamation of future salvation.

So who is speaking here? In terms of the history of the tradition this may be a saying of Hosea—or, as many suppose, it may not be. But that is not the question here. In a synchronic reading, in terms of the step-by-step construction of the text-world along the line of reading, only the author can be speaking here. No one else has been introduced, and no one new is introduced here either, not even indirectly. But now the author is no longer *narrating*. He is *commenting* on the narrative he has just finished, and very simply by contradicting it.

At this point I am not asking where he gets his wisdom or why at the very beginning of the book he so humbly and yet deliberately throws the divine words back at their speaker—no matter how pertinent both questions may be. I am only asking what is happening, at this point in the text, as regards the reader's formative sense of the genre. If readers, on the basis of the book's title, expected prophetic words from God, in the first chapter they have had to recognize first of all that an author is narrating something. Now they also learn that this narrator offers commentary, apparently in contrast to the usual narrators in the biblical books. He expresses his own opinion in his own words, even when it is diametrically opposed to what he has just reported as God's view of things. The book is suddenly electrified. There is an enormous tension between God, as he has appeared so far, and the author of the book.

Moreover, the readers have learned at the break between the first and second chapters that there will be no gradual transitions in this book. In the future, then, they will have to be alert to some rather finely-drawn signals indicating new shifts in mood. And they will soon have opportunity to do so.

The author's commentary assertions about future salvation culminate in 2:1 [MT 2:3] with a new interpretation of two of the children's names.

In good rhetorical fashion the Israelites of the future are addressed joyfully as if they were the prophet's children in the story. Thus the discourse oscillates between Israel and the prophet's family. This very technique is then continued in v. 2:2 [MT 2:4], but with a completely different content: "Plead [conduct a *rib*] with your mother, plead—for she is not my wife, and I am not her husband." Then comes, immediately, the word "whoring," which characterized the prophet's wife at the beginning of the narrative in Hosea 1. Once again we are in the middle of Hosea's family history, which oscillates to a story of God's marriage to Israel, and everything is obscure again. The readers understand that, even when someone or other is speaking, this again is *narrative*.

But two things have changed. For one, the author of the book has withdrawn. He allows his characters to speak as in a drama. It is possible to narrate in this way, without introducing the characters and without going back to describe the situation. The readers themselves must discover from the words that are spoken what the situation is and who is speaking. The author of the book of Hosea will keep to this narrative technique from here on.

On the other hand, the narrative is now multi-layered. God's story is being played out in Hosea's fate. What the children's names only said theoretically before is now accomplished in Hosea's own speech.

I am stretching the analysis. The author has brought the readers so far that they count on finding narrative, and in fact narrative of an unusual kind. The narrator does not construct any further scenes or introduce the speakers individually. He simply allows their voices to be heard, but in such a way that the readers can tell when a new voice begins. On the other hand we must suppose that the narrator can undertake to speak in order to comment on what his characters say, and without any reflexive introductory flourishes.

The speech that begins in 2:2 [MT 2:4], oscillating between Hosea and God, becomes more and more clearly divine speech, and that alone. In its content it also reaches to the salvation that is to come, so that the tension that at first exists between the narrative in Hosea 1 and the commentary at the end of that chapter (beginning of ch. 2 in the Hebrew text) is reduced. The connection to that tension at the beginning of the book is clear because the children's names recur (2:22-23 [MT 2:24-25]). This in turn creates a link by association for the reappearance of Hosea's family story in 3:1.

In 3:1 the narrator again separates the oscillating identity of Hosea and YHWH by beginning, without any transition, a first-person narrative by Hosea. It opens with the statement: "YHWH said to me." Here, then, Hosea *alone* is speaking; he *tells about* YHWH. Between 2:23 [MT 2:25] and 3:1, then, the voice has changed. In the narrative logic, it seems, Hosea is to be heard again simply as a human being. It is only then, apparently, that we can clearly distinguish his other speech, which in fact is not *his,* but God's.

This divine speech is, in any case, introduced again in 4:1, at the beginning of the second part of the book. The readers can now recognize the narrative structural genre in the form that is specific to the book of Hosea. Two great overarching speech-complexes span the rest of the book: Hosea 4–11, concluding with "YHWH's whisper" in 11:11, and Hosea 12–14, ending with the close of the book in 14:9 [MT 14:10]. By taking up the word again at the very end of the book and looking backward over its whole course, the author makes it clear that these gigantic arches are also part of his narrative.

Thus the book's genre can be described as a specific form of narrative. Readers are directed into the genre through a series of steps; then it proceeds freely. Almost in the style of a drama, it allows us to hear only the speaking voices, without any intervening narrative voice between them.

However, this designation of the genre is only preliminary. I have not pursued a particular phenomenon at the beginning of the book, namely the commentary insertion by the author in 2:1-3 [MT 1:10–2:1].

The voices

The great arcs of discourse begin in ch. 4, by which time the readers should have grasped the genre, at least in principle. In themselves these discourses seem like a mosaic. Diachronically this means that a variety of material has been worked together. But what does it mean synchronically? There are certainly some shifts in content that demand interpretation. I will not enter into that aspect in this essay. But before that there are two other irritating phenomena. In the first place, the text shifts constantly between address to Israel and third-person discourse about Israel. Second, God frequently speaks, but just as frequently the text talks about God in the third person; that is, someone else speaks. These two phenomena are connected, sometimes in one way, sometimes in another, without any discernible rule governing the process.

The shifts between address to Israel and speech about Israel seem difficult to explain. They appear simply to have been transposed from the discourse type of real-world prophetic speech into the new major genre of literary prophetic speech. The Israelite prophet spoke before a large audience, but the speech was often aimed at particular persons or a particular group. Thus the prophet would sometimes have spoken directly to the real addressees and sometimes have spoken to the whole audience about those addressees or about the entire audience. That is typical of public speech. Thus there is not a problem of genre here.

The shifts between first-person divine speech and speech about God are a different matter. As far as we can see, this shift was normal enough in the real appearances of the prophets. They used both kinds of speech in combination. To that extent we can also feel content about the book of Hosea. Sometimes Hosea spoke, sometimes he allowed God to speak. We are inclined to read the book with that in mind.

It may be that in fact this multiform prophetic practice was taken over in literary form. But I would like to suggest another possibility. I am presuming that when we read texts synchronically we often have to relearn some things. But we are too easily inclined to bring our diachronic knowledge into the picture, and not only what we know about the original form of the texts, but also what we surmise about their original function. We must continually attempt to read naïvely, shutting out our diachronic knowledge.

In this case the genre analysis we have already conducted may give us some hints about the appropriate technique for reading the book of Hosea. In Hosea 2 the voice of Hosea is slowly submerged beneath the voice of God. The threefold "says Yhwh" (so unusual in Hosea) in 2:13, 16, 21 [MT 2:15, 18, 23]—each time, of course, an aside by the author of the book—underscores, toward the end, what has happened. The sounding of the prophetic voice is made still more deliberate by the fact that then, immediately afterward, in Hosea 3 the prophet himself speaks in the first person, but now as Hosea the man. There is nothing prophetic in him in this narrative. The readers discover the simple human Hosea, to be distinguished from the prophet into whom God has entered, and as such the man Hosea then exits from the book. There is no further first-person speech by Hosea. Could this perhaps be a lighting effect that changes the appearance of everything onstage? Is a new system of coordinates being created here? Does God only speak through Hosea when the divine "I" is speaking? But if that is the case, what voice is speaking when someone talks *about* God?

At the beginning of ch. 2 the author of the book was transformed from a narrator into a commentator. This was not repeated until late in ch. 3, unless one were to read the theological enrichment of the word of God related by Hosea in 3:1b and the words of Hosea to his wife in 3:4-5 as a commentary inserted by the author of the book, who quotes them. However that may be, the possibility that the voice of the author will return with commentary has already been introduced. Can it be, then, that when, beginning in ch. 4, God does not speak, but instead another voice speaks about God, this is again the voice of the book's author?

If so, the author would be doing more than simply commenting. The great rhetorical arches themselves would, in that case, represent texts produced not by God but by the book's author. For in 4:1-3 the major discourse that constitutes Hosea 4–11 opens not with the voice of God, but with another, introductory voice speaking about God in the third person:

> Hear the word of YHWH, O people of Israel; for YHWH has a *rib* against the inhabitants of the land. . . .

The divine "I" appears clearly for the first time in 4:5. Probably from 4:4 onward the discourse gradually shifts into divine speech. On the whole, if we hold with Wolff's determination of the limits of the "God text" in Hosea 4–11, it is about twice as extensive as the "author's text." Still, that is quite a bit of authorial voice.

Likewise, the second major discourse, in Hosea 12–14, begins with divine speech, placed as a kind of "motto" in 11:24–12:1 [MT 12:1-2], followed in 12:2 [MT 12:3] by a voice that speaks of God in the third person:

> YHWH has a *rib* against Judah . . .

The divine "I" appears for the first time in 12:9 [MT 12:10]. Reckoned by the number of verses, in this second discourse the authorial voice speaks for the same length of time as the divine voice.

If we for the moment presume the truth of our supposition, we can say that within the two major discourses, besides the indispensable introductions there are also central passages that belong practically to the authorial voice alone. If we assume, within Hosea 4–11, the structure essentially developed by Wolff, according to which the discourse consists of two sets of five units, in the fifth unit concluding the first half (9:1-9) it is solely the voice of the author that speaks, and similarly in the eighth part, which opens the retrospect on the time when Israel was in its land (10:1-8). Similarly, in Hosea 12–14 almost the whole of the lament is in the voice of the author (12:2–13:2 [MT 12:3–13:2]); only at 13:3, with the threat of punishment, does God begin to speak consistently. In both these major discourses, however, God clearly has the last word (11:11b; 14:5-9).

The author, then—within the world of the text—is shown to be responsible for the new, literary presentation of the "word of YHWH through Hosea." He would not have had any interest in concealing the fact that the message of Hosea appears in the book in a revised and edited form. To make that clear, he has even been willing to take authentic prophetic texts (but not those that speak with the voice of God in the first person) from the prophet and present them in his own name—a fact that perhaps is likewise not intended to be concealed from the readers.

To give an analogy from our own habits of speaking and writing, we might think of the speeches of cabinet ministers and members of Congress as we encounter them every day in the newspapers and television news shows. Without always noting the transition, the journalists offer us literal quotations from the speaker's most important passages along with summary and perhaps even commentary in indirect speech as their own contribution. That is not exactly the same as what I have shown in the book of Hosea, but it is analogous and may help us to understand the internal communicative structure of the book.

Besides structuring the whole book and producing important passages for which there may simply have been no formal word of God available, the authorial voice in the book of Hosea is devoted also to commenting on the divine discourse, especially in the major discourse of Hosea 4–11. However, the author no longer, as in 1:10–2:1 [MT 2:1-3], produces a tension with the commented divine words; instead, he deepens, broadens, and concretizes them. Thus for example the statements that threaten exile in Egypt or Assyria belong to the commenting voice of the author (7:16; 8:13; 9:3, 6; 11:5—and the reversal in 11:11a). The voice goes especially far in almost anticipating the reaction of the readers or at least suggests particular reactions to them. This seems to me to be the case in the prayer of rejection in 9:14:

> Give them, YHWH—what will you give?
> Give them a miscarrying womb and dry breasts.

or the request for confirmation in 9:17:

> Because they have not listened to him, my God will reject them;
> they shall become wanderers among the nations.

This very association with the reader is important for understanding the genre. The shift between direct divine discourse and authorial commentary immediately gives the word of God a dialogical character. It in turn has the power to draw the readers in a sense into itself. The genre itself causes the readers to engage both intellectually and emotionally with the word of God "through Hosea."

Of course, at this point the exegetical analysis of the text would have to examine almost everything anew, something I cannot do here. This proposal about the two principal voices in the book of Hosea apparently involves not only a suggestion for reading, but also a program for commentary. Only when it has been carried through will we know whether the proposal is really valid, or whether its only result is an intellectual game at almost two thousand years' distance. But if the proposal is valid, there is another question to be asked within the framework of narrative analysis.

The "implied author"

When a number of voices are heard in a narrative the question arises: which of these voices has the last word? In the book of Hosea even the voice of God is ultimately only a reality within the world of the text; it is not actually the voice of God, which would have unquestioned authority. Which voice, then, has the last word in the world of the text: that of the author of the book or one of the voices he allows to be heard within the book?

This is the question of the "implied author." The author who speaks in the book, whether as narrator, or commentator, or someone addressing the readers, is also only a voice in the book. It is entirely possible that he will not act properly and that another voice that he himself allows to be heard will prove him false. The celebrated example within biblical literature is the narrator of the book of Joshua. In Josh 21:43-45 the narrator summarizes the conquest and division of the land in his own words and announces that God has given all Israel's enemies into its hands, and that all God's promises have been fulfilled. But in Joshua 23 this narrator has Joshua appear, and Joshua suddenly speaks of the nations who still remain, and the territories that, while assigned, have not yet been seized. Who is right? the narrator or his character? In this example it is clear that we have to get past the narrator or author who appears in the book. Behind him or her there must be an idea of the book itself—still not identical with the opinion of the real-world author, still within the world of the text, but no longer bound to a single voice. Here we speak of the "implied author." Where is the "implied author" in the book of Hosea? Who has the last word: the author of the book (who here has effectively become a divine ghostwriter), or God?

Since only the closest analysis can help us with questions like this, I cannot avoid scrutinizing the text once again. What I will say is extremely abbreviated, but I hope to touch the critical point. At the same time, in doing so I will finally arrive at the thematic area indicated by the title of this essay, the question of "wrath." The "wrath of God" is a central issue in the book of Hosea, no less than in the later letter of Paul to the Romans.

The names Hosea is required to give his three children are names of wrath. The author of the book immediately contradicts them, and in doing so sets himself against God. But not much later he succeeds in proving that he in fact is on God's side, because he again introduces the voice of

God, and at the end of the second chapter God's wrath has ended. God confirms what the author had anticipated. Perhaps this also explains the zeal with which the author three times inserts his "says the LORD," the divine "whisper" in the God-text in the second chapter, as soon as God's wrath has faded.

At this point we should say something about the wavelike character of the book of Hosea. The central problem—wrath or love—has in fact been solved by the end of ch. 3. But it has only been spoken of within the framework of Hosea's family, even though with a very broad perspective. When the waters have flowed away, the next and greater wave washes the strand of the readers' awareness. Now everything is broadened, everything is concrete, the sinner and the sin are named, and now there is a very different retrospective view of history. This is the major discourse in chs. 4–11. But then comes yet another wave in the last three chapters. It laps now at the Jewish strand and brings with it, even more comprehensively, the whole of past history and the foundational myths. Each of these waves is driven by the storm wind of wrath; each one breaks and becomes love. Three times the problem is proposed, and three times it is answered.

Most revealing of all is the interplay between the voice of the author and the voice of God in the central part of the book. As we have said, the author introduces this discourse in 4:1-3. He begins with a kind of preliminary project, an introductory summary. These three verses are unbelievably radical. In the whole book of Hosea there is no harsher judgment on reality. It is a genuine proclamation of divine wrath. Everything that had been positive is denied regarding the inhabitants of the land: fidelity, love, knowledge of God. Everything the Decalogue forbids is attributed to them: They are blasphemers and betrayers, murderers, thieves, and adulterers. Bloodshed is heaped upon bloodshed. The wrath all this evokes can only bring an end to the universe. Even the animals, the birds, and the fish of the sea are destined for destruction. Nothing in the following eight chapters, none of the wrathful words of God or the author's commentary achieves these proportions. The author has, at the very beginning, dared to move interpretatively to the utmost extreme of a declaration of wrath, and thus given his readers a terrifying key for the notes of the musical score. How will he react when God's wrath collapses?

With this question we have arrived at ch. 11; here, in the first verses, God's wrath has already been transformed into mourning. God cannot forget his once-great love for Israel, now so long lost. In 11:5 the voice of the author enters, but it extends the lament tangentially into a new proclamation of punishment, without noticing the curve that is already beginning. He speaks of the rule of Assyria, swords in the cities, an end to all plans for the future. In 11:7 God takes up the discourse again, and definitively asserts the infidelity of God's people. But then the divine wrath burns out. God cannot give Israel up, cannot execute divine anger. God will not come in wrath. In 11:10 it is the author's turn again, and we see that he has understood. He does not hesitate for a second to reverse everything he has just said and to introduce a new tangent. He makes concrete what God has said only in principle, and he encapsulates it in a glowing image:

> They shall go after YHWH, who roars like a lion;
> when he roars, his children shall come trembling from the west.
> They shall come trembling like birds from Egypt,
> and like doves from the land of Assyria.

The author is anticipating; God has not spoken so definitively yet. But immediately, God confirms what the author says. In 11:11b follows the brief, concluding oracle of salvation:

> and I will return them to their homes.

At this critical point in the book it must be clear that the authorial voice subordinates itself to the voice of God. When we ask where the "implied author" of the book of Hosea stands, the answer must be: where God stands at the end. And this God does not come in wrath.

The third *rib* will come to the same end and the image will not be altered, but there will begin to be a breath of what will grow on the other side of wrath, the mystical odor of the divine juniper.

Of course we already knew all these texts about the end of wrath in the past as well. But for the long-familiar technique for reading the book of Hosea they were individual polished stones within a field of gravel. When we considered the historical Hosea we were not so sure whether he was not simply a prophet of wrath. We are no more sure about that today. But to the extent that our interest shifts from the prophet to the book, the divine wrath and its collapse appear in a different and larger configuration. Everything is related in a different way. We can read the book as a book, and decontextualized prophetic words appear in a new context.

That righteousness includes mercy is and was old knowledge. The book of Hosea is also aware of the formulae of its civilization. It can speak in commonplaces in the most offhand way in 14:3 [MT 14:4]:

> In you the orphan finds mercy.

But in a historical moment in which a gigantic catastrophe is crashing upon the land of Israel, the commonplace arises anew into consciousness like volcanic lava, as the wrath of God and its end.

Even the discourse of wrath was probably in the air at that time. In the same century, perhaps even in the same year as the book of Hosea, in Greece the *Iliad* was being written, the epic about the wrath of Achilles, which rose up because of Briseis, the trophy woman whom Agamemnon took from him. God's wrath was kindled because Israel, God's only wife, had made herself a whore. Both forms of wrath collapsed, each in its own way. Two stories of wrath that we have to learn to read again and again, always anew. We probably draw our lives from both of them.

Chapter Six

The Psalter and Meditation
On the Genre of the Book of Psalms

Can we still pray the Psalms, sing them at the daily Office? Modern study of the Psalms makes this a two-edged question. Reform of the Divine Office has sharpened, not blunted it. How would it sound if we turned the question around?

For example: Christian life is not centered on the Torah, and yet the Torah is the theme of Psalm 1. What relationship do we have to the ancient Jewish rituals of kingship? Psalm 2 comes out of them. When should we pray Psalms 3 or 4, if they were once part of the judicial rituals in the Jerusalem Temple? We do not offer daily morning sacrifice by slaughtering sheep. So when can we pray Psalm 5? We could go on this way. The *Sitz im Leben* of most of the psalms is a world in which we no longer live, that no longer even exists. The very study of genres that has contributed so much to our understanding of the psalms makes them strangers to us. It has shown the cultic origins of many psalms. But it was a different cult, not ours.

On the other hand, the psalms are still prayed by many people today. A lot of people can express themselves to God better through the psalms than through other prayers or even their own words. Liturgical fashions wither in a few years, yet monastic prayer in choir has endured. Is it possible that scholarly reflection has overlooked something about the psalms? maybe even the most important thing? This is the question that inspired this essay.

My main point is this: we are really not talking about *individual* psalms, but about the *Psalter,* that is, about a book. In modern biblical scholarship the use of genre analysis has pushed that fact to the margins of our consciousness. Scholars are interested in individual psalms, and in their original state: the oldest form and the oldest use.

Hermann Gunkel, the father of genre criticism of the Old Testament, regarded a great many psalms as late, spiritual poetry. According to him, not all psalms were made for cultic worship. He also doubted whether the Psalter as a collection was only intended for cultic usage. But very quickly scholars, led by Sigmund Mowinckel, asserted the cultic character of all the psalms. That opinion has prevailed, at least at the unconscious level. It still shapes our scholarly work with the Psalter, even though in recent years some things have been written about a post-exilic "spiritualization" of the Psalms. For the most part even that has been done only for individual psalms.

First I want to inquire about the purpose of the psalms at the time when the Psalter was canonically determined, that is, approximately within the century when Jesus of Nazareth was born.

The use of the Psalms in Jesus' time

Some time ago Notker Füglister summarized our present knowledge very well in a thorough essay. I will primarily follow him here.

Undoubtedly the Psalter was the best-known and most-cited book of the Old Testament in Qumran, in the New Testament, and in the witnesses to Hellenistic Judaism. It was of great significance for the religious life of Judaism.

The thesis that the Psalter was the "hymnal of the Second Temple," on the other hand, has been refuted. It is true that levitical choirs sang certain psalms, known to us, for the people during the daily *tamid* sacrifice, and also at certain ceremonies on festival days, standing on the stairs leading from the Court of the Women to the Court of the Men (and thus not at the place where the sacrificial ritual itself took place). They took their signals from trumpeters who were placed so as to be able to observe the progress of the sacrifice. But the number of such psalms is limited, and the priests in the cult proper recited other texts, when they did not carry out their duties in complete silence.

Still less was the Psalter the "hymnal of the synagogue." The rabbinic synagogue liturgy was, to begin with, devoid of psalms. Only in the second half of the first century C.E. was a series of psalms inserted into synagogue prayer, at the behest of pious people and against the will of the rabbinic authorities. The theses of the Karaites may also have played a part.

It was not very different in other Jewish groups. We have no definite evidence from Qumran or from the early Christian communities for the use of the Psalter in worship. Evidence of knowledge and love of the psalms is not, of itself, evidence of their liturgical use, and certainly not as regards the entire Psalter. The Psalms entered Christian worship only toward the end of the second century, and then only individual psalms. At most we may surmise the use of psalms in ritual by the Jewish group of "Therapeutae," who lived in Egypt.

At the same time we must relate this negative liturgical finding to the equally well attested wide knowledge and popularity of the Psalter that we have already noted. I see only one convincing explanation: The Psalter was the fundamental text for personal, individual piety. But how should we picture that concretely?

We know very little about the meditative traditions of early Judaism and Christianity. Those practices were broken off. We now travel to India to learn how to meditate and what a mantra is. Our complete ignorance is reflected even in incorrect translations of the Bible. Thus we read in the text of the "Shema Israel" in many translations:

> Keep these words that I am commanding you today in your heart. Recite them to your children and *talk about them* when you are at home and when you are away, when you lie down and when you rise. (Deut 6:6-7)

The correct translation, somewhat paraphrased, would be:

> Memorize this text that I am proclaiming to you today. Repeat it with your children. Murmur it when you are squatting at home and when you are away, in the evening before sleeping, and in the morning when you rise.

This presumes as a matter of course that one meditates by murmuring memorized texts in the rhythm of one's breath. Deuteronomy 6:6-7 only wants to insist that the meditated (murmured) text should be Deuteronomy.

There is a similar notion in Psalm 1. Our translations read:

> Happy the one who does not follow the advice of the wicked,
> or take the path that sinners tread,
> or sit in the seat of scoffers,
> but whose delight is in the law of the LORD
> and *meditates on* his law day and night. (Ps 1:1-2)

We see the pious as thinkers. The correct translation would be:

> but who is filled with joy by YHWH's Torah,
> *reciting* his Torah day and night.

Jerome translated here:

> *in lege eius meditabitur.*

However, the word *meditari* in the Latin of the monks of his time meant to speak a text from memory. The *meditatio* of the monks in their caves and cells was a soft murmuring of texts while one squatted, rocking to and fro and weaving rush mats. One could also "meditate" by murmuring Bible texts while traveling or working together in the monastery bakery. Even the (always memorized) "reading" of the Psalms at the assemblies for prayer, which everyone listened to while sitting, could be called *meditatio*. Even if one constantly repeated the same biblical phrase over and over, this technique was *meditatio*. That is how the "Jesus prayer" of the Eastern Church developed.

The Hebrew expressions translated differently in the texts cited above all describe the technique of meditation aided by the speaking of memorized texts in a half-voiced rhythmic sing-song. Such action must have been as much a matter of course for pious Jews and Christians at the time of Jesus as is for Muslims today the continuous turning of the thirty-three-bead "rosary" while speaking the hundred names of God. The texts that individuals knew by heart were of course different in length. But in comparison to present-day capacity for memorization we can probably think of more rather than less.

That must have been the *Sitz im Leben* of the Psalter at that time. It was one of the texts that one murmured while "meditating"—unless it was in fact *the* text for that activity.

It is important to note that it was the *Psalter* that was recited. Certainly people must have selected and spoken individual psalms on occasion, and not everyone would have known the entire Psalter. Nevertheless, it was not individual psalms that were the text for meditation, but the whole *book* of Psalms. The Psalter was *one single* meditation text.

There may be an ancient tradition behind the Jewish psalm societies of today whose members promise to begin on the first day of the week by reciting Psalm 1 and to get to Psalm 150 by the Sabbath at the latest. The same may be true of the Jewish people who recite all 150 psalms daily at the Wailing Wall in Jerusalem.

At the moment when the monks' free, personal practice of meditation was augmented by a more sharply ritualized community form of meditation, the earliest monastic hours—and that happened rather quickly—it was at first taken as a matter of course that at least during the night Office the prayer would proceed according to the order of the Psalter. When they got to Psalm 150 they simply began again at Psalm 1, sometimes during the same worship service. This practice can be shown to have been the norm from the Pachomian monasteries until the Rule of the Master at the beginning of the sixth century.

Benedict, who in shaping the daily hours was more influenced by the customs in the Roman basilicas, proposes psalms for Lauds and Compline that are appropriate to the hour of the day, while keeping the order of the Psalter for the remaining hours (though on several parallel tracks). His awareness of the unity of the Psalter is apparent especially from the fact that he prescribes that at all times the whole of it is to be recited every week. Benedict notes that this is very little: "Since we read that our holy Fathers performed the whole Psalter with great labor in one day, let us at least do so in a whole week, despite our tepidity" (*RB* 18, 25).

The similarity of such principles to the Jewish practices of devotion mentioned above, which endure even today, speaks in favor of the notion that the monks in the Egyptian desert had not invented anything new. They had received from the common Jewish-Christian heritage the idea that the Psalter as a whole was *the* text to be recited for meditation.

If this picture of the use of the Psalter seems most probable for the time of Jesus of Nazareth, that is, very soon after the compilation of the Psalter in the form it now has, the question arises whether the *final redaction* of the book of Psalms did not create the Psalter for precisely this purpose, and whether that goal does not play a role in shaping its form. The *linking of key words* in the Psalms also speaks in favor of this idea.

Redactional linking of psalms as an aid to meditation

When Hermann Gunkel speaks of the "ordering" of the Psalms in his *Einleitung in die Psalmen* he notes several things that sound almost tragicomic. Regrettably, he finds, the psalms are not arranged according to genre. That, of course, would have been the ideal thing for the inventor of genre criticism! Then he notes that they are also not arranged according to the "authors" named in the titles of the individual psalms. The rest of the information in the titles is also only of partial use in ordering the psalms. They are not even arranged according to length, with the longer psalms preceding the shorter ones. It is true that all this, and even some other factors such as the "similarity of ideas" in neighboring psalms or "associative key words" between them may have played some role here and there. But on the whole they are really without any order. That was Gunkel's regretful conclusion.

When Gunkel studies the "similarity of ideas" between neighboring psalms and the "associative key words" they share, his principal conversation partner is Franz Delitzsch, whose commentary, appearing first in 1860, was distinguished from all others by the fact that for each psalm he indicated links in content and in key words to the adjoining psalms. No later commentary pursued that line.

In fact, there is a linkage between neighboring psalms throughout the entire Psalter, but our awareness of the fact has almost vanished. Only in recent years have the connections between the psalms been rediscovered, and particularly the associations of key words.

However, awareness of the linkage in the content and language of the psalms is not widespread. In spite of that, I do not want to deal with the fact itself here. I prefer to presume it as proved. I would also like to leave open the question of who created the linkages of content and key words. This was certainly the work of redaction, whether for the whole Psalter or for partial collections. But did that redaction insert additions, replace words, perhaps even compose whole new psalms? Or did it only make skillful use of existing correspondences of content and words? Probably both these things happened. My question—presupposing the facts and simply having sketched them in the above examples—concerns the extent to which such key word linkages, and with them the correspondences in content between one psalm and the others surrounding it, contribute to the reality that the Psalter as a whole became a text for meditation, to be learned by heart and murmured repeatedly over and over.

(a) An initial service of the linkage of psalms, it seems to me, is that we are *led* from one psalm to the next. Sometimes key words from the end of one psalm are simply taken up directly in the next. Thus Psalm 32 ends with the call to praise:

Be glad in Y*HWH* and rejoice, O *righteous,*
and *shout for joy,* all you *upright in heart.* (32:11)

Psalm 33:1 then follows almost like a parallel verse. One verbal root and three addresses are repeated, as well as the divine name:

Rejoice in Y*HWH*, O you *righteous.*
Praise befits *the upright.*

Often the connection is not so immediate. Frequently the key words are only retrieved within the content of the next psalm, or a following psalm continues one line and the next psalm takes up another. Thus at the end of Psalm 7 we read:

I will give to Y*HWH* the *thanks* due to his righteousness,
and *sing praise* to the *name of* Y*HWH, the Most High.* (7:17)

This is followed by Psalm 8, which praises the "name" of God and is in a certain sense the fulfillment of the vow of praise at the end of Psalm 7 (which was a song of lament), but especially as praise of the *name* of God. Psalm 8 begins and ends with the sentence:

Y*HWH*, our Sovereign,
how majestic is your *name* in all the earth! (8:1, 9)

But then Psalm 9 takes up the vow at the end of Psalm 7 in a still broader form, beginning a song of thanksgiving. Much more than simply the key word "name" recurs here:

> I will give *thanks* to Y<small>HWH</small> with my whole heart,
> I will tell of all your wonderful deeds.
> I will be glad and exult in you;
> I will *sing* praise to your *name, O Most High.* (9:1-2)

Thus in its opening verses Psalm 9 develops the end of Psalm 7 still more than Psalm 8 had done.

As soon as the reader or user detects that kind of use of key words or motifs in a literary work as a technique, his or her expectations are raised. From then on, the phenomenon is anticipated. In the case of the Psalter this means that the ending of a psalm does not create a feeling of completion. We expect it to continue, for certain elements of content, certain formulae—even if we do not know which ones—have to find their echo, the continuation of their voice.

By that fact alone the Psalter receives a dynamic that makes it a single text. Meditation need not stand still or break off.

This is intensified when, as often happens, some elements are introduced that require whole groups of psalms for their unfolding. Something of the sort was clearly evident, in germ, at the end of Psalm 7. But these notes can extend much farther, as for example in the last part of the Psalter, Psalms 146–150, the "final Hallel." In 145:21 David, the singer of the preceding group of psalms, announces:

> *My mouth* will speak the *praise of* Y<small>HWH</small>,
> and *all flesh* will bless his holy name forever and ever.

The word *tehillah,* "praise," introduces Psalms 146–150, all framed by the hallelujah-shout: "Praise Y<small>HWH</small>"—that is, the whole remainder of the Psalter. The tension in the parallelism between "my mouth" and "all flesh" anchors the great arch that—with a highly significant retardation of tempo shortly before the reversal—shapes the whole. Psalm 146 begins, in vv. 1-2:

> Praise Y<small>HWH</small>, O *my* soul!
> I will praise Y<small>HWH</small> as long as I live.

Thus David begins his praise of Y<small>HWH</small>. In Psalm 147 the circle of singers expands. Israel/Zion takes up the song of praise. In Psalm 148 the heavenly beings and the whole of the earthly cosmos join in. But at the end of this psalm it is clear that the true reason for praise is that God has raised up a "horn" for the people. This refers to the praise that God's *ḥasidim,* the "faithful" sing in Israel. All this is in the final verse (148:14), which in turn introduces the "new" song in the "assembly of the *ḥasidim,*" in a sense the center of the all-encompassing praise of God:

> Sing to YHWH a new song,
> his praise in the assembly of the *ḥasidim.* (149:1)

In Psalm 150 this song is accompanied by every conceivable instrument, and the final sentence of the last psalm reads:

> Let *everything* that breathes praise YHWH. (150:6)

Here the announcement in 145:21 is fulfilled. David alone began the praise, more and more beings joined in, and now it sounds from the mouth of all flesh, that is, from the mouth of everything that breathes. It is simply impossible to stand still within Psalms 145–150; it is necessary to go on reciting from one psalm to the next.

Perhaps, in light of these observations, which could be multiplied many times over, it is easier to understand why the Psalms are not arranged by genres, primary content, speakers, titles, or length, as Gunkel would have preferred. They cannot be, for that would make the Psalter a boring set of records, a dusty archive. Under all these aspects a constant transition is necessary so that there may be life; every new psalm must be entirely new, different, surprising, and yet at the same time linked, joined. The thing that joins them is on a much more subtle level: that of linking key words, motifs, partial contents, the interplay of loose allusion and its resolution.

(b) Besides producing unity, the first achievement of the Psalms redaction, the same phenomenon of linking of content and key words, produces a second effect: the *interpenetration of aspects.* Let me illustrate this at the beginning of the Psalter.

Psalms 1, 2, and 3 are very different in genre and theme: Psalm 1 is a Torah and Wisdom psalm, Psalm 2 is part of a royal enthronement liturgy (or the imitation of one), and Psalm 3 is an individual song of lament that is at the same time presented as a morning song. The key-word links that are present nonetheless are therefore all the more astonishing.

Psalm 1 begins with a beatitude and Psalm 2 ends with one. According to Ps 1:2 the righteous meditate on (murmur) the Torah, and according to Ps 2:1 the nations conspire (murmur) vain things. Psalm 1 ends with the image of the way: YHWH knows the way of the righteous, but the way of the wicked "will perish." In Psalm 2, in the end the nations are warned that they will "perish" in the way. Psalm 3 immediately takes up the motif of enemies from Psalm 2 (3:1-2; cf. 7). In addition, the image in Ps 2:9 of the ruler who treads on and smashes the necks of his enemies, familiar from

Egyptian portraits of the Pharaohs, recurs in Ps 3:7, applied to God. Moreover, the expression "holy hill" recurs (2:6 and 3:4), though it is scarcely required by the principal theme. It is possible even that the end of Psalm 2, which calls blessed all those who trust in God (2:12), is an introduction to Psalm 3, which begins in vv. 1-3 with a statement of trust.

This linking achieves a very precise effect. In their genre and direct statement these three psalms are quite different, but through the chainlike linking they are, in their very difference, in some sense layered one upon the other or interleaved with one another. The righteous and the wicked, the chosen king of Israel and the nations rising up against him, the persecuted and his or her enemies are suddenly not disparate entities. They are related to one another. The boundaries between the foolishness of wicked individuals, the rising up of the nations against God's plan for history, and the persecution of the righteous in Israel seem to dissolve, as do the distinctions between the righteous, God's anointed, and the one who is unjustly persecuted.

Fundamental structures appear. What in one case the king does, in the other case is done by God: we sense the mystery of the intimate relationship between human and divine action. What in Psalms 2 and 3 appears to be here and now is cast into eschatological light from the perspective of the end of Psalm 1. Thus the anointed one in Psalm 2 is transparent to a Messiah at the end-time, for whom the person praying Psalm 3, oppressed by enemies, yet hopes as much as she or he hopes for God's own action.

The linking of the first three psalms already effects in those who meditatively murmur the Psalter as a whole something like an explosion of the individual statements, a sweeping obliteration of the individual levels of interpretation. One can quickly read each of these psalms on one level or another. Everything is open to insights and still further and more penetrating comprehension. The plane becomes space in which understanding can move freely.

This process of understanding is typical of meditation. It erases the objective limitations of individual objects of contemplation, leads deeper into the foundation of things, approaches non-objectivity. In the Psalter, in contrast to some Eastern doctrines of meditation, this is never the ultimate goal of meditation. The Psalter intends to leave the one murmuring it in the tension between the individual meaning and the non-objective depth. It achieves precisely this through the fullness of its very different texts, full of reversals and exchanges, yet intensively interwoven with one another.

Of course, exegesis must also attempt to describe this will to meaning that is seated at the level of the redaction of the Psalter. As far as I can see we are still very far from such an undertaking.

In a third and final section I will return to the level of the sense of the individual psalms as given in the text. The question is whether, at least in individual cases, the final redaction that linked the psalms has altered their direct meaning by relating certain individual psalms to those nearby.

Alteration of meaning through ordering of psalms to one another

Let me give two examples. In the one case it is a matter of psalm-linking as dialogical dramatization, in the other of psalm-linking as introduction of a new subject—in both cases with massive consequences for what is expressed.

(a) Psalm-linking as dialogical dramatization. The example given is Psalms 137 and 138. We are here at the transition to the last collection of David-psalms in the Psalter, extending from Psalm 138 to Psalm 145. The collection is introduced by the lament of the Babylonian exiles in Ps 137:4:

> How could we sing YHWH's song
> in a foreign land?

This lament intensifies within Psalm 137 in vv. 8-9, culminating in the wish that the destroyer Babylon should be paid back as it deserves, its children seized by enemies and smashed against a rock.

This bitter and despairing abandonment of YHWH's praise in exile is answered by the prototypical David, transparent to the Messiah—according to the superscription of Psalm 138—with an explosive song in praise of YHWH:

> . . . with my whole heart;
> before the gods . . . (138:1)

In the context of the problem created by Psalm 137 the "gods" are of course the divinities that other nations worship "afar, in a foreign land" (137:4). Many translations unfortunately make them "angels," which are completely out of place here. David has thrown himself down in prayer toward YHWH's "holy temple" in Jerusalem, because YHWH's steadfast love and faithfulness, the divine "word," extend farther than YHWH's "name," that is, the realm within which YHWH is known and worshiped by human beings (138:2). David knows from experience that whenever he has called, even from the greatest distance, his God has heard him and "increased [his] strength of soul" (138:3). In the picture of the person praying that develops here, David could dissolve into the image of the legendary Daniel who prayed toward Jerusalem during the Babylonian exile (cf. Dan 6:10).

The sense of this praise of YHWH, sounding in the Jewish diaspora, is to be that it prepares for the praise of YHWH from all the "kings of the earth," which is coming. It will sound when the rulers of the nations have received the words that come from the mouth of YHWH (138:4). The future praise of YHWH on the part of the kings of the nations is then immediately cited in the form of a short hymn (138:5b, 6). It reveals what YHWH has effected by the "words of his mouth" and that results in the conversion of the kings of the nations to YHWH. YHWH regards the lowly (with mercy and aid), and perceives the haughty from afar (138:6). Deciphering this in light of Deutero-Isaiah, we may say that the conversion of the nations to YHWH will take place when they see how YHWH acts through a word of power on behalf of YHWH's poor, Israel dispersed among the nations.

Read in this way, Psalm 138 is a messianic counter-position to Psalm 137, powerful in hope. The two psalms are related to each other as a dramatic dialogue, with victory belonging to the second voice, that of David. With Psalm 138 he introduces a whole collection that continues to sing with his own voice. It will work out in detail much of what is said here in Psalm 138, and at that point it will be evident that the Psalter does not simply obliterate what is said in Psalm 137. The latter expresses a deep-seated experience of persecuted Israel, and it needs to be spoken. But then it must be reversed by the attitude expressed in Psalm 138.

(b) Psalm-linking as introduction of a new subject. The example we shall use here is Psalms 22–26. Psalm 22, the lament whose opening Jesus spoke on the cross, not only ends in hope and vows of thanksgiving (from 22:22 on), but beginning at 22:27 this expands into a future vision of national and world dimensions that in 22:29, according to some interpreters, even surpasses the bounds of death. A reading that takes the psalm as a self-enclosed model of a song of lament can, of course, only speak of the "fictive character" of the statements at this point. The nations are simply "walk-ons" to "round off the praise of God." It is different if the praying person who comes upon Psalm 22 is well practiced in reading the psalms in their linked condition and as mutual keys to each other's meaning. Such a one could read the psalm from the beginning as both an individual's psalm and a psalm of Israel. She or he can also expect that the new theme introduced by the vow of thanksgiving at the end of this psalm will sound the notes of the next psalm.

In fact, Psalm 23:1 takes up the "God is king" statement of 22:28. "Shepherd" is a royal metaphor. This psalm also develops the idea of a rich meal as liturgy of thanksgiving from 22:26 and 30 into a great banquet in the "house of YHWH" (23:5-6). When the person praying 22:22 had promised to "tell" of YHWH's *"name"* to his or her brothers and sisters, and the vision of the psalm culminates in 22:31 with the proclamation that

86 *In the Shadow of Your Wings*

YHWH's "deeds of *righteousness*" [NRSV: deliverance] will be "told" to a future "people" yet unborn, it is almost a probability that Psalm 23 will depict that narrative. For in 23:3 we read:

> He leads me in paths of *righteousness*
> for his *name*'s sake.

If, according to 22:29, the "fat ones of the earth" cannot "keep their *soul* alive," the one who prays Psalm 23 can say:

> he restores my *soul*. (23:3)

There can thus be no doubt about the linking of these two psalms. But does the theme of the nations therefore continue?

That lies at least within the realm of possibility. For at the very beginning of Psalm 23 there is something that ordinarily does not emerge in our translations. We usually translate:

> The LORD is my shepherd.

In our modern languages that sounds as if a believer in YHWH were applying a new title to the God YHWH, whom she or he has always worshiped, seeing YHWH in a new image, that of a shepherd. But according to the rules for word order in Hebrew nominal sentences, what is new here is the divine name. That is: everyone has a "shepherd." The question is only *whom* one has as one's shepherd. In Psalm 23 "David" declares:

> My shepherd is [not Assyria, not Marduk, not one of the other gods of the nations, but] YHWH.

Thus the statement is something in the nature of a declaration of faith pronounced by a new convert who is certain that, led by his or her new divine shepherd, he or she can enter on the (very dangerous) path that will lead to a place where a table is set and the cups are filled. That place is the Temple of YHWH (23:6). Psalm 24 will then immediately speak of entering the Temple. Given that singular and plural have already begun to superimpose themselves on each other within the Psalter, this fits clearly within the perspective of the eschatological conversion of the nations that was introduced at the end of Psalm 22. We can at least say that, as a result of the linking of the two psalms, this is one of the possibilities given for understanding Psalm 23. The theme of the pilgrimage of the nations could be echoed in the path through the dark valley. The nations not yet converted to the God of Israel would be the enemies in the psalm.

With this openness to the theme "pilgrimage of nations," Psalm 23 prepares for Psalm 24, which, as I will show, speaks clearly about that pilgrimage. But first let me say something about the links between these two psalms.

The movement in Psalm 23 ends with the "house of YHWH" (23:6); Psalm 24 takes place on the "hill of YHWH" (24:3) and deals with access to this "holy place." While the one praying 23:3 was traveling on the "paths of righteousness" [NRSV: "right paths"], these are revealed in Ps 24:5 to be paths *to* "righteousness," for "blessing from YHWH, vindication from the God of their salvation" comes to those who are admitted to the sanctuary. Thus the two psalms are indeed linked. What is Psalm 24 about?

In 24:3 the question of the conditions for access to the sanctuary on Zion, familiar to those praying the Psalms from 15:1, is taken up again:

Who shall ascend the hill of YHWH?
And who shall stand in his holy place?

Who are the people whose access to the Temple is in question? After the listing of conditions for access (v. 4) and a promise of blessing and justification (v. 5), they are addressed as follows in v. 6:

Such is the company of those who ask [NRSV: "seek"] him (= YHWH),
who seek thy face, O Jacob [NRSV: "who seek the face of the God of Jacob"].

The verbs "ask" and "seek" are familiar parallels to those who pray the Psalms. But here their objects are not parallel. The second breaks out of the readers' expectations, which have been steered toward a reference to God. If we do not resort to the Septuagint here (as, unfortunately, all our translations do: see the NRSV usage)—which evidently found the statement in these verses unbearable—those whose access to the sanctuary is in question are non-Israelites, people from the "nations." For since they desire to see "Jacob's face," they cannot themselves belong to Jacob (= Israel).

In its Hebrew/Masoretic version Psalm 24 is therefore specifically about the eschatological pilgrimage of the nations to Zion. Together with Isa 2:2-5 = Mic 4:1-5, Psalm 24 may be the most important text on this subject. For that reason, it seems, it also begins with a confession of YHWH, the Lord of the whole world and all its inhabitants (vv. 1-2). Therefore the conditions of access include only purity of heart and hand, together with exclusive worship of the one true God, without reference (as was the case in Psalm 15) to specifically Israelite precepts, for example the prohibition of exacting interest on money.

Hence a major bridge is begun in the final verses of Psalm 22. At least by the time she or he reaches Psalm 24 the person praying is aware that Psalm 23 was primarily to be understood in terms of the approach of the nations to Zion. In turn, in light of Psalm 23 one of the most revolutionary statements in

Psalm 24, little noticed for what it is despite all attempts to reconstruct ritual sequences in it, is contextualized, at least in the broader text.

In Psalm 24 the subject is the entry of the nations into the holy city on the mountain of YHWH (v. 3). There they will receive blessing and justification from YHWH (v. 5). But when, beginning in 24:7, the entry into the sanctuary is played out in a kind of festive liturgy at the portal it is not the nations who enter, but YHWH. It may indeed be the case that an ancient portal liturgy from a time when there were still Ark processions in Jerusalem is being revived here. But in the current psalm it should be the nations who enter. Still, entry is demanded by YHWH, the "king of glory," and it is not immediately granted. As long as YHWH appears as "strong" and "mighty in battle" (v. 8), the gates do not lift up their heads. Only when YHWH appears merely as "YHWH of hosts" can he enter into his own mountain (v. 10). It seems that at this late period "YHWH Sabaoth (= of hosts)" did not designate—if it ever had—a "God of the hosts of war." Instead, we should read the title in light of the parallel in Isa 54:5 ("YHWH of hosts is his name . . . the God of the whole earth he is called") or through the principal translation of the term in the Septuagint, *pantokratōr*, "ruler of all." Then the circle from the beginning of the psalm is closed, and in particular the kerygma of the pilgrimage-of-nations texts from Isaiah 2 and Micah 4 is brought within it: the turning of the nations to Zion is connected with an end to wars. At the eschatological moment of the pilgrimage of the nations YHWH will personally appear on Zion, as if anew, no longer as the warrior hero, but as the Lord of the whole world who peacefully gathers all the nations. This dialectic of the entry of the God to whom the nations come is—and here I again return to the crucial point—already anticipated, since in Psalm 23 YHWH as the "shepherd" goes with the one who prays the psalm to Jerusalem. If the one praying the psalm stands for the nations, the astonishing reversal of aspect in Ps 24:7 has long been prepared for through Psalm 23 as a whole.

In Psalm 23, then, the linking of the psalms has produced a change of *subject*. The same process continues after Psalm 24, which of course is linked forward as well. As in Psalm 15, so in Ps 24:4 the conditions for admission to the sanctuary are listed. The third is:

> . . . who do not *lift up* their *souls* to what is false.

This condition directly corresponds to the opening of Psalm 25:

> To you, O YHWH, I *lift up* my *soul*.

This, in the first place, makes it clear that "what is false" in 24:4 does not refer, for example, to false statements (as our translations seem to imply), but to false, nonexistent gods. But in particular Psalm 25, which opens in this way, proves to be a prayer for the people who, according to Psalm 24, seek admission to Zion's sanctuary. Thus in the minds of those responsible for the Psalms redaction Psalm 25 is meant to show how the people of the nations are to pray there. As a result of the linkage Psalm 25, which in isolation would naturally be read simply in terms of Israel or an individual Israelite, has become a prayer of the nations. As this psalm formulates its prayer, so will the nations speak when "in days to come" they come to the sanctuary on Zion.

I cannot explain in detail what that means. Let me simply draw attention to two points. When Yhwh has forgiven the sins of the one who prays Psalm 25 and taught her or him Yhwh's ways, that person, like Israel of old, will "possess the land" (25:13). In addition, according to v. 14 she or he will even have entrée into Israel as God's holy "assembly" and to the "covenant." The last, especially, is an unheard-of statement, for nowhere else in the entire Hebrew Bible is the "covenant" opened to the "nations."

Since Psalm 26 also refers back to the conditions of access in Ps 24:4 and in addition is closely linked to Psalm 25, even here we can think of a praying person from the nations as the subject of the psalm. But I will only mention that in passing.

Conclusions

The last example was quite extensive. But it may be the only way to show that considering the redaction of the Psalter is not an idle game. If we do not venture it, and instead stick with isolated individual psalms, it may be that important hopes of Israel that are only expressed at this level of the text will escape our notice.

The redaction of the Psalms is still altogether "Old" Testament. But, as we have seen, it achieves an astonishing closeness to the "New" Testament. There remains only a thin wall between the two. The more we enter into the intentions of the Psalter's redaction, the stronger is the impression that there is not a yawning abyss between the "Old" and "New" Testaments, but that the "new" of the "New Testament" is almost nothing but the assertion that what previously could only be formulated as hope and anticipated future has now, in fact, come.

An ordering of the psalms in the Liturgy of the Hours that forces them all into individuality because it does not leave the psalms in the redactionally-created context that represents their immanent hermeneutic not only leads to difficulties in Christians' reading of them. It systematically destroys a true Old Testament reading as well.

If what I have said in this essay is accurate, we cannot avoid a series of practical consequences that I would like to list here in conclusion.

1. It is urgently necessary that biblical scholars pursue in detail the aspects of the Psalter that I have been discussing and that have so long been neglected. At the present time, indeed, they have at their disposal, because of the advances in computer technology, much better research aids for the series of investigations that need to be made than were available in the past.

2. The available translations of the Bible are for the most part unsuitable for indicating to non-scholars the phenomena in the text of the Psalter that have been uncovered here. The images are often reduced to abstractions, the key word correspondences have been lost, the language lacks the density and rhythm that are necessary if people are to learn texts and be able to recite them again and again without their becoming insipid in our mouths. In German, the translation by Martin Buber and Franz Rosenzweig comes closest to what is asked for here. What is needed is an urgent effort to create a better modern-language Psalter than what we currently have.

3. Christians in search of the forms of Christian meditation, especially in contemplative communities, must have the courage to return to the meditative origins of their own tradition. We must learn again to recite the memorized Psalter as "meditation." The last trace elements of this tradition have been preserved, almost to our own day, far down in the much-despised popular devotion of reciting Hail Marys in the rosary. It is no accident that in many places the threefold rosary with its 150 Hail Marys is called a "psalter." Here, and in prayer forms such as the Jesus Prayer, are the starting points for what could take shape once again.

4. If it should happen that something new/old grows in this realm of personal meditative experience, there can also be hope that in another liturgical reform, which will certainly be necessary at some time, the original form of the Liturgy of the Hours in which the psalms were not yet torn apart and isolated can be recovered. Then it will no longer be necessary to mutilate the Psalter by leaving out individual psalms or parts of psalms, because the Psalter will be able once again to take command of its own hermeneutic.

Chapter Seven

The Loneliness of the Just One
Psalm 1

In some of the newer Bible translations the first psalm bears the heading: "The Two Ways." Interpretations almost universally present Psalm 1 in this or similar fashion as well.

It is not inconsequential how Psalm 1 is understood. It is the gateway to the Psalter, and stands there to meet the one who prays it. Only those who feel themselves invited and understood here will enter the gate and wander through the vast garden of meditation that is the Psalter. Does Psalm 1 really speak of "two ways" that divide, and between which a person must decide at some point in her or his life journey? Does this psalm offer two equally real possibilities between which the one praying the Psalter ought to choose? It seems to be so, and yet in truth the psalm is really talking about something quite different.

It does indeed speak of two different ways. At the end it says:

YHWH watches over the way of the righteous,
but the way of the wicked will perish. (Ps 1:6)

In the course of the psalm the mutual existence of good and evil in the world becomes evident (vv. 1-2); the nature of the two forms of existence is illustrated in the images of the flourishing tree and the windblown chaff (vv. 3-4). Ultimately our eyes are directed to the future and the end, and in this, as shown above, the psalm speaks expressly of two ways (vv. 5-6).

It is true that one is not directly challenged to a decision. But that is seldom the case in the genre of "beatitudes." The "blessed" and the "woe" that are contrasted in this genre in themselves imply a call to decision. Modern theory of speech acts has long since made it clear that not every speech act need be auto-explicatory. The situation in which the speaking occurs helps to determine what kind of speech action is taking place. Beatitudes and woes belong in the context of education and human judgment; they are "wisdom" categories. Correspondingly, Psalm 1 is often called a wisdom psalm. But in "wisdom" the impulse to challenge is never lacking. Is it not clear, then, that the first psalm in the Psalter is also a call to choose between two ways?

Still, there are more powerful counter-signals present. Is it true that two groups of people with different ways of life that furnish possible life-contexts for the person who must decide between them are contrasted here?

At the beginning the large group of the "bad" fill the stage. They have various names: the wicked, sinners, scoffers (v. 1). No other group of people is contrasted with them. The word "happy" refers only to a *single* person who apparently *has* long since decided. Contrary to most Bible translations, the first verse of the psalm should be translated in the past tense:

> Happy the person who has not followed the advice of the wicked,
> or taken the path that sinners tread,
> or sat in the seat of scoffers. (Ps 1:1)

The past-tense forms for this person's fundamental decision are all the more striking because in v. 2 the description of her or his positive behavior is shaped in a timeless nominal clause and then a statement about continued action extending into the future:

> This person's joy: in the Torah of the LORD;
> On his Torah this person meditates day and night. (Ps 1:2)

The fact that this distinction between the levels of time is relevant becomes still clearer if we compare this with the biblical texts that are closest to Psalm 1. Apparently it was a text well known to the prophet Jeremiah's audience, since the prophet cites it in his book and uses it as a basis for argument. In that text the prophet speaks in a timeless present or in the future:

> Cursed is the one who trusts in mere mortals
> and makes mere flesh his/her strength,
> whose heart is turned away from the LORD . . .
> Blessed the one who trusts in the LORD,
> And whose hope is the LORD . . . . (Jer 17:5, 7)

There can be no doubt that in Psalm 1 an existing, timeless schema for wisdom sayings has been deliberately transformed. The person who in this psalm is set apart from the world of the wicked has long since made a decision and lives on that basis. She or he no longer stands, like Hercules, at the fork in the road.

In the text Jeremiah cites there are no fixed names for the two sides of the comparison. Both halves are descriptive. In Psalm 1, in contrast, the bad side immediately receives a set of classifying names. Apparently this is a well-known entity in contrast to which the single person who is called happy, the one who has made a different life decision, appears almost as an example of great worth because of its rarity; such a one must be extensively described or defined in a number of relative clauses, followed finally by the image of the tree. There is no multitude of the good. The good as a group, or more precisely as "congregation," appear for the first time in v. 5, near the end of the psalm, in a glance forward to the future. Now, at the moment at which the psalm begins, they do not yet exist. For a world that exists as a matter of course, full of the wicked, sinners, and scoffers, there is at first, in the literary world of this psalm, no counter-world of equal weight.

However, the single, uncategorizable person who stands in contrast to the world of the wicked takes up practically the whole space within the psalm. In the text Jeremiah cites the one who trusts in the Lord only needs half as much text as the one who does not. But here, in Psalm 1, a full three verses speak only of the one who has decided against the dominant world of perception. That is the whole first half of the psalm. Much more succinctly, then, in vv. 4 and 5 the fate of the evil "other side" is described. Only in v. 6, the conclusion already quoted, do good and evil confront one another on a basis of literary equality.

The unequal weight of the depiction is also clear from the imagery. In Jeremiah's text the shrub and the tree are contrasted, both of them full-scale wood-growths—but the shrub is in the waterless, salty desert while the tree is by the water where no drought need be feared. Psalm 1 develops the image of the tree in traditional form for the individual just one of whom it speaks, ending with fruits and green leaves (v. 3). For representatives of the dominant world of meaning, in contrast, there is no effort to supply a wood-image, not even a miserable bush in the desert. The only image worth considering, for their future, is the chaff that the wind blows away when the threshed grain is tossed in the air. There is no independent plant, not even a fruit, but only what with respect to the fruit (the kernels of grain) is worthless and must vanish—nothing green, but only dry cells. And the multitude of those who adhere to the governing world of meaning is visible in the countless bits of chaff that quickly become invisible as they are borne away by the wind.

Thus in Psalm 1 we seem to have something other than a wisdom-style appeal to decide between two possible lifestyles. Apparently what is at issue is a situation other than that of decision. The one who uses the Psalter is meant to be met at this entry gate and feel himself or herself understood.

The Psalter is not for everyone. It is for people who have already experienced an exodus. They have already rejected the maxims of the dominant world of meaning that are followed by so many. They have already recoiled in horror from the prospect of going the accepted way, acting like everyone else. Still less have they entered the circle of those who produce the governing theory of the world—for scoffing is one of the most effective means to set a society apart from others and against those who deviate from it.

These people for whom the Psalter is intended, however, appear to sense at all times that they are lonely individuals. To that degree it is amazing that they have the strength not to go along with what everyone else is doing. That strength comes from within. An internal desire drives them: the desire for and joy in God's Torah. The world they own, then, is not a real world, but a recited one. The Torah is, after all, a project for the world, but in the existing reality it appears not to be realized. It can only be present in the form of someone constantly reciting the text of the Torah, that is, as a "spoken world."

The murmuring of memorized texts was, at that time, the way in which one "meditated." This kind of meditation sets up a contrasted world against the world that exists. If the one meditating were not alone, he or she would be living in a contrast society. But after having departed from the existing society he or she is without a companion, and therefore must continually uphold anew his or her own world, the counter-world. For one must have a "world," even if it exists only in one's own meditation.

If we consider the question historically we will probably arrive in post-exilic Judah. The counter-world of those who love the Torah is not the other nations, but their own people. We are in the time in which the issue of the "true Israel" within nominal Israel became acute, and when groups of Hasidim or Anawim, groups like the Essenes of Qumran or the party of the Pharisees raised the question of where the Israel of God was truly to be found. However, the situation at that time is anything but strange to us today, even within the Church and still more within nations that are only nominally "Christian."

What is crucial is that the person who departs from the governing world of meaning, with God's project for the world at heart and perhaps also on her or his lips, by no means feels automatically included within a social counter-entity that will sustain and shelter her or him. Instead, such persons feel themselves alone.

This is true even though the Torah, toward which such a person's desire is directed, has certainly not arisen simply from the depths of the individual's soul. To speak of the "Torah of the Lord" is to imply that this world-project has a history. The Torah comes from Moses and can only enter an individual's awareness through tradition. Moreover, this world-project is present within an existing society. It is the Torah that was given to Israel. And the people Israel does exist.

Nevertheless the person of whom Psalm 1 speaks feels alone. The Psalter opens the door to such a one for this very purpose: to make this painful situation clear to him or her. Such a person will need the entire Psalter, pacing it, murmuring, from end to end and again and again, to understand her or his loneliness in its very essence. In the process it will be transformed more and more into its opposite, at least with a view to the future. From the perspective of Psalm 1 that is the purpose of the whole Psalter.

The first psalm itself makes a preliminary proposal for what the whole Psalter will develop. The reality "world" seems to exist for the others, the ones from whom the lonely person distances herself or himself. There are lots of them. They constitute a self-defined and self-enclosed "world." This other person has at most an imagined or murmured "world." But it is this one who is told that she or he is a tree.

The symbolic figure of the world-tree played a major role in the ancient Orient. Jesus himself would adopt it when he said that the mustard seed, which only produces a large bush, would become a "tree" in which the birds of the sky would make their nests (Matt 13:32 // Luke 13:19).

> This one will be like a tree
>   planted by streams of water,
>   which yields its fruit in its season,
>   and its leaves do not wither.
> Everything this one does will prosper. (Ps 1:3)

This tree did not grow beside the waterbrook by nature; it was transplanted there. It therefore retains the awareness that an exodus has transpired. But the qualities of the world-tree are now attributed to the lonely wanderer out of the existing world. She or he, and not the many participants in the current world, develops a "world," that is, communication among many. He or she bears fruit (although only in season, when the time comes—the tension toward the future is maintained in the present). She or he endures, living. Here existence succeeds, while the now-dominant world will be blown away by the winds of time.

This is a look into the future at the end of the first half of the psalm. The second half (vv. 4-5) is entirely future-oriented, and is followed only by the brief summary in v. 6 that we have already quoted. The second half has as its subject the bad people, that is, those of the now-dominant world. The counter-image to the tree is only briefly sketched:

> The wicked are not so,
>   but are like chaff that the wind drives away. (Ps 1:4)

In the future here envisioned there will be a "congregation of the righteous." Now the lonely person of the psalm has a name, and not she or he alone, but as member of a congregation.

> Therefore the wicked will not stand in the judgment,
> > nor sinners in the congregation of the righteous. (Ps 1:5)

That is the usual translation, according to which this is immediately about the judgment at death or at the end of time. But it may be that the word "judgment" in v. 5 is only a parallel to "congregation," for an assembly of citizens in ancient Israel was at the same time an assembly for judgment. So this may not necessarily be about God's judgment at the end of the world. It may be that an interpretation toward a more proximate future within history is also possible:

> Therefore the wicked no longer stand at the judgment (at the city gate),
> > nor sinners in the (deliberative) congregation of the righteous. (Ps 1:5)

The designation "congregation of the righteous" for the judgment of the world or simply for the world to come would be unique in the Hebrew Bible. If we adopt this interpretation we need no longer postulate such a thing.

But I do not believe that we need to choose between these two interpretations. Like almost the whole of the Psalter, Psalm 1 remains uniquely open with regard to its statement about the end of history. Throughout nearly the whole Psalter one can read what is said both in terms of present history and of a future beyond the world. This openness was undoubtedly conscious. Those meditating on the Psalter are not to be given a timetable for the future. They are to know only one thing: we have a great, unlimited hope, and that is what we are aiming for. How it looks, and when and where it will arrive: that we don't know. We grasp what we hope for only in images. But here we come to the image of the two ways:

> Yhwh watches over the way of the righteous,
> > but the way of the wicked will perish. (Ps 1:6)

This is the summary of everything the psalm has already said. The "way" is not simply one's moral and social behavior, over which a human being can decide, but beyond that it is the destiny that emerges from these: success or failure. And it is important in this closing statement that now, at the very end of the psalm, God's role is also stated. God appears in the picture of the righteous as infinitely restrained and modest: God "knows" their way. But this statement says everything; it contains all eternity.

To the nothingness into which the way of the wicked sinks, God contributes nothing—at least in this psalm. The mere logic of this "world" leads to self-destruction. Or, as the image in the center of the psalm says it: the winds of history bear it away into the unfathomable.

In the end, nowhere in this psalm do two social worlds stand contrasted within history. At the beginning there is only the evil world, and anyone who does not want to share in it must go into exile and stand alone. In the end there is only the good world, and the evil ones from before are no longer there. The sense of a lonely, good existence is to be the beginning of the full, rich, and just world of the future. All this the Psalter will spell out in a meditation text that is 150 chapters long; like a complicated mosaic, it is skillfully composed out of many of Israel's ancient songs.

The second psalm, closely tied to Psalm 1, will immediately sketch the same basic figure in an entirely new constellation. There the subject is not the individual human being in a surrounding evil society, but Israel in the world-society of the nations. What is exciting is that while on the one side the peoples, and not only the kings and rulers of the earth, rage and the nations mutter plans for revolt, on the other side there is again only one: the Lord's "anointed" on the holy hill of Zion. How easy it is to think that here the psalm is speaking of the Anointed and of God's people Israel—and indeed, that thought is included. But in the literary world that the psalm constructs this does not appear. God only sets God's Anointed One on the holy hill.

Again, this one is alone, and this one alone addresses the kings and rulers of the earth and calls on them to repent. In contrast to Psalm 1, we here behold a conflict between the two sides. But God's side is again occupied by a single figure. Only at the end of Psalm 3, where the lonely individual of the Psalter has already become a suffering and persecuted Righteous One, is there mention, almost in passing, of God's "people" (Ps 3:8). Thus for the Psalter the Righteous One as a lonely individual is a prominent theme.

Of course this loneliness is not identical with the individuality that a postmodern social construction has in a sense made a necessary element of the social structure. It is, rather, the loneliness of the one who no longer fits within the dominant society. But the question is whether our new form of individuality is not contradictory within itself, whether it can be anything more than a passing phenomenon, whether it will not ultimately prove to be community in a (radically inhuman) society, or else be automatically transformed into a state of expulsion from the dominant society—but without a Torah in the heart that proves to be a tree of life planted by living waters. A future, after all, is promised only to that loneliness that stems from exodus, an exodus that happens because of desire for and joy in God's Torah.

Chapter Eight

Introspection and Cosmic Mysticism
Psalm 36

What is closer to us than our own hearts? The question of the nearness of God seems, consequently, to move immediately into the fundamental impulse of every mysticism: to experience God in the depths of one's own self.

Who would want to deny it? But still, things can be different. For example, Psalm 36 stands contrary to such an idea. It seems as if it would like to force us to question our seemingly so obvious talk about "the nearness of God," as if it would say: It is really entirely different.

For according to this psalm what speaks in our own hearts is the temptation to sin, while God's illuminating presence fills the broad spaces of the world. In the course of the psalm both these statements are then developed and refined. Nevertheless, the fundamental experience at the outset remains: in the heart, sin; in the universe, God. Is it true, then, that for those who seek God what is to be desired is not so much the nearness of God as something like the distance of God?

Most likely, such different symbolic experiences of space are not contradictory. There are legitimate leaps in imagery permissible in speaking of religious experiences, connected with the inexpressibility of the transcendent. But for that very reason it is good not to cling to single metaphors. The attempt at an interpretation of Psalm 36 may be of some service to such a loosening of ties.

However, what follows is not specifically a response to this one question, but simply the attempt at an interpretation of this astonishing psalm. Let me first present as literal a translation as possible:

Translation of Psalm 36

[1 To the leader. Of David, the servant of Y{HWH}]

2   The whispering of infidelity to the sinner—
    (it speaks) within the space of my (own) heart.
    Never (is there) any fear of God
    before his eyes.
3   For he has flattered himself (too much) in his own eyes
    (for) his iniquity to be found out, (so that it might be) hated.
4   The words of his mouth (bring) mischief and deceit;
    he is no longer capable of willing good through wisdom.
5   Thus he will (continue to) plot evil while on his bed,
    to travel a way that is not good,
    and will not reject evil.

6   O Y{HWH}, your faithfulness (reaches) to the heavens,
    your trustworthiness to the clouds.
7   Your righteousness (extends) like (as far as) the mountains of God,
    your judgments (press as deep as) the great primeval flood,
    human and animal you constantly rescue, O Y{HWH}.

8   How precious is your faithfulness, O God,
    so that all people take refuge in the shadow of your wings.
9   They feast on the fat of your house,
    and the river of your delights—from that you permit them to drink.
10 For with you is the fountain of life;
    in your light we see light.
11 O continue your faithfulness to those who know you,
    and your righteousness to those of upright heart.
12 May the feet of pride not tread upon me,
    or the hand of the sinner drive me away.

13 There the practitioners of evil lie prostrate;
    they are thrust down and unable to rise.

A first trip through the psalm

Psalm 36 begins, almost stammering, and certainly in the wake of a massive fright, with a surprising statement. The one praying looks deep into her own heart. We should all do that, of course. This one hears oracular whispers and listens more closely. And she discovers that the one whispering is not God. Instead, it is "infidelity." Infidelity addresses the sinner.

So it is as if an oracle were speaking. The one praying hears it deep within, but then discovers that it is the perversion of an oracle. He listens to the whispering of sin, which desires to make him a sinner (2a).

Thus she discovers—not through external observation, but ultimately through insight into what is surfacing within herself—who the sinner is. She now describes him in vv. 2b-5.

This is a disturbingly objective description: to the point, with a clearly logical arrangement. The sinner is a world trapped within himself. He can no longer be any different from what he long has been. He has locked himself within his sinful figure. He is so entrapped within it that he can no longer escape. Anyone could predict his future.

At the end we read: ". . . and will not reject evil" (5b). This negative statement includes, as a necessary condition, its positive counterstatement: it must be possible to reject evil. As is frequently the case in the Psalms, this countermotif, located at the low point of a series of statements and surrounded by negations, initiates the reversal within the text. At this point the text has arrived at the point at which evil is rejected.

That, of course, does not mean that it has arrived at the good person. The psalm has almost nothing to say about any good person until near the end. She is there at the very end, the person "of upright heart" (v. 11). But for the moment such an idea is still very far from the praying person who can hear nothing but the voice of evil in her own heart. If anything is to be said about goodness, then all that can be said is that God alone is good. Thus in the psalm the sinner, cramped and bent by evil, stands in immediate contrast to the good God.

But the text not only leaps from the sinner to God; in doing so it alters its mode of speech. What had up to this point been objective description now shifts to direct address. The literary meditation that sought to express what could be read in one's own heart becomes prayer directed outward: astonished, exultant prayer. It begins with address to God, and here for the first time the psalm speaks the name of God: "O Yhwh!"

Almost all of the rest of the psalm will be a prayer: first a laudatory description of God and God's work (vv. 6-10), followed by petitions (vv. 11-12). At the very end of this part the "I" of the one praying again emerges when, as at the beginning of the psalm, he finds himself once more confronted by sin (v. 12).

The petitions at the end correspond in reverse order to the previous themes. First there was the sinner; then the psalm spoke of the human being in God's light. Now the text first prays for those who "know" God; there follows a petition for aid against sinners. Thus the two petitions chiastically weave together all that has gone before. Consequently, we could propose the following chiastic schema for the entire psalm:

2b-5	A	The sinner	"he"
6-10	B	God's kindness to creatures	prayer
11	B'	Petition for God's enduring kindness	prayer
12	A'	Petition for aid against sinners	prayer

That is not the structure of the psalm as such, not even of the part up to v. 12. Later we will have to speak again about a very different structure against which this present structure is already playing. The other structure will be more static, whereas what we have shown here on the basis of the intra-textual development has a more dynamic character. For as the overview shows, the second part is decidedly longer than the first, and yet the dynamic set in motion by the expanding text is once again brought under control at the point where it becomes petition by their brevity and chiastic ordering in contrast to the preceding major portion. The two structures work together and at the same time are in tension and supplement each other.

That v. 12 represents an ending is also indicated by key framing words. The words "heart" and "sinner" from v. 2 return in vv. 11 and 12 respectively. The ancient reader heard such signals acutely.

But then comes v. 13. With its first word, "there," it steps directly into the center of the question of the place where God is. But no one is quite sure to what this word refers: is it the heart of the person praying (v. 2)? Is it God's temple, where people take refuge (vv. 8-9)? Or has v. 10 already arrived at eternal life, so that the reference is to the world to come? The "there" in v. 13 remains open, as does the whole verse.

This verse is easiest to understand if we see it in contrast to the whole psalm. I see two possibilities.

We could presume that Psalm 36 was also originally used in a cultic context. Then we could imagine that when the psalm was publicly proclaimed it was sung by a soloist while, throughout the performance, a group of singers intoned the single v. 13 in the background as a kind of victorious counter-text.

The second possibility takes into account that the psalm, at least in its present complete form (with superscription and v. 13) was created for its literary context in the Psalter. Then v. 13, together with the superscription in v. 1, would be a kind of literary connecting link to the preceding Psalm 35. There the one praying ("David"), surrounded by enemies, but at the end certain of God's help, proclaims that he, YHWH's "servant" (Ps 35:27), will with his tongue "murmur [meditatively] your righteousness and . . . your praise all day long." In very fact, then, Psalm 36 at its center praises YHWH's righteousness (cf. vv. 7 and 11), and according to the superscription it is from "David, the servant of YHWH" (v. 1). The designation "servant of YHWH" in the superscription of a psalm is most unusual; it undoubtedly refers to the conclusion of the preceding psalm and is meant to say that what follows is the meditation on YHWH's righteousness that David promised to murmur daily. Since in Psalm 35 the plea for help against foes determines everything else, v. 13 in our psalm could be from the same hand as the superscription, and affirm the fulfillment of the plea at the end of the psalm.

This verse's verbal statements form a single metaphor. "Falling" is explicated, in parallelism, by "being thrust down" and "being unable to rise." But all three verbs are taken from Psalm 35: for "falling" cf. 35:8; for "thrust down" cf. 35:5; for "rise" cf. 35:11 and, before that, 35:2. But at the same time this verse lifts Psalm 35, to which it is a response, to a new level of statement. It is no longer a question of a single, concrete encounter with an enemy in the life of an individual, even David; it is now about the crisis of evil in the world as a whole, and the rescue of those who take refuge in God is a matter of being brought into the sphere of light and life as such. The connection of the statements in v. 10 ("life" and "light") with that of v. 13 acts as a kind of hermeneutical key in other parts of the Psalter: cf. Pss 56:13[14] and 116:8-9.

The built-up world of the sinner

Thus at the beginning of the psalm the person praying discovers by looking into her own heart how it is with a person whom sin has grasped. In her own depths she experiences the whispers of temptation. Out of that experience she describes who the "sinner" is. Of course this is not at all to say that everything that follows by way of description of a sinner is simply to be read in one's own heart. What speaks here, instead, is a highly concentrated and multifaceted observation of human nature. But at the same time it is referred to a single heart.

The one praying is, as the introductory sentence shows, deeply aware that the figure of the sinner he describes and so defines is his own possibility. The oracle of infidelity speaks to his own deepest possibilities: those of a rejecting world.

For the world of the sinner is hedged about with denial and rejection. The sinner is by no means in a position to have the experience that could change her and explode her world: the experience of fear of God. This statement begins the first part of the psalm (v. 2b). And the sinner will never again do what could prove her to be a human being possessed of freedom: namely, reject evil. With that statement this section about the sinner concludes (v. 5b).

Between the two palings of "no" there is a description of this figure of possible human existence. The place in the body where the sinner loses the measure of what is human is the eye. The word "eyes" is repeated (vv. 2b, 3a) and thus dominates the beginning of the description. The human being's windows to the world are no longer such. The instrument through which reality ought to be perceived and accepted no longer functions. For when a person has already entered into sin, the fear of God should be before his eyes: God's reaction to the sinfulness that destroys reality, and behind that simply God's absolute Otherness, God's divinity. These eyes can no longer perceive such things. Why?

When the psalm says that sinners "flatter themselves in their own eyes," it apparently means to say that such a person is in love with himself and constantly keeps only himself in view, so that he is no longer aware of any reality other than the self-projected "I." Consequently he loses perception not only of the fear of God, but also of any genuine insight into himself. He cannot even see his own sin, and he certainly cannot begin to hate any sin he perceives in himself.

After this description of the sinner's altered structure of consciousness, the psalm must speak of his behavior (vv. 4-5). Human action develops in a threefold rhythm of plan, speech, and act. He plans at night on his bed, speaks in the morning at the city gate where the citizens discuss their business and their conflicts before going to work, and he then goes on his way through the day to carry out what he has already planned and announced or set in motion in words.

The psalm seems to regard most critically what the human mouth speaks. At any rate, the works of the mouth are addressed first. In fact, two concepts of sin are introduced at the same time here; altogether there are four words used in the description of the sinner. These four concepts will later correspond to the four words for God's kindness. "Iniquity" (v. 3) and "evil" (v. 5) are here enhanced with "mischief" and "deceit" (v. 4). "Mischief" is even repeated in v. 5. All these words—and every translation of course is stretched to its limits in such cases—have an interpersonal, social dimension. Through her action, especially her speech, the sinner brings human community into chaos.

This is now the case, and even for the future there is no expectation that it will be different, because there now exists an inability to turn to good action through insight. The sinner's future lacks any hope of change. In this statement, which now follows, the other stages of sin are repeated: planning at night and movement toward accomplishment during the day.

In the last part of the description of the sinner's world, closed on itself and yet causing mischief throughout all reality, not only is the word "mischief" repeated, but also a second word, though in negated form: namely, "good" (vv. 4 and 5). Even in this negative form the counter-theme is thus announced, and so prepares for the reversal of the psalm in v. 6.

Yhwh's kindness fills the whole world

Verses 6 and 7 are the center of the principal psalm (vv. 2-12). This is true even from a purely quantitative standpoint. Before and after it are an equal number of words (36 in each case, with the central section having 16). Even if one does not count the words, but only the parallel constructions, there is an exact correspondence between the parts before and after the central section (five each, with two in the central part, thus seven in all). The result is the following schema, a static structure that underlies the dynamic thrust of the first part like a fixed framework. (The third column indicates the names for God that are used in each part.)

2-5	I	The sinner far from God	1 x Elohim
6-7	II	Yhwh, filling the cosmos	2 x Yhwh
8-12	III	People with God	1 x Elohim

The two verses in the separate center are praise addressed to God. Their first word is the divine address, as is their last: "O Yhwh!"

To the four words for sin are now contrasted four words for Yhwh's good actions in the world: "faithfulness" and "trustworthiness," "righteousness," and "judgments." Again any attempt at translation limps, but all four once more have a social component. Above all, however, divine goodness has all-encompassing dimensions. If the first part of the psalm defines the unbearable narrowness of the sinful heart, we find here a counter-image of breadth and openness. It is developed through a metaphor of the universe corresponding to contemporary ideas about the world. One is reminded of the place in the letter to the Ephesians where the author desires that the readers "may have the power to comprehend, with all the saints, what is the breadth and length and height and depth, and to know the love of Christ that surpasses knowledge" (Eph 3:18-19).

The universe is experienced as an immeasurably great space containing the totality of all possibilities, and yet bounded according to habitat. God's goodness reaches up to the heaven and its clouds, while the horizontal expanse of God's righteousness is limited only by the "mountains of God." Those are the high mountains that mark off the limits of the earth, bordering the oceans that flow around the continents; the dome of heaven rests on them. And the depths of God's judgments, which are the help of the powerless: these can only be delimited by the infinity of the great primeval flood, the primitive waters out of which every fixed thing in creation was called forth and given its shape, and in whose depths the foundations of the universe are rooted.

The enormous space of all creation is thus filled with the goodness of God. The world in its breadth is the place of God's presence and thus also of the possibility of encounter with God. Here all the living inhabitants of creation encounter the God of Israel, YHWH: not only the Israelites, not only all humanity, but "humans and animals" (v. 7). They encounter God as God "saves" them (v. 7). Thus no matter how sudden and clearly marked was the reversal in v. 6, the theme of sin is still latently, insistently present. God's presence is not a peaceful matter of course. God's creatures are in danger. The inhabitants of the universe must be constantly "saved" from the chaos that presses upon them through sin. God is close to them because God saves them.

This talk about the "saving" of creatures by the God who rules the entire universe also says something crucial about God, without the word itself being used: namely that God is sovereign, for saving was the action of the ruler. The name Hellenistic kings most often preferred as a title was *sōtēr,* "savior." But even when Israel received its first king, a skeptic said of Saul: "How can this man save us?" (1 Sam 10:27). Awareness of the constant peril and danger that theatened social reality was so strong in antiquity that good rulers were needed primarily to "save"—in war, but also in peace. When the psalm, in its first statement about YHWH, speaks of YHWH's saving power for human and animal it is also naming YHWH the ruler of the universe.

YHWH's royal reign was already hinted at earlier. For it is the duty of the ruler to provide justice and law, while fidelity and trustworthiness are the pillars of the royal throne.

Thus at the center of the psalm the cosmic kingship of YHWH is celebrated. How is it exercised? Another image is built up, again without being explicitly named. For what fills the space between heaven and earth, from one horizon to the other? Only the precious and all-illuminating light of the sun. The sun runs daily from one of the earth's boundaries, upward along the dome of heaven, and down again to the other boundary, filling the whole space with light. In the night it slips through the subterranean depths, back to the starting point of its course.

Therefore in ancient religions the sun god was also usually the god of justice. When the sun arises in the morning people see the light, order and law acquire new form, aid against the perils of the night comes to those now awaking, and they breathe new life.

All this is at the center of the psalm. Though not framed in words, it is there for those who understand this kind of language and imagery. What then follows in the third part of the psalm, especially its climax, emerges from this almost as a matter of course: "In your light we see light."

Flight to the shadow of the wings

The depressingly narrowed world of the sinner from the first part of the psalm contrasts, in the third part, with amazement at the opportunities in the lives of those who take refuge in the sun that governs the universe. Allowing oneself to be saved by the sun of justice is effortless, and in fact perfectly obvious.

But why need one flee to the sun, when its light is present throughout the universe? Is it not everywhere and nowhere? In the third part of the psalm the royal-sun-justice-God Y HWH, who permeates and rules the universe, becomes, almost without its being said, the God who is enthroned in the Temple on Zion (though the name Zion is never mentioned).

At the beginning of this part of the psalm there is simply awe (v. 8). The first key word for Y HWH's rule in the universe is repeated, God's "faithfulness":

How precious is your faithfulness, O God!

In light of this richness, the flight of all people to its protective space is quite natural.

Then the picture changes. The winged sun, which flies like a bird in the dome of heaven, becomes a hen taking her chicks under her wings. With this the cultic dimension enters the spatial structure. To a look into the heart and outward to the universe is added the experience of cultic space, which lies somewhere between. For in the Holy of Holies of the Temple on Zion the cherubim spread protective wings over the Ark. In the Psalter the children of Israel flee to the protection of those wings. We are therefore in the presence of the God whose beams illumine the universe, and yet when we flee beneath God's wings we find ourselves on Zion.

Be it noted, however, that it is not the children of Israel, but the children of *humanity* who here flee under the shadow of God's wings. Is the concentration in this psalm so much on the contrast between "sinners" and "those who flee to Y HWH" that the other division, between Israel and the nations, is in some sense forgotten? Or are we already so much within an eschatological perspective that they no longer play any role at all? Zion certainly, though not mentioned by name, plays a decisive role. The all-encompassing God, in order to be a God of nearness, must have a cultic place where contact is possible.

The next verse (v. 9) takes the location on Zion as understood. The house of creation has been transformed into the protective Temple. Temples are always at the center of the world. Whoever is in the center is in the whole.

And whoever is saved can live. People live when they join for meals. The house of God is the place of the festive meal. Therefore this is the theme of v. 9, and the parallelism thus develops the theme of the meal in both components: eating and drinking. Both share the component echo of abundance and delight, but each has its own particular associations, which carry the stream of the metaphor onward.

When people "feast on the fat of your house" we are not only in a world that has meat available only on feast days, where no one need fear becoming overweight from feasting on animal fat and where, in consequence, fat animals can be regarded without anxiety as the most delicious things possible. No, the fat of sacrificial animals also has a symbolic function in ritual, and thus the very phrase about the "fat of the house of God" makes present the world of cultic memorial. In Jer 31:14 it is said of the coming age of salvation:

> I will give the priests their fill of fatness,
> and my people shall be satisfied with my bounty.

When then, in parallel, drinking follows eating, other associations arise. People will drink of the "river of your delights." The Hebrew word for "delights" that stands here is "Eden," the name of Paradise. Even the river that feeds life is one of the symbols of Paradise. Here, then, the cultic perspective developed from the cosmic is extended into the primeval-eschatological perspective of the world of Paradise. It does not come from inner experience, but from experience of the universe.

With "for," then, v. 10 introduces the movement to the close. The thought returns to the internal basis of this developed imagery. Now, for the first time, the crucial key words "light" and "life" appear.

In the expression "source of life" there is a further association with the river of Paradise. When the psalm speaks of "light" it is important to know that "seeing the light" is idiomatically the same as "being rescued from death." Anyone who has to go down into the underworld "no longer sees the light" (Ps 49:19[20]). But at the same time the statement about light closes the circle back to the depiction of the divine sun permeating the whole universe that lies at the center of the psalm.

It is also important that at the end of v. 10 the subject is again given verbal expression. It was present at the very beginning of the psalm, in the reference to "my heart." But then everything was merely objective description, and even later, when it developed into address to and praise of God, the whole discourse remained entirely objective. There was no reflexive side glance of the speaker on herself; everything was directed to God. Here, now, the subject is suddenly present again, both as a final climax and a confirmation: "*we* see light."

Note, however, that it is not "I," but "we." Only when sin was in view was the isolation of the "I" present. When life and light rule the scene in the house of God "we" see light.

Petitions emerging from the experience of God

The verbal emergence of the subject prepares for the petitions that close the psalm (vv. 11-12). Once one has been rescued and brought into the space of divine governance, one can really ask for nothing new or greater. What one can ask is simply that this miracle continue to exist, and not only for individuals, but for all who have experienced it. Therefore the first word in each of the pairs that, at the center of the psalm, described God's governance of the universe now recurs: "faithfulness" and "justice."

There is a peculiar analogy to the first part, which described the sinner. There, too, we looked to the future at the end of the section, and it was found that the sinner was no longer in a position to act otherwise than the way he had fixed for himself: to do evil. Here, in contrast, God is asked for nothing other than that divine, light-filled action will be sustained for God's own throughout the universe. But this is something asked and expected of God; it is not the human being who makes the ultimate decision. That is the difference.

Nevertheless, at the very end there are also some characterizations of those who have taken refuge in God and exist under God's protection and in God's light. These are people "who know you." "Know" and "recognize" can imply much more in Hebrew than they do in our languages—up to and including the kind of "knowing" that only happens between lovers. ("How shall this be, since I do not know a man?") In the universe and in worship the children of humanity who have taken refuge in God "experience" God in the deepest possible way. It is just here that this "knowledge of God" takes root and grows.

Of course it has also marked them, as the second characterization shows. These are "those of upright heart." This is an unfamiliar metaphor, so it may not tell us very much. At least in this psalm it must stand in opposition to the hearts of sinners, cramped and bent within themselves, turning back into themselves, no longer open. In contrast, for the upright of heart their inner selves lie open and smooth, utterly prepared for the light of the world-encompassing God to fall on them.

This petition for the continuance of the Paradise in which the petitioner is already living corresponds to the petition for protection against a new inbreaking of the world of sin that the petitioner recognized, when looking into her heart at the beginning of the psalm, as her own dreadful possibility. In this petition she senses herself once again as an individual. As individuals those who have fallen prey to evil can, from without, snatch her out of the "we" of those who know God. She prays that this may not happen.

The images in which this petition is formulated give the psalm another, final nuance that did not appear previously. Its background is shaped by two typical depictions of the king. On the one hand there is the king seated on a throne with his foot on the neck of a subjugated enemy who lies on the ground before him. On the other hand there is the standing king who raises his arm to smash, with a club, the head of the defeated enemy kneeling before him. We find these images especially in Egyptian pictures of the Pharaohs. They are images of a power resting on violence and compulsion, self-confirming symbols of the state system. Here the reality of sinners is pictured in these terms.

These are the symbols of "pride," of the self-assertion of human importance. They are opposed to the symbol of taking refuge beneath the sheltering divine wings and pure surrender to the power of the all-encompassing light. What they signify can endanger openness to the God who fills all the wideness of reality, because they can drive one out of this space of life.

In your light

Must we not descend into the depths of our own hearts in order to seek the nearness of God? That was the question at the beginning of this attempt to interpret Psalm 36. The one praying and meditating this psalm began with a look into his own heart. But there he saw only the possibility of sin. Out of this first perception won from reflection on oneself the psalm developed the notion of how dreadfully narrow and tiny the world of the sinner is.

To this was contrasted the encounter with God in the breadth of creation and in the "we" of worship. From outside and from the whole, encompassing reality comes "knowledge of God" and "uprightness of heart," not from introspection. The interior space of one's own conciousness, biblically called the "heart," is clarified at the very end of this movement, having from outside, from the breadth of the universe, become a "straight" reality.

In Christian theological and mystical literature the statement "in your light we see light" has often been an occasion for very deep thoughts, but frequently these have tended to otherworldliness. Seen in its true context, it opens the human being to the fullness of creation in order that, within that fullness, she may encounter God. According to this psalm, God is closest to us in the broadest space.

Chapter Nine

Peace Poetry in Israel
Psalm 46

Psalm 46 as a *"peace poem"*? It does not even contain the word *shalom,* so popular among those in the peace movement and indeed with everyone nowadays. And it doesn't exactly begin with great enthusiasm. But it certainly does speak about peace, and does so out of the anxieties of a world threatened by war. To that extent it is not so foreign to us. Peace is its hope.

In fact, peace is also present in this psalm as something experienced, even though the word itself is lacking, because its world includes "Jacob," and because this "Jacob" has a "city of God" and within it a protecting and caring God. Here we have a "peace poem" that cannot manage to say one word about war and peace without at the same time opening up a horizon against which is dawning the mystery of Israel and the Church.

Unfortunately we perceive Psalm 46 in our Bible translations only as if through a veil. Some of it is very hard to put into our languages, and some passages are already difficult enough in the original text. But there are some things that can be said more clearly than the existing translations do. For that reason I will first attempt a translation. It deliberately tries to avoid concealing the hard shifts between speakers, perspectives, times, and images. It leaves slippery groups of words as difficult as it finds them, translates the same words always the same, and indicates some associations given in the original language through paraphrases.

Translation of Psalm 46

I   2   A God is our refuge and fortress
               known as help in trouble from of old.
               Therefore we need not be anxious lest the earth be overturned,
               lest mountains tumble into the depths of the sea.

	3	Its waters toss and foam,
		the mountains shudder as it arises.
II	5	A stream! Its branches refresh a city of God,
		the holy realm of the dwelling of the Most High.
	6	Deity in its midst—it cannot tumble,
		the Sun God at its morning rising will come to its aid.
	7	When the nations tossed, when rulers tumbled,
		he had lifted up his voice, so that the world trembled.
	8	Yhwh of hosts is with us;
		a fortress for us is the God of Jacob.
III	9	Go, behold the works of Yhwh.
		Such is he: He spreads stillness throughout the earth.
	10	He institutes a war-sabbath
		to the ends of the earth.
		He will break bows and shatter lances;
		he will burn the chariots with fire.
	11	Be still and know: I am God.
		I will exalt myself above the nations, exalt myself above the earth.
	12	Yhwh of hosts is with us;
		a fortress for us is the God of Jacob.

The symbolic world

War and peace are aggregate conditions of *society*. This poem, however, speaks primarily of elements of *nature*—earth, mountains, water—their condition and their peril. Only toward the end of the second strophe is it at all apparent that this is also saying something about war and peace. To this point everything is couched in terms of nature imagery. Even the third strophe has a world-spanning dimension.

It would be wrong to say that nature only furnishes imagery here. This is really about the condition of the universe. War and peace produce decisions about the universe itself. It may be that this still very general observation gives us an initial access to the poem. It displaces us into an experiential space where *the social is also cosmic*. Creation is a fixed order ripped from the waters of chaos, an order constantly in danger from the frothing waves of nothingness. A collapse back into the formless primeval condition would be the "overturning" of the universe. In Gen 1:9-10, on the third day of creation, the Creator caused the waters to withdraw and the fixed land, the space for human life, to emerge from chaos; but since then the waters, rising up against order, constantly lick at the mountains, the essence of what is fixed and firm. The mountains are threatened with tumbling down and falling back into the center of the sea. The chaotic powers of war and unrest are in some sense a beginning, experienced in the human world, of the constant licking of the mythic sea.

Even though in our everyday understanding of the universe, shaped by natural science, we think in different terms, still in our *dreams* the same symbols of threatening water and saving rock play their ancient roles. In our dreams we draw pictures with our fears against nothingness. In this world of imagery what is fixed and certain appears more surely for us as the place where we can take refuge. It is a "fortress." It gives our inner self a "city" and "dwelling place," projecting brilliance and holiness against the darkness outside. The image of "Paradise" can develop. Then it may not be a long step to the point where water, this most ambivalent of all symbols, suddenly acquires a quite different character: as a quiet "river" that flows about the city giving sustenance to the plant world and life to all—as the account of Paradise in Gen 2:10-14 begins with the description of the great river that rises in Eden and divides into four branches.

When today again, at last, the words *"justice," "peace," and "preservation of creation"* are associated, spheres that had been separated are once again united. For the peace poem we are considering here, at any rate, these things constituted a unity.

Construction of a communicative situation

The first word of the poem is *Elohim:* "deity." In the Bible this word can almost be a name, the name of the one and only God of Israel. But here in Psalm 46 we must carefully observe how it appears.

Some "we" makes this confession of faith. As readers of the Psalter we know that this must be Israel's "we." Israel's God has a name: it is YHWH. In a confession of faith it is a central point that one mention the name of the god to whom one is declaring allegiance. In the course of the poem, the name of God will be heard. So why not here, in the opening confession?

If, as usual, we translate "God is our refuge and strength," we obscure for ourselves today this amazing fact about the poem's beginning, for we Christians nowadays no longer have a name for God. When we say "God" it is as when Israel said "YHWH." In order to hear the special sound of the way this poem begins we have to translate with the indefinite article: "*a* God."

As soon as we formulate it this way a highly complex and subtle constellation of communication emerges. Then Israel is speaking *in the presence of others*. These others do not know YHWH, the God of Israel. Therefore it says, tentatively: *"a God."* Still more: these others do not seek refuge with a god, but rather with a king, in a well-defended city, with arms and strategies.

A confession of faith that crumbles

In contrast, in the very first sentence Israel affirms: We want to do without such forms of security, because we find our assurance *elsewhere,* beyond all that. We have a *God:*

> A God is our refuge and fortress
> known as help in trouble from of old.

To which should be added: the speakers have not yet revealed their identity. They are simply *"we,"* and that is how it remains until the end of the second strophe. The reader of the poem is free to include herself or himself in the "we," which is still *open* to a variety of possible identifications. This will be important at the end of the poem. What will happen there would not be possible if the "we" had not previously appeared in such an indeterminate form.

To return to the confession: it is not yet finished. Because ultimately nothing else is adequate, those who do not trust in a god are constantly subject to *anxiety about the world's falling back into chaos*. Precisely in order *not* to suffer that anxiety, "we" now assert in the second sentence of the confession:

> Therefore we need not be anxious lest the earth be overturned,
> lest mountains tumble into the depths of the sea.

However, it is remarkable that, at the very moment when such a bold statement is made, the speaker feels doubt, and the reality that has just been denied makes its presence felt. It is not clear which voice continues— whether it is "we" or, perhaps, a narrator. In any case, the confession is at an end. However, it has *initiated a perception* in "us," those making the confession, that now emerges as a perception of the world. The pressure of chaos is at its height. The fear that "we" say "we" can avoid is vibrating in the imperiled mountains:

> The waters of the sea toss and foam,
> the mountains shudder as it arises.

At the end of the first strophe the space is occupied by a confession of a security found with a God that is, however, called into question by shuddering reality and nearly transformed into irresolution, and this in the presence of a worldwide audience that is itself very probably in terror.

The city on the river

Now begins a completely new *second strophe*. The scenery is utterly different:

A stream!

Naturally there is a close connection with the preceding strophe, for the water-image continues. But now it has the opposite symbolic value. There is no more "we" speaking; instead, the lips of a narrator take up the description. Our eyes are drawn over the waves and across the bank of the *stream* flowing toward us, and up to the *city*. Hence there is a second connection with the preceding strophe: in place of the chaotic sea storming against the mountains we are looking at a stream that cheerfully flows about a peaceful city.

A stream! Its branches refresh a city of God,
the holy realm of the dwelling of the Most High.

Thus creation contains the *place of holiness,* the dwelling of the divine in its highest and ultimate form, for in polytheistic thought the title "most high" always belonged to the *highest deity.*

At first this is all a vision. But it is quickly conceptualized. The consequences are drawn as a *response* to the crisis appearing behind the first strophe:

Deity in its midst—it cannot tumble,
the Sun God at its morning rising will come to its aid.

The words "tumble" and "aid" connect to the first strophe. The word "deity," which began the first strophe, now appears three times in the second strophe. The translation has clarified it in the third instance as *"Sun God."* This is not an automatic association for us today, but it was different for the original addressees. The rising sun in the morning puts an end to night, the time of chaos and peril. In religions that see the deity in many forms, the sun is the light-deity, and consequently also the *deity of justice and peaceful order.*

That YHWH is just that is something Israel has *experienced.* This therefore occasions the *historical account.* "We" are not yet speaking again, but the text moves in such a way that this must soon happen. For the account makes clear what was said in the confession at the beginning: "A God . . . known as help in trouble from of old." Succinctly, like everything in this poem, it says:

When the nations tossed, when rulers tumbled,
he had lifted up his voice, so that the world trembled.

Here emerges for the first time that the real problem is not cosmic, but *social:* "nations," "kings." They tossed and tumbled. The text is very indistinct, and deliberately so. The word "king" is contained within the one translated *"rulers."* We could translate "kingdoms, states," in which case the nations would be the ocean and "toss" against a kingdom appearing like a mountain that begins to "tumble." We could equally well translate "kings, realms," in which case the mass of previously obedient subjects would be "tossing" against a solid state power, and revolution would bring its rule "tumbling." *Both* are probably intended. Contrary to the opinion of many interpreters, the report is not about war against the city of God. Verse 6 already said of that city that it never "tumbles." No, it is simply a matter of the insistent social chaos in creation, wherever and however it occurs. That is a matter of experience; then *"he"* comes and sends forth his voice. "He" appeared as the thundering war god whose terror enters into the foes, here in the whole universe. What does that mean? Has "he" set himself on one of the two sides that are locked in struggle with each other? Which one? Why? Or is it that here the war god is not making war at all, but instead putting an end to war?

That is the question, but the text does not give an immediate answer. It is forced in a different direction. The other question must be still more powerful: *who, then, is "he"?* It must have been more and more important that the initial confession, which has somehow been called into question, be formulated anew. Thus *the confession returns,* and this time it names *names.* "We" now speak it in its full form, and when the full name of the God is given it also becomes clearer who "we" are: namely "Jacob," the people Israel. At the end of the second strophe, with the now fully uttered confession (which is often inserted, without reason, at the end of the first strophe), an initial circle is closed:

"Yhwh of hosts" is with us;
a fortress for us is the God of Jacob.

The circle is closed, yet something *presses farther.* The *third strophe* must come, and it, at last, is decisive. It was necessary from the beginning, for the confession apparently was made in the presence of the nations of the world who then, when the world began to shake, could not take refuge in a god. What could the confession mean for them? Moreover, beyond the revelation of the name of Yhwh in the renewed confession the account of Yhwh's action in the tossing world of the nations is still unfinished and demands continuation. That is the purpose of the third strophe.

How do the nations of the world achieve peace?

The third strophe is a dramatic *dialogue*. First "we," the confessors, speak. From the confession that stood at the beginning of the preceding strophe emerges the address to the world of the nations:

> Go, behold the works of Y<small>HWH</small>.
> Such is he: He spreads stillness throughout the earth.

The nations are challenged to see what Israel has already seen. They can perceive everything that Israel perceives: Y<small>HWH</small>, by putting an end to the chaotic unrest of the world through his penetrating voice, has caused *"chilling fear."* The Hebrew world can describe a field of ruins and devastation. Thus the translation here is often "desolation." That would indeed have been the characteristic work of the war god. It can mean "silence," including the eternal silence of the world of the dead. And if the text did not continue we would have to understand it this way, or in some similar fashion. But as the text goes on there emerges forcefully from the potentiality of the word "silence" what is probably more accurately understood in our language in the word "stillness": an end to unrest, an end to noise, "sabbath." Y<small>HWH</small> appeared as a war god, but the opponent, whom he brought to silence with his war-god's voice, was war itself. Literally the next verse speaks of "ending wars," and the word for "ending" is the same as that contained in the word *"sabbath."* In the Hebrew ear the echo is perceptible:

> He institutes a war-sabbath
> to the ends of the earth.

It is certainly crucial here that the end of wars affects the *whole earth.* "We" have seen this; "we" now tell the nations that they will see it. For the following verse is a prediction of the future:

> He will break bows and shatter lances;
> he will burn the chariots with fire.

Will humanity believe this message from the dwellers on Zion? They will ask: *how* will this God do such a thing?

At this point a voice not previously heard enters the discourse: *the voice of God.*

> Be still and know: I am God.
> I will exalt myself above the nations, exalt myself above the earth.

The world's peace does not come of itself. Its *price is knowledge.* This is the knowledge that enlightens through faith in the God of Jacob. Only when the "pilgrimage of the nations" begins—to make use of another biblical image—only when the rule of the God of Jacob is freely accepted will the end of wars come. His voice of thunder is transformed *almost into a plea:* Surrender yourselves to this world of peace! Ultimately everything depends on the response of those who are addressed. How will they answer?

At the end of the third strophe *we hear again the confession* from the end of the second strophe:

> Yhwh of hosts is with us;
> a fortress for us is the God of Jacob.

Who is speaking? Is it again "we," supporting the voice of our God? Or *are the nations taking up our confession* and also confessing the God of Jacob, so that now wars are really at an end? Undoubtedly it is all meant to be at least a preliminary sketch of this answer. Those who pray this psalm constantly hold before their eyes the confession that security is only to be found in the God of Jacob as an ever-renewed hope, and they also hope that it will be taken up by all. Then there will be peace.

Chapter Ten

Three Ways to Talk about Poverty
Psalm 109

Psalm 109—wouldn't it be better to leave it in oblivion? Aren't there better texts to use, if we want to talk about what the Bible says on the subject of the poor and poverty? But if we are going to talk about "poverty" it is certainly true that this psalm is very probably the poorest, most despised, most calumniated of all the 150 psalms. It is considered a *"cursing psalm,"* in fact, the worst of all the cursing psalms. Pope Paul VI threw it out of the liturgy of the hours in 1971. At that time the psalm already had a horrible history. Even in the New Testament it had become the "Judas psalm." Peter quotes it before the election of Matthias: "Let another take his position of overseer" (Acts 1:20). For the Fathers of the Church the whole psalm was the *psalmus iscarioticus*. For the Middle Ages it cursed all the Jews. It was recited during pogroms. In sub-Christian popular magic there were set rules, even in the last century, for "praying to death" (as was said) one's personal enemies by reciting this psalm.

And yet it is not certain that Psalm 109 contains even a single curse. What is usually called a curse is rather a declaration of intent, though rather a dark one. Someone in the psalm makes this declaration. Somewhere in the psalm there is also talk of a curse that a poor person could have uttered. But that is not the passage that is referred to when people talk about this being a "cursing psalm." Instead, the reference is to the declaration of intent. Supposing it were a curse—who utters it? Is this the voice of the one praying? Or is the praying person quoting another voice in order to lament what that other wants to happen to her or him?

Asking about the "voices" in the psalms in this way ultimately means using the tools of modern literary-theoretical analysis to call into question the disastrous interpretations of the Psalms that have been current until now.

At the beginning of a new consideration of Psalm 109 that contradicts previous understandings stands a sharp-eyed Jew from the nineteenth century, Heinrich Graetz, professor in the University of Breslau. In the intervening years it has scarcely been realized that Graetz was the first to observe the real division of voices in the psalm. For too many exegetes the subject has become matter-of-fact. Hence in what follows it is unnecessary to prove anything argumentatively for the first time in the strictest sense of the word. It suffices to introduce the psalm in such a way that it shows what it really is.

I will begin with a working translation of the psalm. It is not in the most elegant English, especially because the same Hebrew words are always translated with the same English words. That is important, because the role that rhyme plays for us is taken, in Hebrew poetry, by word-repetitions and wordplay. They join statements and establish connections of meaning at a distance. The indentations, as well as the emphases in boldface, italics, and capitals will be explained in the course of the subsequent discussion.

Working Translation of Psalm 109

(¹ For the Choirmaster. A Psalm of David.)   (Title)
    God, whose praise I sing, stay not silent!   Address + Petition
² **For** the **mouth** of the wicked   Accusation (lament)
    and the **mouth** of the deceiver   against the enemy
    are opened against me.
    They have spoken to me with lying tongues,
³   beset me with words full of hate,
       attacked me without cause.
⁴   Where I acted in love, they want to **accuse** me,
       there shall remain to me nothing but to plead for mercy.
⁵   They have offered against me evil for good,
       hatred for my love:
⁶   "Let someone demand an account from him, the criminal,
          let an accuser *stand on his right.*
⁷   Let *the judgment of a court* prove him a criminal,
          if he asks for mercy, **may he fall short of it:**
⁸   'May he live but a few days,
             may a **neighbor** take over his office.
⁹   May his children be made **orphans,**
             his wife a widow.
¹⁰   May his children wander about and beg,
             seeking food, because their house lies in ruins.
¹¹   May a creditor sell off all his possessions,
             strangers plunder what he has gained.

12   May there be no one who remains faithful to him,
        no one who takes pity on his **orphans.**
13   May his posterity be despised,
        and his name be blotted out in the **next** generation.'
14   The guilt of his ancestors will be remembered before the LORD,
        the **shortcoming** of his mother will not be blotted out.
15   May the LORD continually see his ancestors before him,
        may their memory be outlawed from the land.
16   Because he did not choose to act faithfully,
        because he persecuted a needy and *poor* person,
        and finally killed the one whose heart was already broken,
17   because he loved *cursing,* and it came upon him,
        did not seek *blessing,* and it was far from him,
18   because he *has put on cursing* as his shirt,
        and it soaked into his body like water,
        like rich oil into his bones—
19   let it remain to him like a garment in which he *wraps himself,*
        like a belt that forever girds him."
20 So they urge, my accusers—the LORD permits it—
    and those who speak evil, that I may come *to death.*

21 BUT YOU, LORD, my ruler,	Address + Petition
act on my behalf for your name's sake!	
Because your faithfulness is goodness, set me free!	"I" Lament
22 For I am needy and *poor,*	
my heart flutters within me.	
23 Like a shadow stretched out I have grown pale,	
I was shaken off like a locust.	
24 My knees are bent with hunger,	
my body has become gaunt.	
25 ME, THEN, who have become a joke to them	"I" Petition
—they shake their heads when they see me—	
26 help me, O LORD, my God,	
save me through the power of your faithfulness!	
27 May they see that it was your hand,	
that you, O LORD, have done this.	
28 IT IS TRUE THAT THEY want to call me *accursed*—	Petition
may you *bless.*	about the enemy
When they have arisen and been put to shame,	
may your servant be filled with joy.	
29 Let my **accusers** *be clothed with* dishonor,	
let them *be wrapped in* shame as in a cloak.	
30 I will thank the LORD with my **mouth,**	Vow of Praise
I will **praise** him in the midst of the great ones.	

³¹ **For** he *will stand at the right hand of the poor,*
   to *save* him from those who would *condemn him to death.*

Genre and structure of Psalm 109

Modern psalm research has given a new definition of the various types of texts or *genres* in the Psalms. That is one of its greatest achievements, and it is fundamental to an understanding of the texts. The Psalms themselves reveal a high degree of awareness of their different genres. Thus Psalm 109 begins with the tension between two genres. God is addressed as the "God whose praise I sing," and yet this address does not initiate a song of praise, but moves directly into petition:

> God, whose praise I sing, stay not silent!

It would be normal to sing a hymn. But now is the hour of petition, of the "song of lament."

The *song of lament* is one of the most important kinds of texts. However, the name does not fully describe the content, for a song of lament does more than lament. It is just that the fact of lament is most striking to us moderns when we view these texts. That is how the genre got its name. A better name would be "prayer of petition." But within the genre of petitionary prayers in the Psalter the song of lament has its definite place. Before a human being in crisis petitions her God for something, she first sets forth the nature of the suffering: She laments.

With this, almost by the very nature of things, we have named the most important elements of the psalm genre "song of lament." The prayer situation begins with *calling on the name of God*. Then the *lament* gives the reason, and from it arises the *petition*. At the end a *vow* lifts its hands high. The one praying promises, when his prayer has been heard, to thank his God in the presence of the assembly ("vow of praise").

This same structure, with some doubling, also shapes Psalm 109. In the translation the parts of the text are designated on the right margin. Here is the schema without the text, with the length of each section in verses:

Address + Petition (I)	1b	1 verse
Accusation (lament) against the enemy	2-20	*19 verses*
Address + Petition (II)	21	1 verse
"I" Lament	22-24	3 verses
"I" Petition	25-27	3 verses
Petition about the enemy	28-29	2 verses
Vow of Praise	30-31	2 verses

The psalm begins in v. 1 with an *address* and a brief *petition:*

God, whose praise I sing, stay not silent! (1b)

Immediately a long description of the petitioner's desperate situation begins to unfold: a *lament.* In v. 21 the psalm begins again with *address* and *petition:*

But You, LORD, my ruler,
act on my behalf for your name's sake!
Because your faithfulness is goodness, set me free!
For . . . (21-22)

—and now the *lament* begins again. Its content differs from that of the first. If the first was about the enemy who wants to bring the petitioner to judgment, the second is about the petitioner's illness. The special exegetical terms for such different laments are *"accusation/lament against the enemy"* and *"'I' lament."*

With v. 25, after the lament, the *petition* begins. Now the themes are reversed. The *"I" petition* follows immediately after the "I" lament: Help me out of my sickness! Out of this develops, in v. 28, the *"Petition about the enemy,"* which refers back to the accusation/lament about the enemy at the beginning: Help me in my trouble with the enemy! With v. 30 begins the concluding *vow of praise.*

Thus we have here a song of lament with a classic structure. That in this analysis the lines between the parts have been correctly drawn is shown by the personal pronouns that begin the individual sections. They are given in capitals in the translation:

BUT YOU	v. 21	Second sequence of appeal + petition + lament
ME, THEN	v. 25	"I" petition
IT IS TRUE THAT THEY	v. 28	Petition about the enemy

This was a conventional signal for a new beginning and would be still more so later, in the songs of praise of the community at Qumran. That toward v. 30 the end of the psalm is drawing near is—also conventionally—signaled by the fact that typical key words from the beginning of the psalm recur. In the translation they are given in boldface in vv. 1-4 and 29-31. This is called "key word framing."

There is only *one* blot on this whole structure. The element "accusation/lament against the enemy" at the beginning is unusually long. However, the Psalter frequently uses this literary technique: where the most important statements are made, an expected form is distorted. Such a calculated affront to expectations disturbs those using the text and renders them alert. So also in Psalm 109: the huge expansion of the accusation against the enemy must mean something.

The quotation from the opponent in verses 6-19

The expansion of the "accusation/lament against the enemy" is carefully signaled, for the enmity that surrounds the petitioner is revealed in speaking, speaking, and more speaking. Thus immediately in vv. 2 and 3:

> . . . the mouth of the wicked and the mouth of the deceiver are opened against me.
> They have spoken to me with lying tongues,
> beset me with words full of hate,
> attacked me [again, no doubt, in speech] without cause.

All this is about speech. What are they saying? we ask. As yet we do not know. Verse 4 says that they seek out a specific forum for their speech, namely the law courts:

> Where I acted in love, they want to accuse me [in court].

Why do they want to make accusations? What punishment are they aiming at? we ask. We still do not know. Then v. 5 is like the introduction to a speech: They have made a wicked, hate-spawned decision. From v. 6 onward the petitioner only quotes this decision. The petitioner is to be brought before the court and thus destroyed. Finally we learn what is being said.

The quotation extends to v. 19. In the translation it is indented and placed in quotation marks. The petitioner himself speaks again for the first time in v. 20. Looking back, he comments on the quotation:

> So they urge, my accusers [v. 4 had said: "they want to accuse me"] . . .
> [so they urge], those who speak evil, that I may come *to death* [v. 5 had said: "they have offered evil against me"].

The repetitions of words signal the framing of the counter-quotation.

But even in the quotation itself it is immediately clear that it is no longer the petitioner who is speaking, but the voices of her enemies. The petitioner had spoken to God. Now God is no longer being addressed. The petitioner had spoken of many opponents. Now the talk is about a single person, namely the petitioner. The petitioner had announced that they wanted to accuse her. Now we find immediately in v. 6 that someone is supposed to "demand an account" of this "criminal"; an "accuser" is to appear. The petitioner had said in v. 4 that they wanted her to be left with no recourse but to beg for mercy. Now it is said, in v. 7, of this plea for mercy: "may it be for nought." Thus it is clear that in our psalm the petitioner develops, within the accusation against the enemy, a description of her own distress by broadly and yet concisely summarizing what those who are threatening her have in mind and what they think of her.

As if to drive this quoting to an extreme, a second quotation is embedded within the first. It is in vv. 8-13, and is doubly indented in the translation above. It is a kind of projection in advance of the judgment the accuser is supposed to achieve in the trial.

This whole complex of quotation represents the text that, according to the traditional understanding of the psalm, the petitioner is supposed to have flung as a curse against his opponents, the betrayed Jesus against his betrayer Judas. But it is not a curse at all. It is a summary, in quotation form, of what the opponents of the petitioner intend for him. It is not the voice of the petitioner that is heard, but the voice of those who want to destroy him, quoted by the petitioner in a lament to his God. He seeks God's help against them.

Images of distress in Psalm 109

Now to the petitioner and her crisis. The accusation regarding the enemy is followed, from v. 21 on, by the *"I" lament*. Both are internally connected. What exactly is the petitioner's critical situation?

When we put the question this way we must be clear about one thing: The Psalms are not biographically-tinged pop songs. They are prayer formulae for constant use, over and over again. People in the widest variety of situations should be able to slip into these texts. Thus the contours of the crises that are articulated in them should not be read too much in individual terms. There needs to be room for a great variety of situations. Indeterminacy must be inherent in the descriptions. These must be more images of crises than concrete critical situations to which names can be given. In fact, every psalm of lament in the Bible should be able to contain every human crisis and need.

According to the accusation against the enemy in Psalm 109 the petitioner is to be brought before the court and condemned to death. This psalm can be prayed by everyone who has been in a similar situation. But others can pray it as well, for such a trial is prototypical for what happens in every situation of human enmity. Perhaps someone who is publicly slammed by the media can also find himself in this lament, or someone in whose family an indestructible enmity between two members breaks forth anew every morning, or a sick person who no longer knows what her visitors are thinking and saying before they open the door and come into her room, someone in whose soul the suspicion is growing that, in fact, the others are only waiting for her to die.

This furnishes a connection to the "I" lament in the psalm, for it appears in vv. 22-24 that the petitioner is deathly ill. His heartbeat is irregular. His strength is dissipated. As one might brush an exhausted locust, blown by the hot desert wind, from one's cloak, life has shaken him off, and he lies in the dust. His own knees are like the inbent joints of the locust; he is skin and bones, a sick man approaching his end.

And yet this sickness is only an image for a great deal more. It can simply be poverty; it can be existence as one expelled from one's group. Perhaps it is the loss of every feeling for life. People experience such things as mortal illness, and they can lament them before God by slipping into the "I" lament of this psalm.

We must take the laments in such psalms as literally as possible. Ultimately it is all about our concrete fate. But at the same time we must not take them literally. The lament simply unfolds primeval imagery from the landscape of suffering. Every suffering finds itself reflected there, no matter how unique it may be.

Analysis of the counterarguments

That needs to be said before we now begin to trace the contours of the mountains of lament in Psalm 109. We belong to a different culture. The person in the "I" lament, pushed to the edges of life, may be easiest for us to imagine and understand. Hence we will begin there and feel our way backwards from that point.

Thus we come, first of all, to the second half of what the petitioner's enemies are saying, vv. 16-19. These verses establish *why the enemies desire the petitioner's death.* The beginning of his guilt, and thus the ultimate reason for the mortal illness in which he now lies, is for them, as they clearly say, that he must have persecuted and ultimately killed *a poor person.* Verse 16:

> Because he did not choose to act faithfully,
>> because he persecuted a needy and *poor* person,
>> and finally killed the one whose heart was already broken . . .

Something like that must be at the beginning of the whole story, they appear to conclude. Otherwise this man would not be so miserable now.

Probably someone really has died. But it may be that people have simply concluded to the fact of an evil deed, as Job's friends did in the book of Job. For here, in any case, someone is deathly ill. Must there not be a corresponding sin? It is very easy to draw that kind of connection.

The *poor* are, in a sense, God's presence in the world. Those who are faithful to them receive blessing. Those who refuse them love receive curses. Indeed, it is all much more concrete: The poor person himself or herself blesses or curses. Nothing is more effective than the curse or the blessing of the poor. Both of these must be intended in v. 17:

> because he loved *cursing* [namely, the curse of the poor], and it came upon him,
> did not seek *blessing* [namely, the blessing of the poor], and it was far from him . . .

That a poor person's curse is at work is evident, according to this argument, from the presence and advanced state of the petitioner's illness. Verse 18, with its incredible imagery, says as much:

> because he *has put on cursing* [of the poor] as his shirt,
> and it soaked into his body like water,
> like rich oil into his bones . . .

Thus when the opponents seek a judgment of death on the petitioner it is for them only the consequence the petitioner has brought on himself. So they take up the image of the shirt of cursing drawn over the head when they formulate their conclusion in v. 19:

> let it [the curse] remain to him like a garment in which he *wraps himself*,
> like a belt that forever girds him.

Thus he will die. And we must accelerate the process by bringing him to trial. That is the logic.

It may seem magical and archaic to us. But is it really wrong? Do not the inhuman things we do, after all, ultimately destroy us and our life? When we sink more and more into misery, into crisis, toward our own end, do not questions about the beginning of our unhappiness and the reasons for it force themselves on us? What else do our psychologists work at day after day?

The petitioner's opponents are consistent to the end. That is clear when we go another step back into the psalm, to the *judgment that the court ought to impose on the petitioner*. It is in vv. 7-13 and is most skillfully formulated. In the translation the basic structure can be recognized from the chiastically arranged key words, which are set in boldface:

128   *In the Shadow of Your Wings*

    fall short of it
      neighbor
        orphans
        orphans
      next
    shortcoming

This corresponds to the content of the speech as it unfolds. Verse 8: the man must die; another will take his office. So: setting aside. Verse 9 tells the consequences: now there is a widow and there are orphans. The family is destroyed. Material collapse follows automatically. This is concretely described in vv. 10-11: the house is in ruins, the children have become vagabonds and live by begging, because debts have quickly destroyed the estate and strangers have plundered them. Now, in v. 12, the eyes turn back to the children: the whole family as a social entity has become nothing; consequently, no one cares about the orphans. Verse 13 goes still farther: society ejects such a family. Even in the next generation the name of this family will no longer exist. At the beginning is the death of the head of the family; at the end the whole family is extinguished. The opponents therefore intend more than the punishment of a single person. They are looking to the *extirpation of a tribe.*

With this, the statement in v. 8 that another is to take this person's *office* at last acquires its full meaning. Not everyone in the land has an "office." Nor was it permissible in ancient Israel simply to exterminate whole tribes. That kind of radical procedure was typical of the leadership class. We read about them in the Bible when there was a change of dynastic regime: thus, for example, that Asa, the son of Jeroboam, founder of the Northern Kingdom, was murdered by one Baasha, who became king in his place:

> As soon as he was king, he killed all the house of Jeroboam; he left to the house of Jeroboam not one that breathed, until he had destroyed it . . . . (1 Kings 15:29; cf. 16:12)

Thus it is important that our psalm speaks about supersession in office. The petitioner in this psalm is not just anyone. He belongs to the *upper class.* Nothing prevents us from playing with the idea that he is the *king.* However, we must also remember that such a psalm remains a prayer formula for many. But just as it is in today's supermarket tabloids, so even then many people of the lower classes understood their own destiny best when they could see it reflected in the fates of the figures above them.

Now let us take a further step: so that the idea of the extermination of a whole tribe may be as deeply rooted as possible, vv. 14-15 are even *theological* in nature. Here for the first time, and only here within the long quotation from the opponents, does *God* enter the picture—quite differently than was the case with the petitioner herself in the psalm, who speaks to her God from the very beginning. Even here the opponents do not pray. They only say what they expect from God in the way of assistance after an individual and that individual's whole family have been extirpated from the earth: namely, that God should ratify the whole business.

God, after all, upholds even the dead, who ultimately are the sustaining ground of a family in its past. Therefore God is to add all the guilt of this family to all its past generations, covering nothing with mercy, but instead holding the whole thing constantly before the divine eyes as in an open heavenly account book. The earthly consequence, then, is stated in v. 15:

> from the land their memory [is definitively] outlawed.

In the quotation from the opponents hate, violence, and the will to destruction are truly combined in a single whole. But at the same time it is all logical and highly moral. After all, it is only a question of aiding the curse of a murdered poor person to achieve its effect.

Psalm 109 as the cry of a poor person

The one praying this psalm knows and understands the whole situation. She presents it as a lament before her God. But from the beginning she does not hide the fact that it is all false. Verse 2:

> For the mouth of the wicked and the mouth of the deceiver are opened
>   against me.
> They have spoken to me with lying tongues.

As logical as it all seems, it is not true. More precisely: the beginning of the logical deduction is wrong. The petitioner did not persecute a poor person, and yet she is sick and everything looks as if the curse of a poor person had fallen upon her; there is no escaping that fact. So out of the lament arises a *petition,* v. 26:

> help me, O Lord, my God,
> save me through the power of your faithfulness!

This plea is itself the cry of a poor person. At the very beginning of the "I" lament, in v. 22, the petitioner had turned all the perspectives of the opponents upside down. If they had presumed that his misery was ultimately caused by his having (v. 16) "persecuted a needy and poor person," he can only say that he is being persecuted by them, and is himself—in v. 22 he uses the precise formulation employed by the opponents—"needy and poor." So he now lays claim to the *privilege of the poor,* the right to cry to God in time of trouble.

Only if God rescues her from sickness and once again surrounds her with blessing and joy will the logic of the opponents collapse. Then, as it says in v. 27, it will be known that it was all God's "hand," that "you, O LORD, have done this." These are clear, but extremely reserved statements. They leave in place the mystery and the incomprehensibility of the petitioner's own misfortune. And yet they anchor it in a different context of meaning, one that rests in God and is neither conceived nor fabricated by human beings.

What the petitioner desires for the opponents

Of course, the rescue of the petitioner, when God accomplishes it, has *social* consequences for the opponents. They themselves sought to carry on their destructive fight in public, and they act in public in other ways as well. According to v. 25 the petitioner has

> become a joke to them;
> they shake their heads when they see me.

When the one they have been opposing is suddenly and fully again in their midst and his anticipated physical destruction, the ultimately conclusive argument, has been stopped, the public's judgment will be overturned—as will the public itself. The action against him will collapse. Automatically, then, they are in an oblique light, in "dishonor" and "shame," as v. 29 says. That is a serious matter in a *shame culture,* which Israel was.

And yet the incongruence between this plea of the petitioner and what was in process against her is striking. One can see in the translation, in italics, how the petition regarding the enemies refers back to what was in the accusation against the enemies. They had spoken of curse and blessing. Now the petitioner asks:

> They want to call me accursed—*may you bless [me]* (v. 28).

They used the dreadful image of the curse that the petitioner must put on like a shirt. In v. 29 she turns the same image on them, using the same words.

However—and this shows definitively how poorly this psalm fits within the usual cliché about talionic cursing psalms and their lust for vengeance—he does not say that God should now clothe them with the curses of the poor and let them penetrate like water and oil. He speaks only of public shaming, which must happen if God rescues him and thus reverses the whole situation:

> Let my accusers be clothed with dishonor,
>> let them be wrapped in shame as in a cloak.

In the *vow of praise* that concludes the psalm another image is taken up from the quotation of the opponents. Their plan was (v. 6) that "an accuser stand on his right." Here (in v. 31) the petitioner knows what he can proclaim in thanksgiving for rescue "in the midst of the great ones": God

> will stand at the right hand of the poor,
>> to save him from those who would condemn him to death.

God shoves the accuser aside and takes his place. God's argument is the healing of the sick person—so the petitioner hopes as she lies, skin and bones, on her deathbed.

Let us conclude the analysis here. Psalm 109 is fully before our eyes. Now we can ask the main question we were aiming toward: How does this psalm speak about poverty?

Three ways to talk about poverty

In Psalm 109 personal fate and social public life constitute a worldly unit of a sort we are seldom accustomed to find in our prayers, and in that world poverty appears to play a crucial role.

A first, superficial observation reveals how central it is. With psalms it is always worthwhile simply to count the words. Then, for example, one can ask where, from a purely quantitative point of view, the center of the text is. If one counts in Psalm 109—in the Hebrew text, of course—91 word units (individual words or words connected by hyphens) from the beginning, and does the same from the end, then vv. 16-17 are exactly in the middle: the accusation made against the petitioner by the opponents, which the petitioner describes from the beginning as a lie:

> Because he did not choose to act faithfully,
> because he persecuted a needy and poor person,
> and finally killed the one whose heart was already broken,
> because he loved cursing, and it came upon him,
> did not seek blessing, and it was far from him . . .

The issue is whether this is true or not. In the world of the Psalms we read of poor people, persecution, the murder of the poor, the curse of the poor, the blessing of the poor—the phenomenon of poverty and living with poverty are of central importance.

This shows us the first way of talking about poverty. In our psalm it does not appear formally, but it is presumed. The society of this psalm does not repress the fact of poverty; it has the courage to speak of it. Moreover, it speaks about it ethically. It contains an ethos of care for the poor.

This the psalm itself takes as understood. Otherwise it would be impossible for anyone to accuse the petitioner of having persecuted and killed a poor person. Dealing with poverty is also seen as an especially ticklish matter. Otherwise there would not be such instinctive fear of a poor person's curse or such obvious desire to obtain a poor person's blessing.

The awareness that in a socially divided community some critical thing is not right, combined with a high ethos of care for the poor, is in fact not only typical of Old Testament Israel, but of the entire Ancient Near East. The reality may have been another question, but the highly developed ethos was present. It was especially an ethos of the elite leadership, particularly the kings. It was their responsibility to defend their land militarily against encroachments from without, to join their people upwardly with the divine world through building temples and providing for divine worship, and within society to promote justice by giving judgment. Again and again in the documents royal judging is characterized as listening to the cry of the poor, accomplishing justice for widows and orphans.

This ethos was also spelled out theoretically: in the prologues and epilogues to the great law codes, in instructional Wisdom literature, in epic narratives containing examples. Thus poverty was addressed in objective description and in ethical demands. I would describe this discourse as the first way of speaking about poverty. Our psalm presupposes it as a matter of course, and as legitimate.

Our own discourse corresponds to theirs when it formulates a social or charitable ethos. In this category are the churches' social teaching as well as the theology of liberation. Here, too, belongs the social document of the German churches published in 1997. Of course teaching and universally challenging speech about social problems also belongs in other milieus, in the widest variety of parties and institutions. Such discourse is fundamental and is a natural thing in a responsible society. It is possible that in antiquity, when there was as yet no theory of a market economy, it was easier to hear than it is today. But it is certainly audible among us as well.

Our psalm thus presupposes such discourse. But the two other ways of speaking about poverty are still more important. They are not only presupposed; they appear in the psalm itself.

There is, first of all, the way in which the petitioner's opponents speak about poverty. They apparently are attempting to get rid of a person—in fact, to eliminate a powerful family. We find ourselves on a political, perhaps also an economic battlefield. There is to be a changing of the guard in the seats of power. It cannot happen unless the public is persuaded, and that is to be accomplished through an activation of their socio-ethical conscience. The opponent they are challenging is accused of injustice toward the poor, of antisocial behavior. In the case of our psalm not all of it is true. But whether true or false in individual cases, in such instances poverty is spoken of very differently than in theoretical discourse about poverty in society or in general admonitions proclaiming an ethos regarding poverty. Here the talk about exploitation and oppression of the poor is part of the ammunition in the power struggle. The one who can best employ it to besmirch his or her enemy will win the contest.

There can be no doubt that this technique for manipulating the theme of "poverty" is omnipresent in our political world, in wage negotiations, and in many other professional and private arenas. I am not saying that there cannot be legitimate occasions for talking about poverty in this way. Poverty is produced, and poor people are oppressed. That has to be combatted. But only too often the existing social and poverty ethos becomes an ideology, a weapon in service not to the poor, but only to one's own acquisition of power and influence.

Precisely where this second way of speaking about poverty appears, a third necessarily emerges as well. It is represented, in our psalm, by the petitioner. As one mortally ill, she has not only entered something like a final, private state of poverty, but is also being publicly ejected into a kind of human outsider status by the accusation of antisocial behavior. One may say that this is something different from poverty, and that the concept of poverty should not be extended too far. But the formulation of the opponents' judgment in vv. 10 and 11 clearly shows that their aim also includes the petitioner's loss of every form of material possession. Nothing but ruins will remain; the children are to go begging. And the petitioner describes herself, at the beginning of the "I" petitions, as "needy and poor," and in the last verse hopes that her God "will stand at the right hand of the poor" and "save" her. Thus the whole psalm becomes a "cry of the poor."

The old German legal term is *Zeterschrei* (murder cry). Anyone in ancient societies who heard the cry of "murder" and did not rush to help made himself or herself a murderer and a criminal. Everyone is addressed by the murder cry, but the particular addressee is the judge, especially the king, and beyond the king, God. Our psalm cries out to this final source of rescue.

Ultimately it is only the murder cry of the poor that is authentic discourse about poverty. All other discourse only speaks of poverty from outside, whether with good or evil intent. Only the murder cry comes from within. Only here does the victim himself cry out, the person who is in misery and who may for that very reason have been made a scapegoat, in order to have peace and quiet elsewhere.

The messianic dimension

Psalm 109 hopes that God will hear the murder cry and stand at the right hand of the poor to save them. Is it only a hope? No, it is a certainty.

To see this in the text itself we have to allow biblical scholarship again to approach, the very newest scholarship with its latest conclusions. We indicated above, in "The Psalter and Meditation," that it is crucial to realize that the Psalter does not belong to the genre of compiled literature; it is not a loose collection of songs (as are, for example, our contemporary church hymnals). Rather, it is constructed out of old songs and hymns, but has been skillfully built into a unified text. Text links to text, profundities call out to each other, the echo of the words, images, themes, fears, hopes, and praises sounds from one end to the other and rings back ever anew from the walls of the individual texts.

Probably the Psalter was intended as a text for meditation. It was learned by heart and continually murmured to oneself, from beginning to end. That is the only reason why it could have been so well known and beloved in New Testament times. When Jesus prayed all night long, those nights would have been filled with the Psalms.

If we presuppose that, then we only have to look at what comes after Psalm 109 in the Psalter. In fact, whereas at the end of Psalm 109 we find the hope that God will stand *at the right hand* of the poor person who cries, Psalm 110 creates the certainty of it. It catches the ball that has been thrown to it, beginning:

> The LORD says to my lord,
>   "Sit at my right hand
>   until I make your enemies your footstool."

With this, of course, we again enter a new dimension. We had read Psalm 109 as the prayer of an individual, but on the synchronic level of the full Psalter God's response is one of the great *messianic psalms,* Psalm 110. This is the psalm out of which New Testament *christology* grew. But in that case we cannot read Psalm 109 simply as the psalm of an individual in ancient Israel.

We should already have been taken aback by the fact that the title designates this as a "psalm of David." At this point in the Psalter David had long ceased to be merely the historical figure. He stands, and has long stood, for the whole people of God in its progress through history, and he is the prototype of the Messiah to come. Thus also the petitioner in Psalm 109 is no longer simply an individual. In him or her the people of God emerges, the people hunted to death throughout history by the nations of the world as "the poor." At the same time this petitioner is the distantly sensed figure of the hoped-for messianic king whom God raises to God's right hand, but who before that time has the destiny of a "poor man" who can only cry "murder" because the mighty of the world seek his death, and only his God can save him.

Chapter Eleven

The Old Testament and the Course of the Christian's Day
The Songs in Luke's Infancy Narrative

Through the Bible we can enter into communication with God. But how often do we reach for our Bibles? One of the most powerful ways in which the Bible enters into Christian lives is through the *Daily Office,* which consists almost entirely of texts from the Bible, and which runs its course through the whole of every day. At least for priests and monastics, it shapes the rhythm of the day. For many others in pastoral work the Daily Office, or Liturgy of the Hours, is certainly at least the model for their prayer. And the group of those who have discovered it as their own way is still greater. In recent years their numbers have rather increased than decreased. In what follows I would like to point to something that may especially help us, in the Daily Office, to walk with the God of the Bible through our days.

In doing this, though coming from the perspective of the Old Testament, I want to turn to some New Testament texts, and specifically the first two chapters of Luke's gospel, which contain Luke's so-called *Infancy Narrative.* I will be asking how this narrative takes up the Old Testament's experience of God and of history. It does so primarily through *hymns and songs* that are distributed throughout. There are four of them, and they are very familiar: the Magnificat, the Benedictus, the Gloria, and the Nunc dimittis. These are the songs referred to in the subtitle of this essay.

In terms of facts, we must first know something about the *literary technique* we observe in the songs of the Infancy Narrative. That technique comes from the Old Testament. Luke's style of writing is deliberately modeled on the Old Testament. Here I can in part refer to some things I have already dealt with in earlier essays in this book. After that we can look at the *Infancy Narrative* itself. We will ask what exactly is happening in the songs so liberally sprinkled throughout this very short story.

Linking of psalms in the Psalter

Our Roman Liturgy of the Hours, especially in the new version since the reform of the liturgy, makes use of the book of Psalms almost like a stone quarry. It regards all the psalms as individual pieces, like building blocks, and it composes the hours of prayer for each day by rearranging these blocks.

It was not always that way. The early men and women monastics prayed the psalms in the sequence in which they stand in the book of Psalms. In the twentieth century it was thought that this was a sign that they did not do much thinking and simply prayed mechanically. The radical new arrangement a quarter of a century ago had its own prehistory, but no one had gone quite so far in rearranging the psalms before that. All the same, what was then done certainly corresponded to the dominant scholarly consensus. It was expressed particularly through the perspective of so-called form criticism. But in the mean time we have exited from precisely that way of thinking.

At the present time biblical scholars are learning again to regard the Psalter as a redactionally conceived, unified book, no longer as a collection of songs or a hymn book in which each song stands alone. As I have already described in a previous essay, the Psalter as a unified text is coming once more into view.

The Psalms are intended to be a running text with an overall message that is more than the sum of the messages in its individual parts. Of course its building blocks were originally, almost without exception, independent songs and prayers. But it appears that the redactors of the book had a different intention. The Psalter was meant to be memorized as a whole and to serve as a text for meditation.

Often the content of the individual psalms refers to other psalms; often they carry forward the statement of earlier psalms or refine what was said before. Key words tie them together. And yet each psalm retains its individuality, so that the one praying the psalms, meditating, murmuring them, retains a great deal of freedom. She or he can draw connections between psalms, sometimes these, sometimes others. But one thing the person praying *must* do, and that is to establish some kind of connections.

We exegetes are in the process, then, of rediscovering this "linking of the psalms." We are just beginning to spell out the effect this has on constituting meaning. Linguistic signals appear to produce a relationship between texts that in themselves are heterogeneous. By this process spaces of meaning are established, with a multidimensionality that could not be produced by a single text with its particular meaning and linear form. The one praying the psalms, meditating and murmuring them, comprehends more than what the particular psalm being recited contains in itself.

Embedding of psalms in narratives

The second matter whose discovery I will report, the embedding of psalms in narrative contexts, also serves the purpose of constructing new dimensions of meaning. This relates to the fact that in Old Testament narratives the narrative proper is interrupted from time to time by songs. Think, for example, of the Song of Miriam after the passage through the Reed Sea (Exodus 15), the Song of Hannah after the birth of Samuel (1 Samuel 2), or the psalm of the prophet Jonah in the fish (Jonah 2). That songs are suddenly quoted within narratives was, of course, well known, but the songs were regarded as nothing more than "embellishment" of the narrative.

Here narrative analysis has advanced a step further in recent years. If we consider not all the poetic insertions in the Hebrew Old Testament, but only those that have the character of psalms, we can first say negatively that the embedded psalms do not serve to advance the action. On the contrary: they are resting places within the action. They often occur at the end of an action unit and thus do not even serve to intensify the tension through a pause in the action ("plot break"). Their function can best be compared to that of the chorus in a Broadway musical, which ideally evokes wild applause from the audience and so becomes a "show-stopper."

The references to the context in content and words vary in intensity within the Old Testament examples. The Song at the Sea (Exodus 15) and the Song of Deborah (Judges 5) relate strongly to the events previously narrated in prose. But Hannah's song in 1 Samuel 2 has no special reference to the sorrow of childless Hannah and her joy when her son Samuel was born. It is a victory song. Apparently such embedded psalms are not necessarily aimed at a lyric recapitulation of the fable, and it is equally questionable whether they are intended to "characterize" the singers in a technical literary sense.

It may be that the song Jonah sings in the belly of the fish serves to "characterize" him (Jon 2:3-10), but if so it would be an exception. It is a traditional cultic song of thanksgiving, carried almost to the point of exaggeration. It would describe Jonah as a fossilized normally pious type who for that very reason is not in a position, later on, to respond to God's new and unheard-of action on behalf of the non-Israelites in Nineveh. It is true that this interpretation of Jonah's psalm is often given, but it remains disputed.

We come closer to describing the real effect of these embedded psalms if we call them "characterizations of God." All the singers, female or male, are somehow prophetically inspired, and all these songs open new theological horizons.

The Song at the Sea draws a parallel between the passage through the stilled waters of the Reed Sea and the entry into the promised land, and ends at the Jerusalem sanctuary. Thus, on the shore of the sea after rescue has been accomplished, there opens a vision of God's all-encompassing historical action, of which God's leading the people of Israel out of Egypt is only the beginning. It draws the reader into its praise and exultation.

A still longer historical view, perhaps extending even to exile and return, is projected by the Song of Moses at the end of the Pentateuch, in Deuteronomy 32. Hannah's song, raised at a time when no one in Israel was yet thinking of a king, ends with a blessing for God's king and anointed one (1 Sam 2:10). There can be no doubt that this is a prelude to the two books that follow. It is not Hannah who is singing here; through her sings the divine Spirit who already sees all things.

It is no different with Jonah's psalm. It is true that it is sung by Jonah in the belly of the fish. But it is about the God who is always a saving God for all creatures, even for the Gentile sailors who had thrown Jonah into the sea, even for the sinful city of Nineveh with its many people and cattle, and even for the readers of the story who may not yet know which of the characters in the narrative they want to identify with. Jonah refutes himself through what he sings. But that sort of thing can happen when the prophetic spirit seizes a human being.

The biblical narrator is always "omniscient," as we say. He knows everything; in a sense he shares in divine omniscience. But within the narrative there are moments of still more comprehensive revelation. When the acting persons, at high points or end points in the narrative, open their mouths to recite a psalm, they themselves become prophets within the story and unlock its larger contexts, at the same time drawing the readers into their own songs of praise.

In the case of Hannah's song of praise this matter is still more evident because, as has long been recognized, this psalm at the beginning of 1 Samuel corresponds to and mirrors David's song of thanksgiving at the end of 2 Samuel (2 Sam 22:2-51). The two songs frame the two-volume Samuel book: that is, practically speaking, the history of the first two kings, Saul and David. They are not related to each other merely by their framing positions at the beginning and end of the literary complex. Instead, they are related to each other in the same way as are two psalms that stand next to each other in the Psalter: namely, they are linked in the most intensive manner by common motifs and words. "Hannah's song could in fact serve as a summary of 2 Samuel 22" (Robert Polzin).

It is almost a matter of indifference who the singers of these two psalms that frame the double book of Samuel are. They need not have been

140 *In the Shadow of Your Wings*

Hannah and David. Nor is it important how much these songs in any sense "naturally" arise out of the respective points in the story at which they occur. Here the Spirit comes upon a person who at this moment is involved in the action, and no one can force the Spirit of God to come or to stay away. All that is important is that these psalms open a higher and more comprehensive sphere of knowledge and invite the reader to an attitude that, while arising out of interest in the story, now becomes praise of God.

In these two phenomena of "linking of psalms in the Psalter" and "embedding of psalms in narratives" we have presented two typical Old Testament literary techniques that will help us to understand what the songs in Luke's Infancy Narrative in fact accomplish, and what is their intent.

The psalms in Luke's Infancy Narrative

Which texts are we interested in? Here is a table that gives an overview of the two chapters at the beginning of Luke's gospel, indicating all the poetic parts:

Section			Poetic Element	
1. 1:5-25	Promise of John	1:13-20		*Gabriel's dialogue*
2. 1:26-38	Promise of Jesus	1:30-33		*Gabriel's dialogue*
3. 1:39-56	Mary and Elizabeth	1:46-55		**Magnificat**
4. 1:57-80	Birth of John	1:68-79		**Benedictus**
5. 2:1-21	Birth of Jesus	2:14		**Gloria**
6. 2:22-40	Presentation of Jesus in the Temple	2:29-32		**Nunc dimittis**
7. 2:41-52	Jesus remains in the Temple	—		—

From among the poetic texts we are interested in Mary's song when she meets her cousin Elizabeth (Luke 1:46-55, the "Magnificat"), Zechariah's hymn after his son John's naming (Luke 1:68-79, the "Benedictus"), the song of the angels in the fields after Jesus' birth (Luke 2:14, the "Gloria"), and Simeon's song of praise at Jesus' presentation in the Temple (Luke 2:29-32, the "Nunc dimittis"). We will consider just those four texts. There are other poetic passages in these two chapters, at the announcement of the two births by the angel Gabriel, but they do not have psalmic character. Just as in my account of the Old Testament, we will only look at the embedded psalms and hymns, and not at all the poetic passages.

In reverse order to the previous section I will speak first of the embedding, and then of the linking of the psalms in the Infancy Narrative.

The relationship of the four songs to the narrative in Luke 1–2

At least the first three of the four songs (in contrast to the poetic parts of Gabriel's dialogue that are to be regarded as action) do not serve to advance the action. The Benedictus may even be seen as standing athwart the course of events, as a kind of postscript. If the narrative structure followed the story exactly it would seem to belong after 1:64:

> Immediately his mouth was opened and his tongue freed, and he began to speak, praising God.

But it is not there; it is inserted later in the text.

The Magnificat could also be a later insertion. In the story it is easy to imagine it as an intermediate reaction within Elizabeth's speech (1:42-45), perhaps after 1:44, when Elizabeth has praised Mary and told her how the child has leapt in her womb. Such a possible dialogue between Elizabeth and Mary within the course of events would then end in 1:45 with Elizabeth's blessing of Mary: "Blessed are you who have believed." But this very dialogue, and thus an "action," escapes the narrative structure of the Infancy Narrative. As long as one is reading the Magnificat, the Benedictus, and the Gloria, the action is arrested.

It was not necessary to quote Simeon's song of praise in full to advance the narrative. It is true that the Nunc dimittis moves the action forward. It awakens the awe of the parents (2:33) and thereby provokes Simeon's further praise of the parents of the child, accompanied by a prophetic word to Jesus' mother (2:34). But in light of this parallelism it is striking that Simeon's praise of the parents is only mentioned, while his praise of God, just before this, is quoted in full. As a result the full reference to the Nunc dimittis in the narrative descriptive action works, at least in retrospect, to put a brake on the action.

The interruption of the action by the hymns corresponds exactly to the Old Testament parallels.

In terms of content, we should properly speak of distance from the context rather than of relationship to the context. The content of the Magnificat is not in continuity either with the angel's message (in 1:28-37) or with Elizabeth's prophetic words (in 1:42-45). The Benedictus only gets around to speaking about the occasion, the birth of John, in the second half (1:76). The Gloria, which is so fundamental in its focus, is clearly demarcated from the preceding, highly concrete message of the angel to the shepherds (in 2:10-12), which mentions Bethlehem by name and even speaks of the child's swaddling bands. The Nunc dimittis develops the theme of revelation to the Gentiles, for which there is no real point of contact in the immediate context. Thus, as in the Old Testament parallels, the four hymns do *not* serve as a lyric doubling of what is narrated in the context.

In terms of the choice of words, too, the ties to the narrative context are measured, though in part they are very deliberate.

In the Magnificat the first parallels use a number of words from the preceding or succeeding narrative, but not always in exactly the same sense. Later there are no such references.

The first words of the Benedictus (1:68: "Blessed be the Lord God of Israel") were anticipated in the narrator's note in 1:64 ("praising God"). Then the word "mercy," which appears at two climactic points in the hymn (1:72, 78), recalls the narrator's words in 1:58:

> Her neighbors and relatives heard that the Lord had shown his great mercy to her.

The reference is to the name "John," which means "The Lord has had mercy." Otherwise the usage of words in the Benedictus is independent. Only at the characterization of John in 1:76,

> And you, child, will be called the prophet of the Most High,
> for you will go before the Lord to prepare his ways,

does material reappear from Gabriel's messages to Zechariah and Mary, and from the family conflict about the name of the child.

The beginning of the Gloria (2:14: "Glory to God in the highest heaven") links to the narrative notice about the appearance of the angels in 2:9:

> and the glory of the Lord shone around them.

Otherwise the song of the angels contains entirely new words.

Finally, the Nunc dimittis is linked not only by the opening thought ("now I can die"), but also by the key word "see" to the narrator's note in 2:26, according to which it had been revealed to Simeon that

> he would not see death before he had seen the Lord's Messiah.

Otherwise the vocabulary of the Nunc dimittis is likewise independent.

Thus in all four songs there are word-links to the narrative context at certain points, but the technique of these word-links is not very strongly developed. This again corresponds to what we find in the Old Testament parallels. There, too, the language of the imbedded psalms develops a different, independent world. This is all the more striking because in Luke 1–2 not only the song material, but the whole narrative text is constantly alluding to Old Testament texts. Luke was a master of the technique of allusion through the use of referent words.

Moreover, one can scarcely say that the four psalms serve to *characterize* their singers. It is true that all four are adapted to their particular singers. The Magnificat is the song of the "maidservant" (1:48), as Mary had described herself to the angel (1:38). The Benedictus belongs to the father of the "child" (1:76) who has just been circumcised (1:59), and over whom the people are puzzling, asking:

> "What then will this child become?" (1:66)

In the Gloria the "glory" of the Lord is in a certain sense self-expressed in the form of the angels whose brilliance shines around the shepherds (2:9). In the Nunc dimittis Simeon is prepared to die (2:29), having been promised by the Holy Spirit

> that he would not see death before he had seen the Lord's Messiah. (2:26)

Thus the association of the individual hymns with certain actors in the narrative is apparent. None of these songs could be placed, without alteration, on the lips of another person. But do they by the same token serve to characterize these particular figures?

At most they do so in the sense that all the singers are presented as salvation-historical, theological visionaries. Their songs open up dimensions of meaning that extend beyond the immediate narrative and the persons within it.

This characterization of the singers as "inspired" people, which is evident from the content of their songs, is prepared by previous descriptions of these persons in the narrative itself, often directly in the introduction to their speeches.

The Magnificat comes out of a situation that is, in truth, impregnated with the Holy Spirit. Elizabeth is filled with the Spirit (1:41) and speaks in a loud voice, that is, prophetically (1:42). She praises Mary, who is already overshadowed by the Holy Spirit (1:35), as the greater person (1:43). Thus the Magnificat, even though the introduction simply reads "and Mary said," is a Spirit-filled, prophetic word.

Zechariah cannot sing until his tongue is loosed by a miracle (1:64). In the introduction to the Benedictus it is also expressly said that he

> was filled with the Holy Spirit and spoke this prophecy. (1:67)

As regards the choir of angels who sing the Gloria above the fields of Bethlehem, the supernatural character is guaranteed by the singers themselves. These are angels, and after singing they return to heaven (2:15).

Of Simeon it is said, not once but three times before he begins to sing, that the Holy Spirit is at work in him (2:25, 26, 27). Anna, who is paralleled with him and also praises God (2:38), is a prophet (2:36).

Hence there can be no doubt: what is expressed in the four songs is not a set of human feelings, but divine realities. If the singers of the four songs are characterized, it is only as their transmitters. In the strict sense what is characterized is, rather, the real actor in the whole narrative: *God*. It is God whom the songs sing about. God's action in history is given voice. That, again, corresponds to what we find in the Old Testament parallels.

How is God characterized? The Magnificat praises God in the language of theology of the poor. God has acted on behalf of the poor. A popular modern German translation uses the present tense, which is wrong: the Greek aorists are to be understood in their usual sense, that is, as past tense. (The NRSV retains the past here.) God *has* acted on behalf of God's servant Israel, as will be clear at the end, in the fulfillment of the promises to the ancestors (1:54-55). The statements about God's action are a mosaic of Old Testament allusions, which combine to show that Mary is singing of God's whole history with Israel, culminating in God's action on behalf of Mary, God's servant. At the end of the song Mary has become the representative of Israel, which speaks through her.

It is only with the Benedictus, then, that the two angelic messages are deciphered, for it speaks of the coming of the Davidic Messiah and his precursor—always in that order, and thus chiastically to the narrative itself. The messianic event is seen on the one hand as the liberation of Israel from its oppressors, and on the other hand as the pardoning of its sins.

The Gloria gives universal dimensions to God's action: glory in the highest, peace on earth. There is a gap at the point where we might inquire who the recipients of this peace will be. One would expect "Israel" here, as previously in the message to the shepherds:

> good news of great joy for all the people (= Israel). (2:10)

But instead the song speaks, more abstractly, of people in general, to whom (divine) "favor" is directed. Into this gap the Nunc dimittis inserts knowledge of the inbreaking revelation to all peoples.

In thus briefly summarizing the content of the four hymns with an eye to divine action, one cannot avoid drawing two surprising conclusions:

By no means do these four hymns appear to be entirely independent of one another. Rather, they build and expand on each other. If we take them together they complement one another in constituting a "messianology," Old Testament in its conception and in terms of its extent apparently aimed at completeness, a "messianology" that is at the same time an "ecclesiology."

The relationship of the content to the situation in which the individual songs are sung and with the persons who sing them is even looser than it has appeared thus far. This is especially true of Mary's song of praise, which has no reference at all to the angel's saying that Mary will be the mother of the Messiah. Elizabeth, who did not even know that message, had been instructed by the Spirit and immediately before this had spoken directly of Gabriel's words to Mary, which she had not even heard (1:42-45). It is only Zechariah, then, who retrieves the Messiah theme in his hymn.

Simeon also speaks strangely. He really has nothing to do with John, the precursor of Jesus. Does he even know of him? But, at least in a way that is recognizable to the reader of the entire gospel, he presents the revelation to the Gentiles as a motif connected to the precursor, when in 2:30-31 he speaks of the "salvation" that God has "prepared" before the eyes of all peoples. "Prepare" in Luke's gospel is a key word connected to John, and the word "salvation," which appears here for the first time, combined with the verb "to see," will return in Luke 3:6 in a quotation of Isa 40:3-5 that at this point characterizes the precursor. There we will read:

> all flesh shall see the salvation of God.

The statement is thus understood in a universal sense, and since at the same time it is applied to the precursor, it appears that here the connection of the precursor with the hope for the conversion of the Gentiles has its roots. But why, then, must Simeon be the one to open up this theme? Would it not have been better to put it in the Benedictus?

Once we take account of all these things, the four songs appear to us as fundamentally one. And so they are. Although they are certainly part of the narrated story, they evidently have their own statement to make, and

146 *In the Shadow of Your Wings*

that agenda has a certain independence of the narrative program of the stories presented in prose.

However, this perception is so unheard-of that one would only wish to affirm it if other proofs are found, independent of the observations made thus far. In fact, there are such proofs. Here what I have said about the "linking" of psalms in the Old Testament Psalter becomes important, for the four hymns are, in fact, linked to one another.

The linking of the hymns in Luke's Infancy Narrative

The linking is accomplished primarily through words common to a number of the hymns. One really should never describe such features of texts without simultaneously analyzing the effects, in terms of the content, that emerge. But at present only some brief indications can be given; if we were to pursue this seriously we would have to present a complete analysis of the four hymns. In what follows I will go through the hymns in the order in which they stand in the story, and I will mention only the most important linking elements. In each case I will first offer a summary table.

Magnificat	**Benedictus**
1:54 Israel	1:68 The God of Israel his people
his servant	1:69 his servant David
1:55 as he promised/spoke	1:70 as he promised/spoke . . . of his holy prophets
our ancestors . . . Abraham	1:73 to our ancestor Abraham
1:47 my Savior	1:69 a horn of salvation
	1:71 saved
1:50 his mercy	
1:54 in remembrance of his mercy	1:72 mercy . . . and . . . remembered

The Magnificat begins the chain. Mary sings her own story in the history of Israel, in a series of allusions. Only at the end does the decisive word appear: "He has helped his servant Israel" (1:54). This concluding key word of the Magnificat is taken up by the beginning of the Benedictus. Zechariah praises the Lord, the "God of Israel," and then draws a distinction, speaking of the "redemption" of God's "people" (1:68) through the lifting up of the "horn of salvation" in the "house of David, his servant" (1:69).

That the second song develops the point reached at the end of the first is shown also by the fact that at both these points there is reference back to a divine promise: "as he promised/spoke" (1:55; 1:70). The addressees of the promise were, in the Magnificat, "our ancestors, Abraham and his descendants" (1:55). In the Benedictus the reference to the promise peaks and is doubled. It takes place "through the mouth of his holy prophets" (1:70) and ultimately refers to the "holy covenant," the "oath that he swore to our ancestor Abraham" (1:73). We see clearly how here, in the first part of the Benedictus, the final statement of the Magnificat has been taken up and developed.

This is also clear from the names given to God's saving action. At the beginning of the Magnificat God is called "savior" (1:47). The body of the song is framed by the key word "mercy" (1:50, 54). Complementing this, in the first part of the Benedictus "salvation" or "saved" appears twice (1:69, 71), and "mercy" once (1:72). This first part does what we miss in the Magnificat: it develops the theme of the coming Davidic royal Messiah; this is the first point in the sequence of songs at which this theme is introduced.

Benedictus	**Gloria**
1:76 prophet of the Most High	2:14 in the highest heaven
1:78 our God	God
the dawn from on high	
1:79 the way of peace	on earth peace

In the second part of the Benedictus, whose theme is John the Baptizer, two key words appear almost as if by accident. These words will be definitive in the song the angels sing over the fields of Bethlehem. John will be called "prophet of the Most High" (1:76), because he will give knowledge of the coming of the "dawn from on high" (1:78). The messianic "dawn" will shine as light in the darkness and guide people's steps "into the way of peace" (1:79). After the birth of the Messiah, the angel choirs take all this up into their song in the light-filled night:

> Glory above in the highest spaces of the universe (now belongs to) God, and on earth (there comes to pass) peace among people of good will. (2:14*)

Thus the angelic choir is directly linked to the Benedictus, and offers in turn, with the key words "peace" and "glory," two central words for Simeon's song of praise (2:29, 32). They recur there in reverse order:

Gloria	Nunc dimittis
2:14 Glory in the highest heaven	2:29 in peace
peace on earth	2:32 glory to your people Israel

In the statement about "light for revelation to the Gentiles" (2:32) Simeon also continues the light-motif from the Benedictus. Moreover, with the key words "servant" (2:29), "salvation" (2:30), and "your people Israel" (2:32) the Nunc dimittis is linked back to the beginning of the lyric chain, to the Magnificat (cf. there 1:48, 47, 54, and in the Benedictus 1:68). One more table will show this:

Nunc dimittis	Magnificat
2:29 your servant	1:47 my savior
2:30 your salvation	1:48 your servant
2:32 Israel	1:54 Israel

All that is necessarily quite superficial. There is no need to see this whole network of key words all at once in all its detail and in some sense to master it intellectually. My concern was to give a real impression of the linking of words that is objectively present. It would be urgently necessary at this point to demonstrate, in terms of content, the dense messianology of this lyric complex, imbued with all the major motifs of Old Testament expectation—from the humble beginning in the Magnificat, with its theology of the poor, through the Davidic, royal messianology of the Benedictus, to the pilgrimage theme of the conclusion, with peace on earth at the center. But that is not possible in this context. We can only draw conclusions.

The songs and the narrative

Athwart the actions in the Infancy Narrative taking place on earth, through the mediation of the four hymns, the cosmic-divine fullness of meaning in these events takes its stance. Individual figures in the story are made aware of it at different points, and speak it prophetically in their songs. None of them was present when the others sang, but one song takes up where the other left off. All of them together make up one whole. Each song, of course, elucidates the point in the narrative at which it is sung, but at the same time it stands in relationship to all the other points in the whole sequence of events.

These two chapters in the gospel are undoubtedly a narrative that is understood to be inspired. Even the omniscient narrator is to be understood as inspired, in the Old Testament tradition. But within his narrative other inspired figures begin to speak, and they open our view beyond the earthly sequence of the story to its heavenly context. This brings a multi-dimensional character to the narrative. The connections revealed in the hymns expand the horizon of the narrative itself. Each hymn clarifies the point in the action at which it occurs, but at the same time it is part of a comprehensive system of interpretation touching the whole story and all its individual points. Here, then, a broader application of meaning through creative participation by the readers can begin.

Despite orientation to the concrete course of the narrative in Luke 1–2, the world of meaning unfolded in the four hymns is so complete in itself that one could imagine it as separable from the narrative and capable of being inserted in other sequences of action—analogous in structure, of course. And with this I come, at the close of my remarks, to the title I have chosen.

The hymns and the course of the Christian's day

In the Church's practice the four hymns of the Infancy Narrative are in fact brought into new contexts. At least in our Western Catholic Liturgy of the Hours the Magnificat is sung at the beginning of the liturgical day, that is, at evening Vespers. In the morning prayer, Lauds, the Benedictus is the high point. The angels' Gloria, in expanded form, stands at the beginning of the eucharistic service that follows Lauds. Compline, the last evening prayer, culminates in the Nunc dimittis. That is to say: the four hymns of the Infancy Narrative are spread evenly over the course of the day, and in their original sequence.

Every day in the long history of humanity is different, is in a certain sense its own story. Again, the same day is different for every individual human being, and again its own story. But for those who pray the Liturgy of the Hours the four hymns are set within the course of events in exactly the same way as they are set within the events of the Infancy Narrative. They stop the action. They open horizons. They combine into an interpretation, spanning the whole of salvation history, of the very events that are taking place in each concrete day of each one's life.

Our day is normally just as simple and human as what takes place in the Infancy Narrative. Families await babies; the babies come; there are sorrows and joys. People are separated and come together again. People look backward; they see signs of the future. Is there, despite all the miracles that run through our Lukan story, anything simpler, more human, more normal than these kinds of events? Everything else that happens to us fits into this picture, too. We think that our daily lives are nothing special, nothing but what they are. But the Church inserts these four hymns that, in Luke's Infancy Narrative, open the horizon of divine salvation history into our days, those days that seem so normal to us. Like a shining row of lamps, they are to accompany us through our day. What is happening?

Apparently the Church presumes that, by the very nature of things, in the course of a Christian's day miracles will happen, miracles like those that are told in the Lukan Infancy Narrative. Therefore we can interpret them with the same inspired psalms and transform them into songs of praise. Once we have understood that, we see that our daily life is meant to be lived within that great divine history that the Bible tells from beginning to end. For the four hymns of the Lukan Infancy Narrative are nothing but a poetic summary of the whole of biblical salvation history.

The question for us is simply whether we will accept the Church's invitation, extended in its distribution of these hymns throughout our day. Perhaps, even before that, it is whether we *can* accept them: whether our daily life is such that it can be interpreted by these accompanying hymns and in light of the Old Testament. If so, then the God of Abraham, Isaac, and Jacob accompanies us through our day, and our day must at every moment become a song of praise to this God.

Chapter Twelve

Children of Abraham from Stones

Does the Old Testament Promise a
New Covenant Without Israel?

"A covenant never revoked"—through Martin Buber that phrase has entered our language, and through the current pope it has made its way into almost every Christian-Jewish dialogue. It presumes certain *agreements:* agreement about something that is by no means a matter of course, namely that God acts in history—and then that God does this work neither in a purely internal fashion in millions of individual souls, nor externally and miraculously in the whole of humanity, but rather that God pursues this work in human history through a people to whom God binds Godself and, binding them as well, takes into God's service. And still more, it presumes agreement that this all began with Abraham and continued in Abraham's children. Finally, it presumes agreement that it still continues today. But where?

Here the agreements end. Has the role of Abraham's children as instruments of God's work been cancelled and promised to another group of people? John the Baptizer said that God could raise up children of Abraham out of stones (Matt 3:9; Luke 3:8). That threatens cancellation—not of the promise to Abraham that he would have descendants, but apparently to those John saw before him, and their descendants. Did God actually bring that about, and awaken a new people for God out of the stony remainder of humanity, while God's first people became blowing sand in the desert of the nations? Here again perhaps there is agreement that we have to ask the question.

In fact, the agreement extends a few millimeters farther. After Auschwitz we Christians are even willing to follow two advanced popes and thoughtfully feel our way into the darkness in which it might be possible to think that God's covenant with the Jewish people was in fact *not* cancelled, and that God still needs this people as God's beloved instrument.

We are seeking proofs of this tentative thesis, and if there are no proofs, let us at least look for open doors. As Christians, we naturally seek within the writings of the New Testament. We are looking for the mistakes that may have been made in dealing with those writings. Those mistakes are responsible for the fact that this truth has not been seen.

That is the *statement of the standpoint* within the framework of which the following reflections belong.

The task

We are concerned, then, with theology in the strict sense. But for the sake of that theology we will enter into its preliminaries: history and literary textual analysis. Can we find there a basis for the theological point of view we secretly desire? Or do the texts bar us from it?

Within the historical-literal question, I as an Old Testament scholar am interested here in a kind of *pre-question*. The New Testament writings were created within the world of Judaism. In this process the Sacred Scriptures of that time played a special role. This is true in any case, even if we are uncertain about their exact content and the nature of their authority. In spite of that, we can turn our attention to them. We are confident of a certain core, and we are certain that they were regarded as the words of God and of the prophets.

How did this body of texts see the future of the people Israel? Did it contemplate the possibility that God would one day abandon the people Israel as God's instrument in history? Or is it certain that God will always accompany Israel through history? Even in the latter case, of course, it would be possible to suppose that, beyond these writings, God could have acted differently in the messianic age. Thus what I will present really decides nothing about the question proper. But it is a preliminary to the statements the New Testament will make, whether agreeing, transforming, or rejecting.

Two *restrictions* are connected with this definition of my task. First: I am really restricting myself to the *canonical* body of the New Testament. Obviously this does not deny the importance of the rest of early Jewish literature, and that is presupposed every time I extend my regard into historical matters. Second, I can dispense with all types of descriptions of *developments* within the Old Testament. I must only attempt to read what the New Testament authors read. What they read was the end product, at that time, of the literary developments that led to the canon. They understood it as a coherent body. Call this a "canonical approach," if you will. But it is neither a Christian "canonical approach" nor a Jewish "canonical approach" in the contemporary sense. It is at most the historical reconstruction of the "canonical approach" of that time. I am going to stay within history.

A difficult problem arises out of the discrepancy between the thing and the word. Buber and the Pope spoke of the "covenant," the *one* covenant, the *old* covenant. The term comes from the Hebrew Bible, and it is also in the New Testament. It is a key concept. But the thing itself does not depend on the word; it is spoken of from beginning to end without the use of the word. The word may appear, but the same text can speak of the same thing in other words. We dare not lose sight of the word "covenant," but it would be equally wrong to freeze onto it, and it alone.

Consequently I think it is best if I divide my remarks into two parts. First I will deal, independently of any fixed terminology, with the statements of Israel's Bible about this question, and then with the assistance they provide and the difficulty they raise for speaking of the question in terms of the covenant metaphor.

God's ties to Israel

That Israel is YHWH's people, and that YHWH is Israel's God, that this situation drives history from within itself and ever onward, that even when this history one day will encompass the world of the nations, Zion will remain at the center—all this is omnipresent in Israel's narrative writings. Texts from times of crisis play it out. In retrospect it is commented on; in anticipation it is projected. It is the principal theme not only of the opening movement but of the entire symphony. Nowhere is there any hint of a definitive cancellation of this prerogative of Israel at any time in the future.

It would be pedantic to offer citations to prove this. Let me quote just *one* passage pointing to the future—found, incidentally, immediately after Jeremiah's words about the "new covenant":

> Thus says the LORD,
>   who gives the sun for light by day
>   and the fixed order of the moon and the stars for light by night,
>   who stirs up the sea so that its waves roar—
>   the LORD of hosts is his name:
> If this fixed order were ever to cease from my presence, says the LORD, then also the offspring of Israel would cease to be a nation before me forever.
> Thus says the LORD:
> If the heavens above can be measured,
>   and the foundations of the earth below can be explored,
> then I will reject all the offspring of Israel
>   because of all they have done, says the LORD. (Jer 31:35-37 MT*)

But we should not take all this too much for granted or think of it lightly. Therefore in what follows I would like to speak, in four stages, of the harshness, the angularity, and the burden of this matter.

The many predictions of the end

This is about history, and therefore about freedom. For that very reason nothing can be taken for granted here. More than once the relationship between God and the people hangs by a thread. It looks as if the sword is about to fall. God is already announcing the end of the relationship. God's word is so clear and so loud that the reader can scarcely believe that the end will not come, and yet afterward it turns out otherwise. The threat remains only a threat.

Threats are not prophecies, even when prophets proclaim them. Other things may yet happen, and then perhaps what is threatened will not come to pass. Those who miss the genre of such texts will of course not be so sure that God has never cancelled the covenant. For in any case threats imply that God *could* cancel it, and moreover, when they are uttered, that God is already in the process of withdrawing from it. But according to the Bible, God never did that to Israel back then.

The basic pattern can be found at Israel's first fall: at Sinai, in the case of the golden calf. God says to Moses:

> Now let me alone, so that my wrath may burn hot against them and I may consume them; and of *you* I will make a great nation. (Exod 32:10; cf. Deut 9:14)

That strange "let me alone!" is the thread by which everything hangs. God demands the assent of the new tribal ancestor, but he refuses it. He makes himself the advocate of the people destined for death and persuades God to regret those words. Moses is supposed to substitute for Israel and initiate a new people. If his loyalty had not remained with Israel, the end would have come then.

The prophetic books are also marked by a rising threat that then, at the end, does not come to pass. This is clearest in the eleventh chapter of Hosea, a book we spoke of in one of the previous essays in this book. Here there is not even an advocate, to say nothing of repentance on the part of the people. The drama plays itself out solely within God. From ch. 4 onward God conducts the trial against God's people in a cosmic auditorium. God the prosecutor demands the death sentence. Guilt is piled upon guilt. Every penitential act on the part of Israel is shown to be mere appearance. When dawn comes, the king of Israel will be destroyed—so ends ch. 10.

In the eleventh chapter everything is reversed. God's voice begins to lament. Memories of the Egyptian beginnings arise. Israel's rejection becomes God's pain. In v. 8 we read:

> How can I give you up, Ephraim?
> > How can I hand you over, O Israel?
> How can I make you like Admah?
> > How can I treat you like Zeboiim?
> My heart recoils within me;
> > my compassion grows warm and tender.

God's wrath is exhausted. Immediately, a vision of the future unfolds: God roars like a lion into the vastness of space, and those who have already been thrust into exile come flying back like birds from every direction and dwell again in their houses. The common history will go on.

It is the same everywhere in the books of the prophets. Historically oriented exegesis, however, has embedded a different image of the prophetic books in our minds. "Amos's No" was the title of a 1963 essay by Rudolf Smend that can stand as representative of many others. One crucial sentence read: "From Yahweh's 'no' to Israel's behavior and attitude follows his 'no' to the existence of the people itself." This is intended as a summary of *Amos's* message. A second sentence referring to this first one reads: "This is said categorically; it is not accompanied by any prophecy of salvation; there is simply no future for Israel at all." We can leave it open, historically speaking, whether Amos himself understood his "no" as an irrevocable announcement of Israel's end, or whether it was only a threat in the guise of a proclamation. But in the book of Amos as it now stands there is no final and irrevocable "no," and certainly there is none in the canon as a whole. But if, since Wilhelm Martin Leberecht de Wette, and above all since Julius Wellhausen, the "no" of a historical Amos and other similar prophetic figures constitutes the dominant historical picture, according to which the positively-weighted pre-exilic "Hebraism" yielded, in exile, to the negatively-colored figure of "Judaism," and if one understands that whole complex as a salvation-historical and theological statement, one arrives very quickly at what Klaus Koch has repeatedly called the *"Prophetic Annexation Theory":* Israel, as people of God, collapsed at least half a millennium before Christ, and then God began something new in history, starting from historical Judaism certainly, but discontinuous with it and with completely different people. This point of view, lying in the depths of our socialized knowledge, probably shapes our thinking more strongly than we can appreciate. It positively impels us to formulate substitution theories to explain the relationship between the Church and Israel.

The Bible that precedes the New Testament is not aware of any empty centuries in which there was no people of God. Its "no" is threat, not fact. This "no" witnesses to the disturbing character of freedom in this history, to a nightmare passage along the abyss, but not to a fatal plunge. However, this conclusion probably still covers the horrors of this history too gently. The wine that fills it is much cloudier. Nevertheless: even if we admit to still greater horrors, we do not see any ultimate and final end.

The catastrophes that happened

It is not the case that the threats were not fulfilled. They happened all too often. Because Israel, after leaving Sinai and being urged to enter the land of promise, lost its nerve and did not believe, it had to remain in the wilderness for forty years, until none were left of the generation of those who came out of Egypt. A new generation under Joshua entered the land. Not even Moses came in (Num 14:10-35; cf. also Deut 1:34-40).

In this case the continuity through time was secured by passing over a fallen generation, which had thereby dropped out of God's story, and making a new beginning with the next generation. There is also a second pattern in the scheme distinguishing, within the people, between the guilty and the (usually very few) others. This is found especially in the prophetic books. It works with the concept of the escapees, the "remnant" after the catastrophe. With them, God continues the story.

These things are too familiar to need further explanation. I want at most to point to an extreme case of this historical pattern, proposed by the book of Zephaniah. In Zephaniah's vision God's wrath strikes Jerusalem as well as the other nations. The only ones who have a chance to be rescued, as a "remnant," are the poor people outside the city, in Judah (Zeph 2:3). But their rescue is effected by the fact that the "people of the isles," that is, the people from the uttermost limits of the earth, there in their own place convert to YHWH and call on YHWH's name. Then all the peoples come with their gifts to Zion, and here it appears that the "remnant of Israel" God had left was the poor and lowly people (Zeph 3:12-13; cf., in preparation, 2:11; 3:9-11). Here all the bearers of the tradition have disappeared; the continuity of Israel's tie to its God is rescued almost entirely from without.

In both these thought patterns—the jump to the next generation and the rescue of a "remnant"—the threats appear because Israel has failed. But both patterns result in a situation in which Israel as such nevertheless remains. On the other hand, catastrophe follows catastrophe. This history is only salvation history in a limited sense. It also encompasses a great deal of evil: deserved, but nevertheless evil. God has attached Godself to a people that is never really with God, and yet God remains with it. Even if at some time, after many centuries, of the twelve tribes of the original group only Judah remains, it still counts as the whole of Israel, and Jesus, to establish a claim to the continuity of Israel, would create the symbolic group of the Twelve.

That, for example, is a challenge to the certainty with which Christian proclamation is accustomed to conclude from the destruction of Jerusalem predicted by Jesus in the gospels that the events of the year 70 signified the end of the Jewish people as the people of God. All that had happened before. When the first Temple fell and Jerusalem was destroyed there was, nevertheless, a surviving remnant, and new generations that followed from it. Such catastrophes, as brutal as they are, are not simply the end of God's history with Israel.

But is that end perhaps, in a completely different way, to be expected in the eschatological future, when in spite of all the windings of the path and delays in the tempo the peoples of the world have converted and united with Israel? Can the old, used-up instrument of God then perhaps be, if not thrown away, at least dissolved in the new and greater reality?

Israel in the eschatological fulfillment

Here again we can learn something. The discourse about a reign of God in the end-time that will encompass the world of all peoples goes farthest in the books of Isaiah and the Psalms. As regards the Psalms, they must of course be read in their canonical text and as an entire composition if we are to ask about their intention. But in such a reading it becomes clear that although the human-royal "messianic" theme of the first three books of Psalms (up to Psalm 89) is replaced by the divine-royal "theocratic" theme of the fourth book (beginning with Psalm 90), and remains in the background also in the fifth book (beginning with Psalm 107), which unites both themes, nevertheless, and despite these shifts in emphasis, the role of Israel and the central position of Zion is never dissolved. In the great concluding Hallel (Psalms 146–50), the concluding "hermeneutic of the Psalter" internal to the book (Erich Zenger), the symmetrically arranged Psalms 147 and 149 emphasize that even in the final reign of God the center of divine praise remains on Zion. There God's ḥasidim will sing their songs of praise.

It is not very different in the book of Isaiah. Its final chapters speak of a new heaven and a new earth. They discern in Israel and among the nations a final division. But they remain centered on Zion, even insofar as, according to Isa 66:21, men from the people streaming to Zion will be chosen as priests and Levites. As for what remains of "Israel" at the end: "For as the new heavens and the new earth, which I will make, shall remain before me, says the LORD; so shall your descendants and your name remain" (Isa 66:22). One could at most object that within the two literary complexes there are individual passages that more sharply play down Israel's role at the end of history. I am thinking of Psalm 87 in the Psalter, and in Isaiah of Isa 19:18-25. But on close examination it cannot be said, even in these passages, that at the end of history, among the converted nations, Israel will be simply without a function—even apart from the fact that the New Testament certainly deciphered these passages as an integral part of the one great painting shown it by its Bible.

According to Psalm 87 not only Israel, but now people from all the nations of the earth will say that they were born in Zion. That is a removal of boundaries. But the center of this new world is all the more clearly revealed: it is Zion, God's foundation on holy mountains, the eschatological mother of all nations.

In Isa 19:25 YHWH will bless the three nations of Egypt, Assyria, and Israel (with Egypt and Assyria apparently representing all the nations of the world) as follows:

> "Blessed be Egypt my people,
> and Assyria the work of my hands,
> and Israel my heritage!"

It is evident that all three, in parallel variations, are promised the same quality, namely that of being God's people. Thus at the end of time that will no longer be Israel's prerogative. From the original concept of the people of God emerges the paradoxical miracle that all peoples will each individually be God's people. Nevertheless, even in this text Israel retains a special position.

We can see this with regard to Egypt, for its conversion is told at length. Among those dwelling in Egypt and the Israelites again oppressed there the events that led to Israel's exodus at the beginning of its history will be repeated, except that this time when YHWH is made known to Egypt, Egypt will truly recognize and acknowledge YHWH and give YHWH cultic worship (Isa 19:20-22). Thus it will become a people of God, and for that Israel is instrumental.

This blessing of God on the three nations is also followed by the statement that Israel will be "a blessing in the midst of the earth" (Isa 19:24). That certainly does not simply mean that it lies on the road between Assyria and Egypt as a kind of land-bridge between the great nations; instead, it makes this central geographical position a symbol for the fulfillment of the promise of blessing that once was given to Abraham (Gen 12:2-3). Even when Israel's special status among the nations is removed, at the same time this remains.

As the major bodies of Christians emerged in the first centuries, nothing ultimately remained of Jewish Christianity. I do not believe that this process corresponds to what is said of the eschaton in the book of Isaiah, especially not in ch. 19. On the other hand, the texts of the Psalter and of Isaiah certainly do not recognize any definitive antagonism at the end of history between the descendants of Abraham and the nations that have received Abraham's blessing. What they see is far from that kind of lurking presence alongside one another that seems to be our idea of the normal relationship between Judaism and Christianity. Does Israel's Bible perhaps have some interpretive pointers for such an antagonism, in case it should emerge?

God's long patience with a divided people

Among the horrors of the reality of "God's people" in Israel's Bible is the fact that it can be divided, and to such an extent that its unity is no longer perceptible. I will speak only of the most concrete example: the divided kingdom.

Our historical picture is perhaps clearer than we sense when we take our lead from the books of Chronicles. For this author it was clear, from a long historical perspective, that the thread of divine history had only continued, beyond the Babylonian exile, with Judah. Consequently, only Judah was interesting for the author of Chronicles. Between Solomon and the fall of Jerusalem there is nothing said about the history of the northern kingdom. But even if this author may have written with a hermeneutics of canonical finality, the books of Kings remained in the canon. Their essentially more complicated point of view retains its canonical weight. They show, at least, how long the true red thread of history could remain invisible.

Through the sins of Solomon and the arrogance of his son Rehoboam, the kingdom of David fell. Further sins, such as the new cult inaugurated by Jeroboam I, deepened the division. The deuteronomistic redactors of the books of Kings certainly asked themselves on which side the legitimacy stood. They did not answer in favor of one side or the other. Instead, God had given kingship over Israel (= the whole people), through the oracle of Ahija in 1 Kings 11, a kind of new Nathan-oracle, to Jeroboam, while through the same oracle the Davidic dynasty, because of the merits of David and the Temple at Jerusalem built by Solomon, retained power over the separated tribe of Judah. Part of God's heart was with each side, and God continued to accompany both. This was also apparent later, even though both sides behaved badly again and again, worse and worse. In the North—at first, at any rate—more prophets appeared than in the South. What really should have happened, that the two halves reunited, did not happen. Only centuries later came the end first of the North, then of the South. That the story would ultimately continue with the rescued remnant from the South is almost outside the horizon of the books of Kings.

Thus for several centuries the Bible cannot really decide in which historical group the people of God subsisted. When human sin unravels the divine fabric of history, God's patience is long. As long as God remains patient, God's people are present in a number of forms, and not entirely in any of them. That was not anticipated, or intended as an enduring situation. It was an untenable condition that could only end in catastrophe. Nevertheless: it appears that for the Bible something like that is within the realm of the dramas that human sin can produce.

The authors of the New Testament had no need to refer to such thought models. For them, the end of time had come. It could only be a short while until everything came together. But as it became apparent that after the first coming of the Messiah the time until his parousia would extend somewhat longer, that there would be some real history to live through—didn't they have to consider such possibilities again?

The only New Testament author who could have suspected something like this was Paul, in Romans 9–11. But even if he only touched the tip of this model we cannot remove it from our arsenal of interpretative possibilities. It may be that God is still being patient in our own history, because once again the people of God has been torn apart and therefore its identity cannot be clearly determined.

Here I will conclude the first part of my remarks. The topic has been addressed. But there are still the words, especially the word "covenant," by means of which the Bible and we ourselves attempt to express the subject itself. That, unfortunately, leads to further complications, to which I will now turn.

God's "covenant" with Israel

I will presuppose that the spectrum of opinions of Old Testament scholars regarding the topic of "covenant," with all its wealth of extreme positions, is at least generally familiar. At the present time we seem to be at the end of a phase of "silence about the covenant" (Erich Zenger; similarly Eckart Otto). The shift is being brought about by new knowledge gained from comparative legal history and narrative textual analysis. Above all, the genetic connection between deuteronomistic covenant theology and Neo-Assyrian legal forms is again apparent. But the development of Christian-Jewish dialogue has also contributed to the return of the "covenant" theme. At the same time, new questions have moved into the foreground. Consequently, it may be that not all the older matters that led to "silence about the covenant" have really been dealt with. This is true especially of the broadly conceived and detailed semantic work—one could almost say *life's* work—of Ernst Kutsch. Therefore I would like to begin with some remarks about the Hebrew word *berit* and its English translations, without, of course, being able to go into detail.

Difficulties with the word "berit"

From a great many discussions with Ernst Kutsch as well as from his publications I am rather certain that his semantic studies were driven by a theological impetus. He saw in the legal form of a contract, when applied to the relationship between God and the human being, a reduction of God's sovereignty. One of his books *(Neues Testament—Neuer Bund? Eine Fehlübersetzung wird korrigiert)*[1] ended as follows:

> Thus instead of "new covenant" we should say "new settlement," which is not only philologically and theologically correct, but also gives honor to the gracious action of God to which the phrase refers.

Lothar Perlitt seems to be writing from a similar religious conviction (in his influential book *Bundestheologie im Alten Testament)*[2] when he says of Exod 24:9-11:

> This vision of God grounds a relationship in which God is the giver and humans the receivers. Any breath of mutuality would take away from the sovereignty of the God who thus appears. Every association with any kind of contractual relationship is excluded by the text itself . . . . Anyone who, in view of this scene, uses the word "covenant"—in whatever sense—corrupts it.

Here we are touching on the basic sources of the new "silence about the covenant." They deserve respect, but they also reveal a certain cluelessness about what is called *"law."*

Of course there are "associations" among human beings. It may be that legal relationships arise even, in a very remote sense, between a criminal

---
1. New Testament—New Covenant? Correcting a False Translation.
2. Covenant Theology in the Old Testament.

and the accessories to his accessories, or between those who bend an elbow in the same bar every night: promises of fidelity or expectations of confidentiality that may be demanded, although scarcely in public. But we certainly cannot reduce law to that level. In reverse: giving and accepting a gift—what Perlitt contrasts with "contract"—is, juridically speaking, also a contract, of course. And what jurist would ever assert that in such a contract the partners are *eo ipso* equal? That statements about God and relationships between creatures and God have only analogical character is an additional factor—but here I simply want to insist that a great part of the semantic literature on the Hebrew word *berit,* and probably also on the Greek *diathēkē,* two words from the world of juridical language, appear to lack a sense and sensibility for the law. For that reason alone, a good deal needs to be examined.

But now for the *semantic* analysis itself! In this regard it would seem that James Barr, in Zimmerli's Festschrift toward the end of the 1970s, put his finger clearly enough on the questionable methodology of Ernst Kutsch and others, although he was concerned with the specific difficulties surrounding the word in any semantic study. With studied caution he avoided presenting a theory of his own, as will I. But I would like at least to point to a term in ancient textual theory that may be helpful for the word *berit* (usually translated "covenant") and the idiomatic expression *karat berit* (usually translated "make a covenant"), but that I have not yet found in the discussion: the concept of *metonymy* ("naming-with").

Metonymy is the designation of a more general thing in terms of a characteristic partial element. To introduce idiomatic examples from our own language right away: When we say that a man "turned to the bottle," of course his reaching for the bottle is only a significant part of the human transformation that we describe with metaphors from the language of love or war when we say such things as "he surrendered himself to drink." If we say that a woman has "taken the veil," this minor ritual element from the consecration of virgins says that she has become a nun. The man who turns to the bottle acquires a behavioral habit. The woman who takes the veil enters into a new social and legal complex of relationships. In both cases we are using the language of metonymy.

Could it be that the expression *karat berit* ("to cut a *berit*), opaque in itself, refers to a (normally ritualized) act of obligation, but is metonymically used for the entire relationship, usually a legal relationship, into which the act of obligation binds? According to the context, attention may be focused more on the relationship coming into existence or on the act itself. Both the act in its concrete form and the relationship thus formed, in its concrete structure, could allow for a number of variations. In individual cases only the situation and the textual context would provide more detailed information.

The English word "covenant" (German "Bund") and our expression "make a covenant" are then in many cases the appropriate translation, but certainly not in all instances. Kutsch's translation "settlement, obligation" is somewhat correct, but has to be metonymical in modern languages if it is to cover all cases. However, our language will surely not do him the favor of allowing it to be metonymy, since we are not talking about a present, living reality. So it is inappropriate, and can be left lying on the roadside of the history of research.

My next remark takes us almost more into the realm of modern German or English semantics than of Hebrew. It concerns the expression *hefer berit,* a metaphor. The word-for-word translation would be *"to break a covenant."* But when we say that someone has broken the marriage bond we do not mean that he or she has annulled the marriage, so that it has ceased to exist. We only mean that she or he has not adhered to the marital obligation of exclusivity. The marriage still exists. It may from here on have a shakier history. At most in the further course of things it might come to a divorce or an annullment. Again, breaking a contract, in our language, is not the same thing as cancelling or calling off a contract, unless such a consequence of breaking the contract was specifically stipulated in the contract itself. To that extent it is—in terms of English or German—surprising that in our exegetical literature the statement that Israel broke the covenant with God is almost automatically equated with the covenant's ceasing to exist.

This is especially important in the exegesis of Jer 31:31-34, the text about the "new covenant." God promises it because the first covenant partners or the later Israelites have "broken" the covenant of the Exodus. Often that is understood as if the Exodus covenant had thereby ceased to exist. But that is using the metaphor "break a covenant" contrary to English or German usage. If one is persuaded by that exegesis, one should use a different translation of *hefer berit,* and avoid the image of the breaking of a staff in English or German. One should say something like: "They (the ancestors/the Israelites) have dissolved the covenant." But I ask myself whether *hefer berit* has to mean that. No one has yet clearly demonstrated it. If we want to hold to the image and assert that the covenant has been annulled, we should at least avoid the expression "break a covenant," with its fixed meaning, and create a new one, something like "shatter a covenant." But as I have said, I would consider that a false interpretation of Jer 31:32.

If we see things that way, then the controversial question whether the new covenant in Jeremiah 31 is a *new* or a *renewed* covenant may take on a different aspect. Here again, by the way, I would recommend that we be careful about our modern-language formulations. Our languages can speak of a "new" contract or a "renewed" contract, but also of something else: a "fresh" contract.[3] Has this possibility been tried? But it may be that none of these three possible expressions is useful for Jeremiah 31 without additional notes. For example, in German or English when a sick person's dressings are "changed" or "freshened" the wound remains the same, but the bandage consists of "new" gauze and tape. It may be that not even the expression "renew the covenant" will do what its defenders say it does.

Enough of these semantic marginal notes! I only wanted to call for a little caution. But now to the contribution that the idea of the covenant makes to the formulation of a conviction about the continuity and identity of the people of God.

The plurality of covenant theologies

"Covenant" is undoubtedly the most important category that serves to crystallize the idea of the continuity and identity of Israel as the people of God. But it does not always happen in the same way. *Berit* is a key word in a number of theological initiatives that are individually very different from one another, and that apply the word in very different ways. These initiatives arose sometimes in succession and in light of others, and were meant to be distinct from one another.

Thus the "covenant theology" of the Priestly document is one of irrevocable divine "promises." In using the word *berit* for this, coupling it with the word *ʾolam* ("eternity"), and introducing it in history not at Sinai, but with (Noah and) Abraham, it intends to correct the deuteronomistic *berit* theology of a *berit* between God and the people Israel that is more strongly oriented to the analogy with vows of fidelity, and that consequently could in the end lead to the destruction of the one, unfaithful partner and hence also the end of the "covenant."

However, other proposed systems developed out of the deuteronomistic initiative, using the word *berit* and having as their purpose, as in the Priestly document, the overcoming of the historical-theological weaknesses of the deuteronomistic view of the future. To these belong, within Deuteronomy itself, for example, the statements of certain very late layers in chs. 4 and 30, and in the book of Jeremiah the saying about the "new covenant" in ch. 31, to which may be added other comparable texts in the prophetic books.

---

3. The author is playing with different meanings of German "erneuern" and "erneuen," a strategy that is not directly reproducible in English.—Tr.

In later texts of Israel's Bible, and also in the New Testament, statements using the words *berit* and *diathēkē* are often allusive. In these cases there is reference to the statement of a basic text already within the canon. This in itself has as a result that the plurality of covenant ideas in the Old Testament passes into the New. If there is no unified application of the category "covenant" in writings that were canonical Scripture for the writers of the New Testament, we can scarcely expect to find such an application in the New Testament itself.

I will not attempt to give a more detailed characterization of the various covenant theologies in the Old Testament. More important is the question whether, within the framework of the Old Testament canon, which became fixed at some point or other, there came to be something like a synthesis of covenant theology that was then available to the New Testament. This question has arisen anew in recent years, and at the present time it is quite controversial.

Is there a "canonical" covenant theology?

Recently, in his study on covenant theology in early Judaism and Christianity (*Das Heil des Bundes: Bundestheologie im Frühjudentum und im frühen Christentum*[4] [Tübingen: Francke, 1996]), Manuel Vogel has shown that in the Book of Jubilees "the priestly covenant thought of the Priestly document and Ben Sira is introduced within the narrative and theological horizon of the Sinai covenant." The priestly concept is accepted as a beginning, but with a view to the danger that Israel could destroy the prescribed order of salvation through disobedience toward the Torah, Jubilees reactivates the "deuteronomic-deuteronomistic concept of the legally covenantal Sinai-*berit*," and does so by introducing a regular "renewal of the covenant" at the Feast of Weeks. Here we appear to have, in a post-Pentateuchal writing, a systematic historical project that unites the several very different concepts of covenant in the Pentateuch itself in a single, though of course very complex, idea. Thus the project is not *per se* impossible.

Should something of the sort be sought also in the putting together of the Jewish canon? Since the canon, despite the division into Torah, Nebiim, and Kethubim, is ultimately twofold—Torah and the other books—it suffices to put the question to the Torah. If it works with a single system of covenant statements, then the statements about the covenant in the other books should be read in those terms.

---

4. The Salvation of the Covenant: Covenant Theology in Early Judaism and in Early Christianity

First of all, though, we have to answer a preliminary question: Does the Torah, and the whole Jewish canon, have any interest in putting together its own statement under the category of "covenant"? I myself have come to this answer: the real central category of the Torah and the whole Old Testament canon is, in fact, not "covenant," but "Torah," and that seems to correspond generally to Jewish opinion. From the point of view of "Torah" the five books of the Pentateuch are seen, within the canon as a whole, as an internal unit. Of course Torah and covenant are closely connected, and one can say that the Pentateuch aims to be a Torah existing within the context of covenant. But does that go so far that a unified concept of covenant is constructed, and are the individual statements about covenant systematically related to one another?

The fact that text complexes such as the Priestly document and Deuteronomy have been combined into a single literary fabric does not in itself force this conclusion, since the texts of the individual works were scarcely affected. The fact that there are some texts, and all of them at strategically important points, that apparently link the different covenant concepts and intend to adjust them to each other takes us somewhat farther. Among these are Exod 31:12-17, Leviticus 26, Deuteronomy 4, and Deuteronomy 29–30. Walter Gross has recently given his attention to texts of this type. In addition, there is the question whether certain fixed linguistic elements that belong within the context of these statements about covenant have been systematically applied at the level of the overall Pentateuch. Rolf Rendtorff finds in the final text of the Pentateuch, when read synchronically, a "structuring function for the covenant formula."

How far do these studies-in-progress bring us? Walter Gross comes to a reticent conclusion: "Traces" can be observed of how "well formulated concepts of covenant are further developed or combined with other existing covenant ideas." This is the work of redactors, who have linked disparate material not for the purpose of a "systematic theological attempt to combine just any conceptual ideas of covenant." Rolf Rendtorff appears rather to reckon with a situation like that in the Book of Jubilees. In any case, these two scholars have chosen different methodologies. Gross determinedly restricts himself to the redaction-critical perspective, which leads "to an irreducible multiplicity of OT covenant theologies." Rendtorff, with equal determination, interprets the canonical final text synchronically. It may be that this in itself explains their different results.

I myself believe that the final text of the Pentateuch, at certain points, indeed insinuates that the different concepts are related. But in its highly tradition-conscious manner it lets the existing blocks of text remain as they are. Their true unity appears to lie beyond conceptual and systematic assimilation. The Pentateuch, with its different systems of expression, was constructed for one particular audience situation. It ends with the death of Moses, before the entry into the Land. Thus also post-exilic Judaism lives far from the Land or is again in a Jerusalem that by no means glows with eschatological light. The very different covenant theologies in the Pentateuch speak to this audience situation. The deuteronomic theology transforms sin and presents the Torah that will be valid even in the eschaton. The prophetic theology, with its universal extension (also represented in the Pentateuch) contains hope. The Priestly document offers the ultimate ground for hope: God's eternal fidelity, not to be abolished by any human infidelity. For the background to these considerations let me refer readers to the first essay in this book.

In the New Testament as well, different covenant concepts are used as needed. Therefore I believe that even if Rendtorff's position regarding the Old Testament proves the most tenable, nothing can be extrapolated from it as regards the New. At least we may accept for the New Testament the idea of a common audience situation that includes everything, but of course is no longer exactly the same as in the Old Testament. Nothing more is really necessary. The matter at issue does not depend on the word "covenant."

Texts about the "new covenant"

Nor does everything by any means depend on the phrase "new covenant." In Matthew's gospel, for example, not only is the adjective "new" before the word "covenant" lacking in the Last Supper account (likewise in Mark), but also in the Gentile mission that begins after the Resurrection the element of "teaching" is so essential that a Matthean reference to Jer 31:31-34 is really unthinkable. The latter text too clearly emphasizes that handing on the Torah through teaching will no longer be necessary in the new covenant. Thus in the New Testament the eschatological new thing that has come with Jesus can be formulated without reference to any talk of a "new covenant."

Nevertheless, texts about the "new covenant" are highly significant for the New Testament. I speak of "texts" in the plural, because while there is only one, Jer 31:31-34, that uses the expression "new covenant," a reception-aesthetically oriented, canonically intratextual reading of the Old Testament will group a series of other texts, by means of allusions and cross-references, around this sole reference to the new covenant.

In the book of Jeremiah itself we find Jer 24:5-7 and 32:37-41. These two passages themselves compel us, through the fact that they also speak of return from exile, to link Jer 31:31-34 at least with Jer 30:1-3; 31:27-30, and in fact to read the whole of Jeremiah 30–31 as the full text regarding the new covenant. Thus in view of these parallels the saying about the new covenant is closely joined to the saying about return from exile and the conversion of Israel, even though in Jer 31:33 it may be located in a later historical layer than the other two elements.

In the book of Ezekiel we find, corresponding to these texts in Jeremiah, Ezek 11:17-20; 36:22-32; 37:21-28. Here the critical motifs from Jeremiah recur, in part translated into a somewhat different anthropology, in part enriched with new but similar elements. Still more loosely related are Ps 51:12-14; Deut 30:1-10, and Bar 2:30-35. One may suspect that for the authors of the New Testament all these texts already belonged together with the Jeremiah text about the new covenant and were read in such a way that they mutually illuminated and enhanced one another.

It is more difficult to answer the question whether the texts in Ezekiel 36 and 37 already furnished the New Testament writers with a link to the promises of the eschatological conversion of the nations, existing elsewhere in the Old Testament as independent prophetic tradition. In Jeremiah 31, after all, the new covenant is promised only to Israel, and the parallels previously described speak constantly and only of a covenant with Israel newly gathered in its Land. In the New Testament, by contrast, it appears that the new covenant is understood almost as a matter of course as also a covenant for the Gentiles. According to Ezek 36:23, 36; 37:28 the Gentiles will "recognize" from the gathering of Israel and the new covenant in its Land that YHWH has acted. Was that the bridge for the New Testament authors to the texts about the pilgrimage of nations and the other texts grouped around them?

But now with regard to Jer 31:31-34: I want to go back to the proposition that the word *berit* represents a metonymy, with the act of donation standing for the entire relationship established by the gift. Both the idea of "breaking the covenant" and the association between the God-given covenant formula as reality and the Torah that is to be observed by Israel speak in favor of the idea that here, also, the "covenant" is regarded as a legal relationship (of course to be conceived analogously). None of the components or structures of an ancient legal relationship are changed. Instead, the word "new" refers to a repeated act of donation or establishment. It presents a new form of assurance of the endurance of the covenant. While the covenant with the ancestors was outwardly proclaimed, written on material substances, and had to be handed on through teaching, the same covenant will now be given as something internal, written on the heart, so that handing it on through teaching will be superfluous. This, then, is a renewed gift, a different kind of establishment, of the old relationship. There is no doubt that here the language takes another stride into the realm of analogy, for no legal arrangements between human beings are arrived at in such a way. That cannot happen. But at the level of the covenant relationship itself the legal image is preserved. In an earlier essay in this book I have given more detailed attention to the statement of this important text about the "new covenant."

Only in the New Testament itself can we find an answer to the question whether those parts of the New Testament that work with the expression *kainē diathēkē* ("new covenant") have in view only the fact that the making of a covenant can be repeated, or whether this radically new way of repeating the covenant-making, which leads to a transformed anthropology, also plays a significant part.

Is Israel still in the covenant?

So—does the Old Testament know of a future "new covenant" that will be accomplished without Israel? No: that was already our response in the first part of these reflections. The Old Testament never releases Israel, even at the end of time, from its original relationship to God. The second part of my remarks spoke of the linguistic means most often used to express this conviction in Scripture. Essentially this had to do with the word "covenant," which is not a univocal form of expression for this conviction. In the Old as well as in the New Testament, wherever it occurs, it must be examined anew. But however it is used in individual texts, it always aims to preserve the historical bond between God and the descendants of Abraham, even to the end of history.

John the Baptizer threatened that God could raise up children of Abraham from stones, and that the axe was already laid at the root of the trees. That was no empty threat. It named a real, historical possibility. But how much had it already been deconstructed at the very point at which the gospels introduce it! In Luke, John says it to the crowds that come out to him, already intending to be baptized as a sign of conversion, and who ask him three times with heightened intensity: "What shall we do?" (Luke 3:7). In Matthew, who already here—and even more so in the case of Jesus—distinguishes very carefully among the various groups of addressees when it is a question of the assignment of guilt, John uses these words to threaten not all the people, but only the Pharisees and Sadducees he sees among those seeking baptism (Matt 3:7). Nothing is being said about Israel as a people.

Beyond this, it is natural to read these words in light of the book of Isaiah, according to whose program John appears (all the evangelists cite

Isa 40:3). All the descendants of Abraham are born from stones. When they look to him and their mother Sarah they see a childless rock, a quarry out of which they are hewn. But just there lies their hope in the days of wrath (cf. Isa 51:1-3). When, on the day of wrath, the Lord of Hosts fells the mighty trees and uproots the thickets of the wood with iron, there will be a "remnant." From the root of Jesse will spring a shoot (Isa 10:21, 25, 33-34; 11:1). Children of Abraham from stones? There are no other children of that ancestor than those raised up from stones—and even the savage rage of the axe need not put an end to the truth that the ancient tree yet brings forth shoots.

Notes

The following notes contain information about the occasions on which the ideas in the several chapters of this book were first presented as well as about their original publication. In the notes on each chapter there are also, in most cases, suggestions for further reading, and occasionally information on the larger scholarly discussion of the topic. In this collection I have included only a few notes on sources, whether my own publications or the work of other authors that is quoted, used as a basis for my remarks, or that brings the discussion farther.

Chapter One: Death at the River Frontier

This chapter contains my farewell lecture at the Hochschule Sankt Georgen in Frankfurt, July10, 1996. It was first published as "Moses Tod, die Tora und die alttestamentliche Sonntagslesung," *Theologie und Philosophie* 71 (1996) 481–94. On the questions of the sequence of pericopes touched on in this essay see Hansjakob Becker, "Wortgottesdienst als Dialog der beiden Testamente. Der Stellenwert des Alten Testamentes bei einer Weiterführung der Reform des Ordo Lectionum Missae," in Ansgar Franz, ed., *Streit am Tisch des Wortes? Zur Deutung und Bedeutung des Alten Testaments und seiner Verwendung in der Liturgie.* Pietas Liturgica 8 (St. Ottilien: EOS Verlag, 1997) 659–89; Georg Braulik, "Die Tora als Bahnlesung. Zur Hermeneutik einer zukünftigen Auswahl der Sonntagsperikopen," in Reinhard Messner, Eduard Nagel, and Rudolf Pacik, eds., *Bewahren und Erneuern. Studien zur Messliturgie. Festschrift für Hans Bernhard Meyer SJ zum 70. Geburtstag* (Innsbruck and Vienna: Tyrolia, 1995) 50–76; Norbert Lohfink, "Perikopenordnung 'Patmos.' Gedanken eines Alttestamentlers zu dem Leseordnungsentwurf von Hansjakob Becker," *Bibel und Liturgie* 70 (1997) 218–32.

Chapter Two: "Go from Your Country . . ."

This chapter contains a lecture given at the diocesan pastoral conference in Brixen on August 25, 1998. It was published as "Ein Gott, der Menschen zu Fremdlingen macht," *Konferenzblatt für Theologie und Seelsorge* (Bolzano) 110 (1999) 31–40.

Chapter Three: Conquest or Return?

This chapter developed out of several lectures given in 1996 and 1997 in Nuremberg, Mainz, Benediktbeuern, and Erfurt. It was first published as "Landeroberung und Heimkehr. Hermeneutisches zum heutigen Umgang mit dem Josuabuch," *Jahrbuch für biblische Theologie* 12 (1997) 3–24. For information on Palestinian Christians and their self-understanding cf. Mitri Raheb, *I Am a Palestinian Christian*. Translated by Ruth C. L. Gritsch, with a Foreword by Rosemary Radford Ruether (Minneapolis: Fortress, 1995); Ulrike Bachmann and Mitri Raheb, eds., *Verwurzelt im Heiligen Land. Einführung in das palästinensische Christentum* (Frankfurt: J. Knecht, 1995). For the basic theme cf. Norbert Lohfink, *Krieg und Staat im alten Israel*. Beiträge zur Friedensethik 14 (Barsbüttel: Institut für Theologie und Frieden, 1992); Moshe Weinfeld, *The Promise of the Land. The Inheritance of the Land of Canaan by the Israelites*. Taubman Lectures in Jewish Studies 3 (Berkeley: University of California Press, 1993) 76–155. For the analysis of the final chapter of Deuteronomy see especially Georg Braulik, "Die Völkervernichtung und die Rückkehr Israels ins Verheissungsland. Hermeneutische Bemerkungen zum Buch Deuteronomium," in Marc Vervenne and Johan Lust, eds., *Deuteronomy and Deuteronomic Literature. Festschrift C. H. W. Brekelmans*. Bibliotheca Ephemeridum Theologicarum Lovaniensium 83 (Leuven: Leuven University Press/Peeters, 1997) 3–38.

Chapter Four: Jeremiah and the Sacred Heart of Jesus

This chapter follows the festival address at the Festival Academy of the Canisianum, Innsbruck, on the feast of the Sacred Heart of Jesus, June 19, 1998. It was published in *Korrespondenzblatt des Canisianums* 132 (1998/99) 2–10. The works from other fields that are mentioned are: Karl Richstätter, *Die Herz-Jesu-Verehrung des deutschen Mittelalters. Nach gedruckten und ungedruckten Quellen, mit 18 Tafeln altdeutscher Herz-Jesu-Bilder* (2nd ed. Regensburg: J. Kösel & F. Pustet, 1924); Hugo Rahner, "Flumina de ventre Christi: Die patristische Auslegung von Joh 7,37.38," *Biblica* 22 (1941) 269–302, 367–403; idem, "Grundzüge einer

Geschichte der Herz-Jesu-Verehrung," *Zeitschrift für Aszese und Mystik* 61 (1943) 61–83; idem, "Ströme fliessen aus seinem Leib. Die aszetische Deutungsgeschichte von Joh. 7,37.38," ibid. 141–49; Gustav E. Closen, "Das Herz des Erlösers in den heiligen Schriften des Alten Bundes," *Zeitschrift für Aszese und Mystik* 18 (1943) 17–30.

Chapter Five: Hosea and Wrath

This chapter contains a guest lecture I gave in Heidelberg on December 15, 1995. It was published (with extensive documentation) under the title "'I come not in wrath.' Sketch for a Synchronic Method of Reading the Book of Hosea," in Raymond Kuntzmann, ed., *Ce Dieu qui vient: Études sur l'Ancien et le Nouveau Testament offerts au Professeur Bernard Renauld à l'occasion de son soixante-cinquième anniversaire.* Lectio Divina 159 (Paris: Cerf, 1995) 163–90.

Chapter Six: The Psalter and Meditation

This chapter originated with a guest lecture given in Mainz on January 17, 1991. Its scholarly publication, with extensive documentation, was entitled "Psalmengebet und Psalterredaktion," *Archiv für Liturgiewissenschaft* 34 (1992) 1–22. Let me refer especially to Notker Füglister, "Die Verwendung und das Verständnis der Psalmen und des Psalters um die Zeitenwende," in Josef Schreiner, ed., *Beiträge zur Psalmenforschung. Psalm 2 und 22.* FzB 60 (Würzburg: Echter, 1988) 319–94; Georg Braulik, "Christologisches Verständnis der Psalmen—schon im Alten Testament?" in Klemens Richter and Benedikt Kranemann, eds., *Christologie der Liturgie. Der Gottesdienst der Kirche—Christusbekenntnis und Sinaibund.* QD 159 (Freiburg: Herder, 1995) 57–86; see also the recent publications by Frank-Lothar Hossfeld, Erich Zenger, and Gianni Barbiero.

Chapter Seven: The Loneliness of the Just One

The ideas contained in this chapter were presented for the first time in a lecture given in November 1997 during a study year at the Dormitio in Jerusalem. The text was published in French in *Christus* 45 (1998) 433–41 under the title "La solitude du juste dans le Psaume 1."

Chapter Eight: Introspection and Cosmic Mysticism

The ideas in this chapter were presented in 1990 in a number of Catholic and Protestant pastoral conventions at the time when Eugen

Drewermann was dominating the religious scene in Germany. It was published under the title "Das Böse im Herzen und Gottes Gerechtigkeit in der weiten Welt: Gedanken zu Psalm 36," in Paul Imhof, ed., *Gottes Nähe. Religiöse Erfahrung in Mystik und Offenbarung. Festschrift zum 65. Geburtstag von Josef Sudbrack SJ* (Würzburg: Echter, 1990) 327–41.

Chapter Nine: Peace Poetry in Israel

This chapter rests on my work on the Psalms with the Little Sisters of Charles de Foucauld in Frankfurt. It was published as "'Der den Kriegen einen Sabat bereitet.' Psalm 46—ein Beispiel alttestamentlicher Friedenslyrik," *Bibel und Kirche* 44 (1989) 148–53.

Chapter Ten: Three Ways to Talk About Poverty

This chapter was originally a lecture for the Thomas-Akademie on January 26, 1997, at the Hochschule Sankt Georgen in Frankfurt, on the occasion when Bishop Franz Kamphaus of Limburg was presented with a Festschrift. It was published as "Drei Arten, von Armut zu sprechen. Illustriert an Psalm 109," *Theologie und Philosophie* 72 (1997) 321–36. For the history of reception of Psalm 109 cf. Walter Dürig, "Die Verwendung des sogenannten Fluchpsalms 108 (109) im Volksglauben und in der Liturgie," *Münchener Theologischer Zeitschrift* 27 (1976) 71–84. The commentary by Heinrich Graetz that is mentioned here was entitled *Kritischer Commentar zu den Psalmen nebst Text und Uebersetzung, II* (Breslau: S. Schottlaender, 1883). The newest systematic analysis of this psalm in English is in Erich Zenger, *A God of Vengeance? Understanding the Psalms of Divine Wrath*. Translated by Linda M. Maloney (Louisville: Westminster John Knox, 1996) 55–61.

Chapter Eleven: The Old Testament and the Course of the Christian's Day

This chapter contains a public lecture I gave on July 27, 1993 in Münster at the International Meeting of the Society of Biblical Literature, although it was then in an earlier version aimed at a different audience. The publication of that lecture with scholarly apparatus can be found under the title "Psalmen im Neuen Testament. Die Lieder in der Kindheitsgeschichte bei Lukas," in Klaus Seybold and Erich Zenger, eds., *Neue Wege der Psalmenforschung. Für Walter Beyerlin*. Herders Biblische Studien 1 (Freiburg: Herder, 1994) 105–25. This essay continues some ideas from Chapter Seven of the present book. On psalms embedded in Old Testament narratives see James W. Watts, *Psalm and Story. Inset Hymns in Hebrew Narrative.* JSOT.S 139 (Sheffield: JSOT Press, 1992).

Chapter Twelve: Children of Abraham from Stones

   This chapter was originally a lecture at the meeting of the organization of German-speaking Catholic New Testament scholars, March 17–21, 1997, in Innsbruck. It was printed under the title "Kinder Abrahams aus Steinen—wird nach dem Alten Testament Israel einst der 'Bund' genommen werden?" in the Congress Volume edited by Hubert Frankemölle, *Der ungekündigte Bund? Antworten des Neuen Testaments.* QD 172 (Freiburg: Herder, 1998) 17–43. The most important publications of the authors mentioned here by name regarding the concept of covenant are: Ernst Kutsch, *Neues Testament—Neuer Bund? Eine Fehlübersetzung wird korrigiert* (Neukirchen-Vluyn: Neukirchener Verlag, 1978); Lothar Perlitt, *Bundestheologie im Alten Testament.* WMANT 36 (Neukirchen-Vluyn: Neukirchener Verlag, 1969); James Barr, "Some Semantic Notes on the Covenant," in Herbert Donner et al., eds., *Beiträge zur alttestamentlichen Theologie. Festschrift für Walther Zimmerli zum 70. Geburtstag* (Göttingen: Vandenhoeck & Ruprecht, 1977) 23–38; and especially Norbert Lohfink and Erich Zenger, *The God of Israel and the Nations. Studies in Isaiah and the Psalms.* Translated by Everett R. Kalin (Collegeville: The Liturgical Press, 2000). The work by Rolf Rendtorff mentioned is *Die "Bundesformel." Eine exegetisch-theologische Untersuchung.* SBS 160 (Stuttgart: Katholisches Bibelwerk, 1995). The newest study, used by me before its actual publication, is Walter Gross, *Zukunft für Israel. Alttestamentliche Bundeskonzepte und die aktuelle Debatte um den Neuen Bund.* SBS 176 (Stuttgart: Katholisches Bibelwerk, 1998).

General Index

Abraham as alien in God-given land, 15
Abraham's call from God, 18–19
Alacoque, Margaret Mary, 56
alteration of meaning of psalms, 84
Amir, Yigal, 30
Amos, book of, 57
Andersen, Francis I., on Hosea, 60
Arab Christians and Joshua, 28–29
Arab-Israeli conflict, background of, 28–32
arrangement of psalms, 82
Assmann, Jan, 62
authorial voice in Hosea, 69–70

Babylonian Exile, 34, 35, 47
Barr, James, 162
barriers that prevent typological reading, 37–42
Benedict and the Psalter, 78–79
Benedictus, in Infancy Narrative, 146–48
    linking to other hymns, 146–48
    in Luke's Gospel, 141–50
    sung in Liturgy of the Hours, 149
Berit, 161–62, 164, 165, 168
Bible as nonhistorical, 36
Bible-oriented Israelis, 29
biblical narrator, 139
blessings given to Abraham, 19
books replace scrolls, 8–9

Braulik, Georg, 14
Buber, Martin, 151, 153, 90
burning bush, 2

Canisianum in Innsbruck, 44
canonical structure of Old Testament, 41
Cassuto, Umberto, 58
chain-like linking of Psalms 1–3, 83
Chajes, Hirsch Perez, 58
characteristics of God, 138
childlessness, 17
Christians, duties of on behalf of Arab Christians, 43
Closen, Gustav, 45
communicative structure of Hosea, 61–63
congregation of the righteous, 95–96
conquest of Israel as gift of God, 33
covenant, 165, 166
    broken and pardon, 47–48
    with Israel, God's, 160–61
    theology rooted in Pentateuch, 46
cursing psalm, 119

Daily Office, 136
David, psalms of, 134
Decalogue, 48
Delitzsch, Franz, 79
distress, images in Psalm 109, 125–26
divided kingdom, 159–60
divine speech in Hosea, 66–67

178   *In the Shadow of Your Wings*

divinely willed violence in Joshua, 31

Elohim, 113
end, predictions of the, 154–56
eschatological pilgrimage in Psalm 24, 87
Essenes of Qumran, 94
evil in Psalm 1, 91–93
Exodus from Egypt, 2

faith, power of, 21
foreign lands, movement to, 20
foreignness, as a Christian path, 20
   of the chosen people, 23
Freedman, David Noel, 60
freedom as ability to respond to Torah, 50
   story of, 55
Füglister, Notker, 76

genre of the psalms, 75–76
Gloria, in Infancy Narrative, 146–48
   linking to other hymns, 146–48
   in Luke's Gospel, 141–50
   sung in liturgy, 149
God images, 16
God's patience, 159–60
God's ties to Israel, 153–54
good in Psalm 1, 91–93
Graetz, Heinrich, 120
Gross, Walter, 166
Gunkel, Hermann, 76, 79

Hail Mary, 90
Hannah's song, 139
heart of Jesus, 54, 55
   devotion to, 45
hefer berit, 163
"holy hill," 83
Holy Land, ownership in biblical times, 27
Hosea, author's commentary in, 65–66
   book of 57–58
   as commentator, 66–68
   communicative structure of, 61–63
   genre of, 63–67
   implied author of, 71–74
   "inaugural sketches of," 60
   narration by author, 65
   as narrator, 66–68

human and divine action in story of Joseph, 25
human freedom, 50
hymns in Luke's Gospel as summary of salvation history, 150

Iliad, 74
"In your light we see light," 109–10
Infancy Narrative songs, 149
Islamic conquest of Israel land, 35
Isocrates' *Panegyric*, 64
Israel, as a state, 34
   Christians related to, 42
   in eschatological fulfillment, 157–59
   of the Exile, 52
   land of in New Testament, 41
   people of in Scripture, 152
   "remnant of," 156
   role at end of history, 158
   story in Joshua, 32–38
Israeli/Palestinian conflict, 28
Israelis and Christian Palestinians, 28

Jacob and Esau, 22
Jacob flees to foreign places, 21–24
Jacob's reconciliation with Esau, 23
Jeremiah in Old Testament, 50
Jeremias, Jörg, 60–61
Jerusalem destroyed by Babylonians, 33–34
Jesus and "gathering of Israel," 41
Jesus Prayer, 78, 90
Jewish Christian community in Jerusalem, 42
Jews who reject state of Israel, 30–31
Jonah's psalm, 139
Joseph in a foreign land, 24–26
Joshua, as Moses' successor, 3
   not part of Pentatuch, 40
   two ways of interpreting, 30
Josiah of Judah and Torah scroll, 6
Josiah's plan to win back lost land, 33
Judah in Hosea, 62
Judas psalm, 119
justification, from faith alone, 55
   in Old Testament, 51–52

karat berit, 162
key word framing, 123–35
kindness of YHWH in Psalm 36, 104
king images in Psalm 36, 109
knowing and experiencing God, 108–09
Koch, Klaus, and *Prophetic Annexation Theory*, 155
Kutsch, Ernst, 161, 163

Laban as exploiter of Jacob, 23
light and life in Psalm 36, 107–08
linkage of Psalms 22–26, 86–89
linking, key words of psalms, 82–83
  of psalms in the Psalter, 137
Liturgy of the Hours, 136, 137, 150
Liturgy of the Word, structure of, 13
Lowth, Bishop, 59
Lukan writings, division of, 12
Lutheran World Federation and justification, 51

Magnificat, in Infancy Narrative, 146–48
  linking to other hymns, 146–48
  in Luke's Gospel, 141–50
  sung in Liturgy of the Hours, 149
Maimonides, Moses, 31
meal, theme in Psalm 36, 107
meditating on the psalms, 77–78
meditatio, 78
messianic dimension in Psalm 109, 134
metonymy, 162, 168
Meyer, Hans Bernhard, 14
Meynet, Roland, 59
miraculous moments of divine guidance in Joseph story, 25–26
moledet (kindred), 18
Moses, 1
  death of, 11
  death as literary boundary marker, 4
  failure to reach his goal, 3
Mowinckel, Sigmund, 76
Muilenburg, James, 59
murmuring of memorized psalms, 94

narrative genre in Hosea, 63–66
narratives, psalms in, 138–40
new covenant, 48, 49, 167–68, 169
  contrasted with old, 47

  in Jeremiah, 46, 55
  unfulfilled, 55
New Testament as definitive commentary, 12
non-linear connections between books of Bible, 8–10
Noth, Martin, 4
Nunc dimittis, in Infancy narrative, 146–48
  linking to other hymns, 146–48
  in Luke's Gospel, 141–50
  sung in liturgy, 149

old covenant, 47
Old Testament canonical structure, 10
  as primeval history, 10
order of readings at Liturgy of the Word, 14
Otto, Eckart, 160

Palestinian Christians as Jewish Christians, 42
Palestinian Christians, in eyes of modern Israelis, 42
Palestinian/Israeli conflict, causes of, 42–44
Pentateuch, as manual for actors in Joshua, 5–6
Pentecost, as church beginning, 53–54
Perlitt, Lothar, 161–62
personal knowledge, growth of from within, 20–21
petitions emerging from experience of God, 108–09
Philo of Alexandria, 11
pilgrimage of nations to Zion, 42
plurality of covenant theologies, 164–65, 167
poetic verses in Luke's Infancy Narrative, 140
Polzin, Robert, 139
poverty in Psalm 109, 131–33
power struggle among Jacob's sons, 24
power, transfer from Moses to Joshua, 4–5
privilege of the poor, 130
proclamation of divine wrath, 72

promise of new covenant fulfilled, 54
promised land, 2
Prophetic Annexation Theory of Klaus Koch, 155
prophetic books of Old Testament, 63
Psalm 1, as gateway to Psalter, 91
   good and evil in, 91–93
   as "the Two Ways," 91
   as wisdom psalm, 92
Psalm 36, description of sinner in, 104
   human behavior in, 103
   image of a king, 109
   kindness of YHWH, 104
   light and life, 107–08
   as linked to Psalm 35, 102
   meal theme, 107
   sin and goodness in, 104
   sovereignty of God, 105–06
   translation of, 99, 100
Psalm 46, confession of faith, 114–16
   elements of nature in, 112
   end of war in, 117–18
   sun god in, 115
   translation of, 111–12
Psalm 109, analysis of counterarguments of, 126–29
   as cry of the poor, 129
   for general use, 125–26
   genre of, 122
   images of distress in, 125–26
   messianic dimension in, 134
   poverty in, 131–33
   structure of, 122
   translation of, 120–22
psalm-linking as dialogical dramatization, 84
   as introduction of new subject, 85
psalms, connected to Pentateuch, 8
   in Christian worship, 77
   used for meditation, 77
Psalter, 75–76
   as hymnal of Second Temple, 76
   as hymnal of the synagogue, 76
   intended for certain persons, 93–94
   and need for better modern language, 90
   significance in Judaism, 76
   as single meditation text, 78
   as single text, 81

Qoheleth and King Solomon, 9

Rabin, Yitzhak, 28, 30
Rahner, Hugo, 44, 45, 46
redaction of the psalms, 89
redactional linking of psalms, 79–80
relationship of Psalms 137 and 138, 85
"Remnant of Israel," 156
Rendtorff, Rolf, 166
reparation, 56
Richstätter, Karl, 44
Roman Catholic Church and justification, 51
Rosenzweig, Franz, 90

Sacred Heart devotion, basis in Old Testament, 45–46
Sacred Heart of Jesus, devotion to, 44
salvation history, 4
scroll of the Torah, 6
Second Vatican Council, 44
Self-understanding, Christian, 53
Septuagint canon, 11
Sermon on the Mount, 54
Servant of YHWH, 102
Sin, as cause for division, 22
   theme of in Psalm 36, 103–05
Smend, Rudolf, 155
song of lament, 122
sovereignty of God in Psalm 36, 105–06
stranger in one's own land, 15–16
strangers in a foreign land, 20–21
sun god, 106
   in Psalm 46, 116
Sunday liturgy of the Word, 14
Sunday readings, order of, 13

Temple of Jerusalem, 34–35
Terah's failed journey to Caanan, 18–19
"Therapeutae," 77
Torah, 48, 94, 165, 166
   as canon within canon, 10, 11
   in Christian canon, 11
   and justice for oppressed, 7

motifs in Malachi, 8
newly defined in Joshua, 6
scroll in Joshua, 6
tension between two in Isaiah, 7
transfer of property in Roman law, 1–2
tree as symbolic figure, 95
trust, lack of, 2
twins, conflict between in Scripture, 22
typological reading of the Bible, 36
typological view of Israeli/Palestinian conflict, 31

Vogel, Manuel, 165

war, end of in Psalm 46, 117–18
wavelike character of Hosea, 72
Wellhausen, Julius, 155
Wette, Wilhelm Martin, Leberecht de, 155
wisdom psalm, Psalm 1 as, 92
Wolff, Hans Walter, on Hosea, 59–61, 69
world-tree as symbolic figure, 95
wrath of God in Hosea, 71–72
Würthwein, Ernst, Festschrift, 61

Y$_{\text{HWH}}$ as shepherd, 86

Zenger, Eric, 157, 160
Zeterschrei (murder cry), 133
Zionist movement, 35

Scripture Index

Genesis		26:8-10	2	1:3	95
1:9-10	112	28:47f	37	1:4	95
2:10-14	113	29:6-29	37	1:5	96
3:19	9	29:22	38	1:6	91, 96
11:10-32	17	29:23	7	2:10	7
12:1	17–18	29:78	38	7:17	80
12:2-3	19	30:1-10	37	8:1, 9	80
39:7-10	25	30:6	52	9:1-2	81
45:5	24	31:9	6	22–26	85–86
50:19-20	25	31:24	6	22:29	86
Exodus		32:1	7	23:3	86
3:8	2	34	5	24:3	87
23:32	30	34:1-6	1	24:4	88
32:10	154	34:10-12	3	24:5	87
34:12	30	*Joshua*		25:1	88
Deuteronomy		1:7-9	5	25:13	40
1:32	2, 33	1:7, 8	7	32:11	80
1:37	2	9:27	38	33:1	80
3:25	2	21:43-45	33, 71	35:27	102
3:26-27	2	*1 Samuel*		36	108–110
4:25-31	37	8:5	3	36:5b	100
5–28	6	10:27	105	36:8	106
6:6-7	77	*1 Kings*		46:5	115
7:1	28	15:29	128	46:6	115
7:1-2	33			46:7	115
7:2	30	*Psalms*		46:9	115
9:5	51	1:1	92	46:10	117
20:10-20	33	1:1-2	7, 77	46:10b	117
20:15-18	33	1:2	92	46:11	117
				46:12	118

Scripture Index

109:2	129	66:21	40	19:4, 8	54
		66:22	158	28:20	41
Psalms					
109:2-3	124	*Jeremiah*		*Mark*	
109:4	124	8:7	50	1:22	54
109:15	129	12:16	40	1:27	54
109:16	126	17:1	50	10:5-6	54
109:16-17	131	17:5, 7	92		
109:17	127	17:9	50	*Luke*	
109:18	127	31:14	107	1:58	142
109:19	127	31:31-34	46–47	1:64	141
109:20	124	31:35-37	153	1:66	143
109:21-22	123			1:67	144
109:25	130	*Ezekiel*		1:68	142
109:26	129	20:35	10	1:76	142
109:28	130			2:9	142
109:29	131	*Hosea*		2:10	145
109:31	131	4:1-3	69	2:14	148
110:1	134	9:14	70	2:26	143
137	84–85	9:17	70	3:6	145
138:1	84	11:8	155	3:7	169
145:21	81	11:10	73		
149:1	82	11:11b	73	*John*	
150:6	82	12:2	69	3:23, 36	12
		12:3	62	7:38	44
		14:3	73	19:34	44
Isaiah					
1:2	6	*Micah*		*Acts*	
1:10	7	4:1-5	40	1:11	12
2:2-5	40			1:20	119
14:1-2	40	*Zechariah*			
19:24	158	9:13-16	35–36	*Ephesians*	
19:25	158			2:14	41
54:5	88	*Matthew*		2:19	41
61:5	40	5:5	41	3:18-19	104
		7:29	54		